THE THISTLE AND THE PEN

THE
THISTLE AND THE PEN

An Anthology of Modern Scottish Writers
chosen and introduced
by
ERIC LINKLATER

THOMAS NELSON AND SONS LTD
LONDON EDINBURGH PARIS MELBOURNE
TORONTO AND NEW YORK

THOMAS NELSON AND SONS LTD
Parkside Works Edinburgh 9
3 Henrietta Street London WC2
312 Flinders Street Melbourne C1
5 Parker's Buildings Burg Street Cape Town

THOMAS NELSON AND SONS (CANADA) LTD
91–93 Wellington Street West Toronto 1

THOMAS NELSON AND SONS
385 Madison Avenue New York 17

SOCIÉTÉ FRANÇAISE D'EDITIONS NELSON
25 rue Henri Barbusse Paris Ve

———

First published 1950

The prose text of this book is set in
12-point Bembo

CONTENTS

CONTENTS

CONTENTS

vii

CONTENTS

ACKNOWLEDGMENTS

THANKS are due, and are hereby tendered, to the following authors and publishers for permission to use copyright poems and extracts from the volumes named hereunder :

John Allan and Messrs Methuen & Co Ltd for *Farmer's Boy* ; George Blake and William Collins, Sons and Co Ltd for *The Shipbuilders* ; Jonathan Cape Ltd for three poems from *Collected Poems* by Lilian Bowes Lyon ; James Bridie and Messrs Constable & Co Ltd for *Mr Bolfry (Plays for Plain People)* ; Ivor Brown and Jonathan Cape Ltd for *Say the Word, Just Another Word, A Word in Your Ear, I Give You my Word* ; Kenneth Buthlay and The Ettrick Press for 'The Salmon' from *Scottish Student Verse 1937–47* ; F Fraser Darling and William Collins, Sons and Co Ltd for *Natural History in the Highlands and Islands* ; Norman Douglas and Messrs Chatto & Windus for *Looking Back*, *Paneros* and *Together* ; Norman Douglas and Martin Secker & Warburg Ltd for *Old Calabria* and *South Wind* ; Adam Drinan for a passage from *The Men of the Rocks*, published by The Fortune Press ; Bernard Fergusson and *Blackwood's Magazine* for 'Across the Chindwin' ; James Fergusson and Messrs Oliver & Boyd Ltd for *Scotland 1938* ; G S Fraser and The Harvill Press Ltd for 'The Black Cherub' from *The Traveller has Regrets* ; Sir Alexander Gray and Messrs Longmans, Green & Co Ltd for *The Socialist Tradition* ; Sir Alexander Gray for 'Scotland' from *Gossip*, published by The Porpoise Press ; Neil M Gunn and Messrs Faber & Faber Ltd for *Morning Tide* and *Young Art and Old Hector* ; George Campbell Hay and Messrs Oliver & Boyd Ltd for three poems from *Wind on Loch Fyne* ; Maurice Lindsay and The Serif Books Ltd for three poems from *At the Wood's Edge* ; Eric Linklater and Jonathan Cape Ltd for 'Rumbelow' from *A Dragon Laughed* ; Eric Linklater and Rupert Hart-Davis Ltd for *Sealskin Trousers and Other Stories* ; Hugh MacDiarmid and William Blackwood & Sons Ltd for four poems from *Penny Wheep*, 'O Wha's been Here' from *A Drunk Man*

ACKNOWLEDGMENTS

Looks at the Thistle, and ' Bonnie Broukit Bairn ' from *Sangschaw* ;
Colin MacDonald and The Moray Press for *Highland Journey* ;
Compton Mackenzie and Messrs Chatto & Windus for *The North
Wind of Love* ; Moray McLaren and Gerald Duckworth & Co Ltd
for *Return to Scotland* ; Donald G Macrae and William Maclellan
for ' The Pterodactyl and Powhatan's Daughter ' from *Poetry Scot-
land* No 3 ; Bruce Marshall and Messrs Constable & Co Ltd for
Yellow Tapers for Paris ; George Millar and William Heinemann
Ltd for *Horned Pigeon* ; Naomi Mitchison and Jonathan Cape Ltd
for *When the Bough Breaks* ; Edwin Muir and George G Harrap
& Co Ltd for *The Story and the Fable* ; Edwin Muir and Messrs
Faber & Faber Ltd for ' The Good Town ' from *The Labyrinth* ;
Will Ogilvie for ' The Blades of Harden ' from *Whaup o' the Rede* ;
Alexander Scott for ' The Gowk in *Lear* ' from *The Latest in Elegies* ;
George Scott-Moncrieff and B T Batsford Ltd for *Lowlands of Scot-
land* ; Sydney Goodsir Smith and William Maclellan for two poems
from *The Deevil's Waltz* ; Andrew Young and Jonathan Cape Ltd
for ' Hard Frost ' from *The Green Man* and two poems from *The
White Blackbird* ; Douglas Young and William Maclellan for three
poems from *A Braird o Thristles*.

x

INTRODUCTION

THIS collection of prose and poetry by living Scottish authors is designed neither as an omnibus nor as a dairy. It does not offer a place to everyone, and it is not a deliberate skimming of the cream. In making the selection I felt no desire to be fair and inclusive ; and I have not been dominated by a critical anxiety to show my chosen authors at the tallest and most immaculate flowering of their several talents. My purpose was rather to make an attractive and, I hope, expository array of contemporary writing, and my method has been to rely on the arbitrary taste of an indifferent memory. I began, that is, with the reflection on my mind of a landscape, sufficiently coloured and showing the proper variety of scene to make a literary portrait of Scotland, and then cast about in my memory for passages in the work of the authors whose prose and poetry had, in the ordinary course of my reading, helped to create that landscape. I filled my imagined map with what I thought would suit it.

Some very respectable features of the landscape have been deliberately omitted. I decided to exclude books and authors whose primary intention was informative or critical, though the decision to do so deprived the anthology of much that would have enhanced its value, and in the few instances where I have broken this rule I have done so for a specific but arbitrary reason. Fraser Darling, for example, is a scientific and therefore informative writer, but I have included his description of the Atlantic Seal because seals are a relevant detail in the Scottish landscape, and I have always regarded them with interest and affection. *A Father of Socialism*, again, is critical and instructive writing, but I remembered it for the sheer

INTRODUCTION

pleasure it had given me ; it is Sir Alexander Gray's
unusual gift to write of political and economic matters
with such grace and wit as few authors command whose
only purpose is entertainment.

But though I have avoided instructional works, and
restricted my choice—or nearly so—to writers who are
primarily imaginative, my plan required that I should take
from their books what would illustrate the Scottish scene
and temperament ; or to be modest, my view of them.
There are rural pictures by John Allan and Edwin Muir
to set beside the urban scenes by Edwin Muir and George
Blake ; and there is a chapter from Compton Mackenzie's
immense novel, *The Four Winds of Love*, that I chose
deliberately in preference to many passages of a more
purely literary interest because it tells a good deal about
the ideas implicit in Scottish Nationalism and about the
sort of people one may hear discussing it. In *Up from the
Sea* there is something of Highland Scotland, unspoiled
by the vulgar world and lighted by the translucent sky
of Neil Gunn's cosmography ; and in *Stone Walls* and
Across the Chindwin there are other provinces, very
turbulently full of the world, where Scots revive their
long history of war.

I have not, it will be observed, confined my choice of
scenery to native heath nor borrowed only from authors
who still pay taxes on their own soil. To have done that
would have been to show an imperfect and most mis-
leading view ; for the tale of Scotland is no more to be
told between Carter Bar and the Pentland Firth than the
history of Jewry between Dan and Beersheba. The true
parties to the Caledonian antisyzygy—Mr MacDiarmid's
impressive word—may be, indeed, not Highlanders and
Lowlanders, not Jacobitish romantics and hard-headed
Whigs, but forth-faring Scots and home-keeping Scots.
A remarkable sentiment for their own country dominates

the latter, a vigorous preference for far places appears to inspire the former—but blood is thicker than the estranging seas, and on two noisy nights of the year in a hundred towns from Auckland to Seattle there are many thousands of otherwise orthodox and disciplined citizens who, in a vast emotional confession, proclaim the breeding that environment, often happily, occludes. I cannot think it likely, I admit, that Norman Douglas makes a habit of attending Burns Suppers, but even against a Mediterranean background the ancestral bone shows clearly in his countenance and work. Even the English climate, in some ways a more subtle menace than Capri, does not often quite obscure a Scottish origin, at least not for a generation or two ; and if in his sentimental consciousness a Scot may continue so in the pervasive airs of Hampstead and Nottingham and Bournemouth, then the confines of Scotland are assuredly not limited by geography.

The aggressive out-and-out Scottishness of the poets in this anthology who, as the disciples of Hugh MacDiarmid, write in the Lallans dialect, is a recent development in our history ; for though there has been much physical combat between Scots and English, Scottish writers have not, until lately, shown hostility to the English language. Such redoubtable figures, indeed, as John Knox and David Hume assiduously cultivated its style and idiom, and neither Smollett nor Sir Walter Scott, Carlyle nor Stevenson, doubted their liberty to use English as their own. But some five and twenty years ago Hugh MacDiarmid published a book of lyrical poems that started a small revolution. It was patriotic as well as literary. MacDiarmid, and those who accepted his lead, were resolved to show their independence of the English tongue as a preliminary to independence of English rule. Of their politics I shall say nothing, but of their poetry it is right to say that some of it is genuine poetry of no

mean order, and the impulse to fashion a new language—
or find contemporary expression of a somewhat hypo-
thetical old language—is evidence of the modest liveliness
that, for the last few years, has informed the Scottish
scene.

I do not want to exaggerate the several appearances of
a renewed vitality in Scotland that many observers,
sympathetic with the country, have lately spoken of;
for Scotland is a small country, and we who live in it are
naturally inclined to see the local view through the
magnifying glasses with which every parish council is
equipped.—That even the greatest powers encourage
their citizens to wear parochial glasses is of course equally
true, but no concern of mine. I cannot amend their
ways, and I may be optimistic in striving to discipline my
own.—But discount as you will the material evidence
of what has hopefully been called a Scottish Renaissance,
there remains throughout the land a strange confidence,
an assurance of its future that often sounds as cheerful
and irrational as the ringing shout of the anvil against the
hammer that belabours it. What justification there is for
confidence, except the spirit of confidence, I do not know
and I shall not pretend to ; but certainly it exists, and
between these present covers there is, for the time of day,
a remarkably good appetite for life, and a strangely small
flavouring of pessimism or disillusion.

This finally has to be said in explanation of the anthology : I hope it will make money—not for myself, alas—
but for the Scottish Centre of the P.E.N. Club, whose
burden and honour in 1950 is to entertain in Edinburgh
the International Congress of the P.E.N. To this end
a great deal of money is required, and to raise a fraction
of it the publishers of this book have offered me all
the resources of their historic organisation, while some
twenty writers, to whom I appealed because I was already

indebted to them for much abiding pleasure, have given me permission to take what I wanted of their work. Here is good will to start with, and good value, I think, to second it. But good things in their best array come three by three, and something is still needed to supplement the givers and ripen their gifts.

What next ? Customers, please. . . .

ERIC LINKLATER

PITCALZEAN HOUSE
EASTER ROSS, *January 1950*

THE THISTLE AND THE PEN

JOHN ALLAN

The Family

I WAS born on the afternoon of the day on which my grandfather signed his third trust-deed on behoof of his creditors . . . the only form of literature in which our family have ever achieved distinction. Though the circumstances of my birth were not such as to cause him any great pleasure, and though his own circumstances were even more involved than usual, the Old Man abated nothing of his usual intransigence in the face of fortune. When the creditors and their agent had departed, the midwife, an ancient and disillusioned female, presented me to the Old Man. The two generations, I am told, looked at each other in silence across the vastness of seventy years, then the Old Man delivered his grim judgment :

' Gin it gets hair an' teeth it winna look sae like a rabbit.'

And so she left him.

' Aw weel,' said the Old Man, thinking over the events of the day, ' we'd better jist mak a nicht o't.'

He thereupon invited a few old friends, neighbouring farmers long tied in the mischances of this world, to come over that night for a game of nap. They came. They hanselled the new child and the new trust-deed in the remains of the greybeard, and the Old Man collected thirty shillings at nap before morning. Such was the world into which I made my entry on a chill December morning about thirty years ago.

Our family could boast of age if not of honour. We could go back for five generations to one James who was reputed to have been hanged for sheep-stealing about the middle of the eighteenth century. All my researches have failed to prove the authenticity of the legend, but I am

3

quite sure that if James existed he deserved hanging, whether or not that was his fate.

It was in the first years of the nineteenth century that my grandfather's grandfather came to Dungair. At that time it was no more than a windy pasture between the moss and the moor. By the terms of his lease he had to bring so many acres under the plough within a term of years and make certain extensions to the steading. Nothing at all has survived of this ancestor beyond the fact that his name was John, that he married a wife by whom he had three sons and that he died in 1831 in the sixty-second year of his age.

Did I say nothing of his personality has survived? I was wrong, for he took in sixty acres from the moss and the moor, manured and ploughed them and gathered ever increasing harvests from them. He died in the middle of October, and his last picture of this earth may have been the stooks row on row in the Home Field, twenty acres of grain where there had been only rashes and heather before he came. The stooks were his memorial, and every fifth year they stood there to his honour, and so will stand as long as harvest comes to Scotland.

John had three sons—Alexander, David and William. David was a good youth, who grew up into a pious man. He was a potter to trade, a great reader in a muddled sort of way and a model to the community in all things. Unfortunately he was left a widow man with one child when he was forty. As there were no unattached female relations available (our family has never bred daughters), David had to engage a housekeeper. Bathia was a rumbustious creature of forty-five who completely altered David's life. She believed in the Church, was a connoisseur of funerals, but she could not be doing with books. David's muddle-headed studiousness and respect-

4

ability appalled her. She set about changing all that. A lot of nasty things were said about her, but I think she had only the best intentions. Anyway, she certainly jazzed up David a bit. First of all she gave little tea-parties. Then porter- and ale-parties. Then they had a grand wedding—at which only the fact that one of the police was best man saved the whole crew from being run in. David's second go of wedded bliss was not exactly one long sweet song, because there were too many mornings after, but he and his good lady certainly did add to the gaiety of the village in which they lived. And David enjoyed it. When anyone spoke of his first wife he used to sigh,—but people were never quite sure that he wasn't thinking of the years he had wasted on her goodness.

William was altogether a simpler case. He was a roisterer from birth. If there was any mischief to do, he did it. If there was blame to be taken, he took it. If there were girls to be kissed, he kissed them. He took no thought for the morrow, but ate and drank and flourished like a sunflower. He was tall, broad and red-faced—a masterful jolly man, fit to be a publican. And a publican he became in a sort of way—at least he also married a widow, and together they ran a discreet little ale-house in a discreet back lane. William was one of his own good customers, and thereby achieved his great distinction, which was half a nose.

It happened this way. William had been drinking all morning with his friend Sandy the butcher, and when Sandy announced that he was going back to the shop to cut up a beast, William insisted on going with him. After the usual amount of drunken argument, they decided that William would hold the beast in position while Sandy hacked it up with the cleaver. They got to work. Unfortunately William's legs were not as steady as they might have been, nor Sandy's aim as accurate. No matter whose was the blame. Sandy fetched the beast a mighty whack with the cleaver, but missed, and sliced off the point of William's nose instead. . . . Sandy was terribly sorry of course, but William always made light of the accident, though his wife used to say that he never looked the same man again.

Alexander was a better man than his brothers. He had the same physical appearance which persists in the family even today—the hard round head covered with thick black hair, the broad shoulders, the deep chest, the rather short legs and the general aspect of an amiable bull. He liked good living, by which I mean dancing, drinking, putting sods on the tops of neighbours' chimneys and courting every pretty girl within ten miles. He was a roistering young man who seemed destined for the Devil, but he had one great passion which gave him a true bearing among the devious ways of his pleasure. He loved Dungair with a constancy and devotion that he never showed towards any human being. He was extravagant ; he was splendidly generous, and he was an indifferent business man, with the result that he was always poor, but no matter who should have to make sacrifices it was never the farm. It would have been easy enough for a husbandman of his skill to have cut down the supply of guano for a year or two without doing any great damage or showing the nakedness of the land. He would far sooner have gone naked himself. Good husbandry was his point of honour—a point cherished to idolatry. It was his religion, perhaps the only religion he ever had. It was his one ideal and he never betrayed it. When he came to die he too left his memorial in the sixty acres he took in from the moss and moor, and in the richness which he had added to John's rather grudging fields. He left more than that, for all his descendants inherited

6

something of his care for his beloved acres. John was the pioneer, but Alexander was the great ancestor. He died in 1878, aged sixty-nine.

I am loth to pass from Alexander, for he is the one member of the family who has had anything of greatness in him. It was not only in his devotion to Dungair that he was great. He could go into any company of men as equal. Remember that he was only a working farmer —not even a bonnet laird—yet he was one of the best-known figures in town. He took his Friday dinner in the Red Lion at the same table as the provost and the dean of guild. He carved his portion from the same joint as men who could have bought and sold a thousand of him, because they respected his craftsmanship in the art of life as much as they enjoyed his broad salt wit which never spared them. Of course life was simpler then. Our town was more intimate, more domestic. A man could find his proper place and be at ease in it. It was the golden age of personality and bred a race of worthies, but none was worthier than Dungair. Take him where you like, he was a whole man. His descendants are only weskits stuffed with straw.

Alexander had six children, four sons and two daughters. There had been five others, but they died in childhood, none of them surviving beyond eight months. They would not have been unduly lamented, for stock-breeding teaches a man to face life and death with a certain realism. Perhaps their mother wept for them a little when she had time. That's what women were for. Susan is a shadowy figure about whom her children had very little to say. She died when she was fifty, being then a little queer, which is not altogether surprising.

Alexander's sons were John, Francis, Simon and George, and his daughters were Jean and Margaret. George, the baby, was a delightful person, a natural of the most

7

engaging kind. If he had been less happy he would have been a poet. As it was, his life was a blameless lyric. He had no inhibitions, no morals and fortunately no great appetites. His passion was animals. Cattle, horses, sheep, pigs, goats and mongrel dogs were all alike his little brothers. Like a wise elder brother he protected them, and like an elder brother he quite frequently thrashed them. But there was no malice in the thrashings and they seemed to have understood it. Certainly he never meant to be cruel—a kinder and more benevolent little man never lived—and if he saw anyone maltreating an animal he became almost homicidal. I never met him, but I have heard so much about him from my grandmother, who loved him and loved to tell me about him, that I feel as if I had known him all my life. He seldom left Dungair, for he was a little shy of strangers, though perfectly self-possessed if he *had* to meet them. He preferred to stay at home, where he was cattleman, singing as he worked in the byre or fraising with the beasts with whom he was on the most familiar terms. His only incursion into society was his attendance at the dancing class held every winter in the smiddy barn. He attended that class for twenty-two years and never managed to learn a step, which was very peculiar, for he often used to dance a minuet to his own whistling when things were going by-ordinary well with him. I rather think he went to the dancing class in order to show off his grey bowler hat of which he was very proud, because he ceased attending the class about the time when a family of mice made their nest in it and he became so devoted to them that he could not bear to turn them out. A lot of people, including his brothers and sisters, thought George was mad. Only his sister-in-law understood that he was beautifully sane. He adored her and was always giving her little presents of flowers. Sometimes, when she had

8

been more than usually kind, his gratitude became embarrassing, as on the day when he presented her with an orphaned hedgehog of an extremely anti-social temper. Of course George had no idea of taking care of himself. One winter night when he was in bed with a cold he became worried about a score of ewes folded up on the moor. He rose at once and, with only a coat over his nightgown, went up to them through the slashing rain. That finished him. He took pneumonia and died in the thirty-ninth year of his age. Everybody mourned for him, especially his elder brother, for he had been a wonderful cattleman and never asked for wages. His sister-in-law mourned for him too, for there were no more flowers, nor any grim unsocial hedgehogs.

Simon was another remarkable character. Like his grandfather he was a pioneer, but in a very different way. He took to learning. Not that he ever became a scholar, but he had ambitions in that direction. He got the same schooling as the others—the privilege of hearing old Mother Kay damn the weather, the crows and himself till he was twelve. Then he was taken home to work on the farm. The good brown earth that the novelists write about took him to herself for twelve hours a day, and after twelve such hours a man had little taste for anything but a chair by the ingle or a walk in the gloaming with a young woman. Yet Simon had the strange impulse to learning in him. Maybe he had the ambition to wag his head in a pulpit ; maybe he wished to be a schoolmaster ; maybe he just wished to know. Whatever it was, he began to study the Latin when he was twenty, struggling with the rudiments at the bothy fire while his companions played the fiddle or told strong country stories. We must feel very humble, we who get our learning handed to us on a silver plate, when we think of Simon sitting down to unravel the vagaries of the subjunctive after

9

twelve hours at the hoe. He could never have hoped for any real reward. His must have been a pure love of learning for itself, without any motives of preferment—unless he was like an old shepherd I once knew who collected terms like '*quantum sufficit*,' '*e pluribus unum*' and '*reductio ad absurdum*' in order to swear the most effectively at his dogs. Simon did not get very far with Latin. At twenty-three he married a wife who taught him that life was real and life was earnest when you had to get meal, milk and potatoes for a family of nine. His brother John helped him into a very small farm, where he spent a laborious life sweetened only by an occasional taste of the wonders of science as revealed in odd corners of the still very occasional newspaper. He was a kindly simple man to whom the world was full of unknown but dimly apprehended mysteries, occluded by a voracious and too self-evident family. He died in 1905, aged fifty, leaving behind eight children who never did much to justify themselves except produce children of the most conventional urban type.

Great-uncle Francis was another family pioneer. He discovered the trust-deed racket which my grandfather was to carry to perfection. His father settled him in a small farm, but did not give him enough capital to make a success even remotely possible. Somehow he managed to carry on for fifteen years until his affairs became so embarrassed that he had to sign a trust-deed on behoof of his creditors. He then found himself cleared of all financial worries, a situation so strange that he died of it. This is all there is to be said about Francis. It required the superior wits of his brother John to see the trust-deed as a perpetual haven of financial rest. Francis died in 1884, aged thirty-nine. His widow married a plumber in Dundee and was never heard or thought of again. He had six children, all of whom went to foreign parts.

Only one, as far as I know, achieved any distinction, he having been bumped-off by an almost famous gangster in a speakeasy in Chicago a few years ago.

My grandfather was the eldest son and inherited many of Alexander's enduring qualities, such as his love for Dungair, his contempt for business, his generosity, his philoprogenitiveness and his short strong figure. When I knew him he was an old man whose sins were coming home to roost on his dauntless shoulders, but they tell me he was a splendid man in his potestatur. When I was a not-so-little boy we used to drive to church every Sunday, the Old Man and I, in a pony and trap drawn by an old white mare. The venerable old gentleman sat high above me on the driving seat, with his antique square hat—something between a bowler and a tile—and his square white beard, a ripe old pagan casting a wise eye over the fields he loved so well and the people he despised so truly. The church-going was a rite which he always honoured, though he held all religion in contempt, and I am sure those Sunday-morning drives through the woods, while the bell sounded so graciously across the shining river, were the pleasantest hours of his life. During the sermon he would lean back in the pew, fold his hands across his stomach and, fixing the evangelist in the south-east window with a hard blue eye, would enjoy in retrospect all the wickedness of his diverting life. When the service was over we went out in the sunlight again, yoked the white mare into the trap and drove home through the woods, while the jingle of the harness mingled so melodiously with the cooing of the pigeons. Every now and then the Old Man would mention some worshipper who had been in church that morning and add a biographical note of which I was too young to understand anything except that it was scandalous. To this day I have never understood why the Old Man went to church, but he may have thought that his presence would be a strong antiseptic against the parish becoming too much infected with religion. On the other hand, church may have been just another place to go to, and he was a great goer-to-places.

He had been a famous figure at fairs and markets since ever he became a man. Any fair or any market came alike to him, but his favourite diversion was the Aulton Market, held in the beginning of November on the glebe of St Machar in Old Aberdeen. The fair was of very great antiquity, and even when I was a child it was one of the leading events of the social year. The war killed it as it killed many other ancient institutions. The last time I saw the Aulton Market there were no more than a dozen horses on the field, and no gingerbread and no whisky tents. How different thirty or forty years ago. Maybe a thousand horses changed hands that day. The whisky tents seethed with roaring drunken crowds. Great piles of gingerbread and chipped apples (a handful a penny) melted off the stalls like snow wreaths in thaw ; roistering farmers staked their shillings in hopeless attempts to find the lady or spot the pea ; fiddlers played reels, pipers piped laments, boxers took on all comers for a guinea and ballad singers made the afternoon hideous with the songs of Scotland. As the evening came on gas flares lit up the lanes between the booths, making the shadows yet more drunken as the wind troubled the flames. The townspeople now came in for their evening's fun—engineers from the shipyards, paper-makers up from the Don and hundreds of redoutable ladies from the Broadford mill. Though the twin spires of St Machar stood raised like pious hands in horror, and though the tower of King's College maintained her aloof communion with the stars, the saturnalia roared and swirled unheeding on the glebe. And in the middle of it all, where the pipers and the singers and the fiddlers were their noisiest, you would find Dungair.

The Aulton Market was the scene of his greatest ploy —certainly of the one which gained the greatest renown. Strangest among the strange creatures attracted to the market was a crazed evangelist known as the Pentecostal Drummer, so named by Dungair because he used to beat a drum at street corners and call on the nations to repentance. Now it so happened that the Pentecostal Drummer had marked down Dungair as a brand specially allotted for him to pluck from the burning. On this particular market-day he took to following him round and round the field, so that as soon as Dungair stopped to have a dram or pass a joke the Pentecostal Drummer pitched his stance at his side and called on him to repent, banging the drum the while. Not only that, but he had a board on which there was a lurid drawing of Hell, and in red letters—'Beware of the Wrath to Come.' No matter where Dungair went he found the board stuck up in his face. There is only a certain amount that a man will stand even at the Aulton Market. Dungair grew so annoyed with the Pentecostal Drummer that he suddenly caught up the board and gave him the weight of the wrath to come full on the top of his head. The Pentecostal Drummer showed fight by aiming a kick at Dungair's stomach, but the Old Man side-stepped, caught the drum in his two hands and brought it down with such force on the Drummer's head that it burst and jammed right over his shoulders. He then gave the Drummer a smart crack over the ankles with his staff, which so alarmed the poor man, blinded as he was by the drum, that he let out a hollow booming yell and set off with a bound, crashing into people right and left, till he finally came to rest in the ruins of a gingerbread stall. Dungair now felt that he had done enough for honour's sake, and left the

Drummer to square matters with the gingerbread woman, after impounding his board as a souvenir. Some time later in the night he made a tour of all his favourite change-houses, bearing the board aloft, like a banner with a strange device. And that was how he came to be known for many years as 'The Wrath to Come.'

My grandfather was thirty when my great-grandfather died. As he inherited the lease of Dungair and the headship of the family, he found himself under the obligation to take a wife. That can have presented no difficulty, for he had already a notable reputation as an empiricist. Within the year he chose the daughter of a neighbouring farmer, obtained favour with her parents and married her. There is no record that she loved him. There was even a legend that she had a romantic passion for a landless youth from the next parish. And yet I am not so sure, for I once heard her confess, half a century later, that he was a braw man in his big black whisker. It was considered a good match, because if a girl got everything else she should not expect fidelity. The strange thing is that however much she had to go without in the hard years to come she always did get fidelity. It is no business of ours what passion there was between them, nor was I ever privy to their tenderness, for embraces are unseemly on old shoulders and they had an inviolate native dignity. She respected even his faults, and he respected the greatness that could respect them. Perhaps there were storms when they were younger, but they were lovely in their age. There was peace in their house when their children left them, and the love with which they cared for me must have sprung from some splendid faith in life, for they were old and could never hope for any reward, nor, as far as I know, did they ever get it.

A few years ago I met an ancient gentleman who used to be our neighbour. He was one of the oldest men I have ever seen, a tiny old man, dried and blanched, like a wand of grass, so that if the north wind had passed over him surely he would have been no more. It was a summer day when I went to see him. He was sitting at the window of a blue sunny room, looking over a small garden full of violas and yellow tea-roses, and warming in the great sun the tiny silver flame of life that still burned in his ancient body. He knew me as soon as he saw me. I might have been the young Dungair of seventy years ago, he said. Then we fell talking of those distant years when he had ridden a horse and danced at weddings. He mentioned my grandmother. 'What was she like as a young woman?' I asked him. 'The handsomest farmer's wife that ever came to town on market-day,' he said, and I'll swear that the life burned stronger far down in his sunken eyes. 'The handsomest wife that ever drove tae market,' he said. We had buried her two months before on a stormy afternoon. We expected few people at the funeral, for we had left Dungair, and the family were scattered beyond the seas, therefore it was a surprise to find how many old men had turned out that day. I thought at the time that they were paying their respects to Dungair and to the family which, the old woman gone, must now be lost forever in the great world. I was grateful to the old men in the antique coats, and strangely proud that I had been part of Dungair. But now that I saw that tiny gleam in the old man's eye, I began to wonder if it were not the pride and beauty of the young wife that had called the old men to her grave after fifty years.

Farmer's Boy

LILIAN BOWES LYON

Man

ONCE you were molten geology, heave and collapse
Of a monster genesis ; once, in the oozy groves
Begotten of ocean, you coined accusative shapes
Who cracked the dusk like an apple in glistening halves.
Once you were shepherds and loved your deliberate lives,
Looked down for advice into wells with limestone lips.

You imposed your will upon clay, cut angry laws
In the simpleton rock, soon yoked the ox-eyed rivers
To turn the mills of your massacred-innocent wars ;
Your cruelties towered as high as the kestrel hovers ;
And yesterday, Earth may sigh, you were pristine lovers,
Whose candour pleased the corrigible stars.

New Earth may sigh for you pressed to the breast of
    Mammon,
For tyrants crowned, the gold and the senile head,
For souls against tingling falls like the spring-bent salmon
Who leap and are hurled back vomiting rainbow blood ;
Your luckier seed shall expound the bewildering dead
Who were enemies locked with a luminous goal in common.

Then burn like stubble ; crash ; tuberculous towns.
You, grim with child, the brood your child may bear,
Daughters of Hesperus, Himalayan sons,
Shall comprehend man's age of brief despair :
Who once adored a moss-green world, aware
Of the slumbering doe and her mild original fawns.

Collected Poems

16

Mr McCrimmon and the Devil

CULLY : I see. Yes. That's very interesting. But, you see, Mr Bolfry, we have got a little away from the conceptions of good and evil that were prevalent in . . . well, in your time. We have rather a different orientation, if you see what I mean.

BOLFRY : I see exactly what you mean. Your generation is not what you call orientated at all. Your scientific gentlemen have robbed you of time and space, and you are all little blind semi-conscious creatures tossing about in a tempest of skim milk. If I may be allowed to say so, it all comes of thinking yourselves a little too good for your priests. You went prancing away from your churches and schoolrooms. And the first thing you did with your emancipated state was to hand yourselves over body and soul to a number of plain-clothes priests whose only qualification was that they were good at sums. That was very foolish of you. [to MORAG] Wasn't it, my dear ?

MORAG : Yes, sir.

BOLFRY : You can't organise and expound the sentient universe simply by being good at sums, can you ?

MORAG : No, sir.

BOLFRY : Just as I thought. And then you found that even sums were a bit too difficult. If you can't do a quadratic equation, all these pages of incomprehensible figures are too much of a strain on simple faith. You went to a new sort of old gentleman who said to you, ' Life, my dear brethren, is one long smutty story.'

' Aha ! ' you said, ' this is a bit of all right. Why wasn't I told this before ? ' But no amount of licentious conversation with serious-looking professors could cure the ache and restlessness in your souls. Could it, my darling ?

MORAG : Whatever you say yourself, sir.

[*He helps himself to another drink*]

BOLFRY : That's an admirable whisky you keep, Mrs McCrimmon.

MRS MCCRIMMON : We only keep it as a medicine. Mr McCrimmon is a teetotaller.

BOLFRY : Everything is a medicine, Mrs McCrimmon. Everybody in this world is sick. Why is everybody in this world sick ? A most profitable line of inquiry. Why are we all sick, Morag ?

MORAG : I think it is because we're all a bit feared of you, Mr Bolfry.

BOLFRY : Feared of me ? Feared of me ? Dear, dear. Come, come. You're not afraid of me, are you, McCrimmon.

MCCRIMMON : Get thee behind me, Satan !

BOLFRY : What did you say ?

MCCRIMMON : Avoid thee. Get thee behind me, Satan !

BOLFRY : Perhaps I should not have allowed you to get within that comfortable ring of chalk. You must not speak to me like that.

MCCRIMMON [*throwing over his chair as he stands up*] : This is nonsensical. It is an evil dream. Presently I will be waking up. What do they call you, sir, you masquerading fiend ?

BOLFRY : I have told you, sir. My name is Bolfry. In the days of sanity and belief it was a name not unknown to men of your cloth.

MCCRIMMON : You are dressed like a minister. Where is your kirk ?

BOLFRY : In Hell.

MCCRIMMON : Are there kirks in Hell ?

18

BOLFRY : Why not ? Would you deny us the consolations of religion ?

McCRIMMON : What I would deny you or grant you is nothing to the point. You are a liar and the father of lies. There cannot be a kirk in Hell.

BOLFRY [*twisting suddenly round to look at the portrait of a clergyman hanging on the wall*] : Who is that ?

McCRIMMON : That is the worthy Doctor Scanderlands of Fetterclash.

BOLFRY : How do you know ?

McCRIMMON : It is an engraving of a portrait taken from the life.

BOLFRY : The portrait was bitten into a plate with acid and printed in ink on paper. The black ink and the white paper were arranged according as the light and shadow fell on the Doctor's face and bands and gown ; so that the Doctor's friends cried in delight, ' It is the very lineaments of the Doctor himself that we behold ! ' Would you recognise it as the Doctor if it were all black ink or white paper ?

McCRIMMON : If you came here, sir, at the back-end of midnight to give us a lecture on the Art of Engraving, I can only observe——

BOLFRY : Keep your herrings for the Loch, and do not drag them across my path. Without this black and that white there would be no form of Doctor Scanderlands that we could see ?

McCRIMMON : Maybe you are right.

BOLFRY : The artist could tell us nothing about the Doctor without them ?

McCRIMMON : He could not.

BOLFRY : And neither you nor I nor anyone else can tell anything about Heaven or Hell, or this very imperfect makeshift of an Earth on which we stand, without our blacks and our whites and our greys, which are whites mixed with black. To put it in simple words, we cannot conceive the Universe except as a pattern of reciprocating opposites, [to MORAG] can we, my love ? No, of course we can't. Therefore when I tell you that there are kirks in Hell, I am telling you something that is at least credible. And I give you my word of honour as a gentleman that it is true.

McCRIMMON : What do you preach in your kirks ?

BOLFRY : Lend me your pulpit and I will show you a specimen.

JEAN : Oh, Uncle Jock, do ! You may never get such a chance again.

McCRIMMON : Sleeping or walking, dream or no dream, I'll have no blasphemy in this parish.

BOLFRY : Blasphemy ? I should never think of committing blasphemy. I think I may say that I know my position better. I am a Duke and a General of Legions. Only gutter devils are impertinent to the Deity. . . . But won't you sit down ?

McCRIMMON [sitting] : I can make nothing of this.

BOLFRY : You disappoint me. You are a Master of Arts. You are a Bachelor of Divinity. You are a theologian and a metaphysician and a scholar of Greek and Hebrew. What is your difficulty ? Don't you believe in the Devil ?

McCRIMMON : He goeth about like a roaring lion.

BOLFRY : Not when I am sober. Answer my question.

McCRIMMON : I believe in a personal devil.

BOLFRY : And in good and evil ?

McCRIMMON : Yes.

BOLFRY : And in Heaven and Hell ?

McCRIMMON : Yes.

BOLFRY : And body and soul ?

McCRIMMON : Yes.

BOLFRY : And life and death ?

20

McCRIMMON : Yes.

BOLFRY : Do you believe in the truth and inspiration of the Bible ?

McCRIMMON : Yes.

BOLFRY : Have you read the Book of Job ?

McCRIMMON : Yes.

BOLFRY : ' Now there was a day when the sons of God came to present themselves before the Lord, and Satan came among them.'

McCRIMMON : The Devil can quote Scripture for his own purpose.

BOLFRY : An entirely suitable purpose in this case. . . . Mr McCrimmon, I believe also in the things of which I have spoken.

McCRIMMON : And tremble.

BOLFRY : Not infrequently. But the point is this : Why, if we hold all these beliefs in common, do you find anything odd in my conversation or my appearance ?

McCRIMMON : I don't know.

BOLFRY : Tuts, tuts, man. Pull yourself together. If the Creator Himself could sit down peacefully and amicably and discuss experimental psychology with the adversary, surely you can follow His example ?

McCRIMMON : Mr Bolfry, or whatever you call yourself, it is plain to me that you could talk the handle off a pump. If you have a message for me, I hope I have enough Highland courtesy to listen to it patiently, but I must ask you to be brief.

BOLFRY : Mr McCrimmon, I am not charged with any message for you. Indeed, I think it will turn out that you and I are in agreement on most essential points. But these young people have summoned me on a cold and dismal night from my extremely warm and comfortable quarters. If you had instructed them properly all this wouldn't have been necessary. But we'll let that pass. Do you mind if we go on from the point at which you rather rudely ordered me to get behind you ?

McCRIMMON : Go on from any point you like. You are whirling about like a Tee-to-tum.

BOLFRY : Highland courtesy, Mr Cully.

McCRIMMON : And keep your tongue off the Highlands.

BOLFRY : Mr McCrimmon, I may be only a Devil, but I am not accustomed to be addressed in that fashion.

JEAN : Mr Bolfry——

BOLFRY : One moment, please [to McCRIMMON]. Unless, sir, you are prepared to exercise a little civility I must decline to continue this discussion.

McCRIMMON : The discussion, sir, is none of my seeking —no more than is your intrusion into my house and family circle. So far as I am concerned, you are completely at liberty to continue or to sneck up.

MRS McCRIMMON : Oh, John ! That's an awful like way to speak to a guest.

McCRIMMON : He is no guest of mine.

BOLFRY : That is true. I am Mr Cully's guest. Why did you send for me, Mr Cully ?

CULLY : I'm blessed if I know, now you come to ask.

BOLFRY : The likeliest reason was that you were unhappy and afraid. These are common complaints in these days. Were you crying for me from the dark ?

JEAN : No. We weren't. My uncle thinks he has got divine authority. And he was using his confidence in that and his learning and his eloquence and his personality to bully us. We wanted a little authority on our side.

BOLFRY : I see. Thank you very much.

JEAN : He's got the advantage of believing everything he says.

BOLFRY : A great advantage.

JEAN : You can't meet a man like that on his own ground if you think he's talking nonsense.

BOLFRY : You can't discuss what brand of green cheese the moon is made of unless you accept the possibility that the moon is made of green cheese. I see. In what *do* you believe, Miss Jean ?

JEAN : I believe that the Kingdom of Heaven is within me.

BOLFRY : Is that all ?

JEAN : That's practically all.

BOLFRY : So far as it goes, you are quite right. But you are also the receptacle of the Kingdom of Hell and of a number of other irrelevances left over in the process of evolution. Until you can reconcile those remarkable elements with one another you will remain unhappy and have the impulse, from time to time, to raise the devil.

JEAN : Then we ought to study these what-do-you-call-'ems—these elements, and try to reconcile them ?

BOLFRY : I didn't say you *ought* to. I said you won't be happy till you do.

JEAN : Then we ought to, oughtn't we ?

BOLFRY : If you want equilibrium. If you want happiness.

CULLY : But surely the pursuit of happiness——

BOLFRY : Yes, yes. The pursuit. A very different thing from catching your electric hare. The happiest man is a general paralytic in Bedlam. Yet you do not envy him. He is in a state of death in life. You naturally prefer life in death—probably because you are used to it. . . . You are not favouring me with much of your attention, Mr Cohen.

COHEN : Sorry, sir.

BOLFRY : Why not ?

23

COHEN : Well, sir, if you want to know the honest truth, I'm bored bloody stiff.

BOLFRY : You say that with an air of some superiority. You must not be proud of being bored stiff. Boredom is a sign of satisfied ignorance, blunted apprehension, crass sympathies, dull understanding, feeble powers of attention and irreclaimable weakness of character. You belie your lively Semitic countenance, Mr Cohen. If you are alive, Mr Cohen, you should be interested in everything—even in the phenomenon of a devil incarnate explaining to you the grand Purpose in virtue of which you live, move and have your breakfast.

COHEN : It's all hooey, that. There's no such thing as a purpose. It's a tele—teleo—teleological fallacy. That's what it is.

BOLFRY : Dear me ! *Dear* me ! Mr McCrimmon, you are an amateur of blasphemy. What do you say to that ?

McCRIMMON : The man is wrong.

BOLFRY : Another point on which we are agreed.

COHEN : I can't help it. I'm entitled to my opinion.

McCRIMMON : In what sort of a world have you been living, man ?

COHEN : In the Borough Road. Do you know it ?

McCRIMMON : Even in the Borough Road, do you find no evidence of eternal purpose ?

COHEN : Not a bit.

BOLFRY : My dear goodness gracious me, I know the place very well, and it's simply bursting with eternal purpose.

McCRIMMON : There's not one brick laid on another, there's not one foot moving past another on the dirty pavement that doesn't tap out ' purpose, purpose, purpose ' to anybody with the ears to hear.

BOLFRY : Every one of your higher faculties is bent to

JAMES BRIDIE

some purpose or other. You can't make anything happen without a purpose. There are things happening all round you on the Borough Road. How in the world do you think they happen without a purpose behind them?

McCRIMMON : Do you deny to your Maker the only respectable faculty you've got?

COHEN : All I can say is, if I've got a Maker and He's got a purpose I can't congratulate Him on the way it works out.

BOLFRY and McCRIMMON [*talking together*] : But my dear good chap, you can't possibly sit there and—— How can you have the presumption to sit there and——

BOLFRY : I beg your pardon.

McCRIMMON : No, no. Excuse me. Please go on.

BOLFRY : Not at all. After you.

McCRIMMON : It is not for you to congratulate or not to congratulate. Who is able to judge the Creator of Heaven and Earth?

CULLY : Well, who is?

COHEN : Yes, who is? Mind, I don't admit there's any such person. But if there is and he give us a critical faculty, we got to use it, see?

JEAN : Conk's absolutely right. You tell us to praise Him. What's the good of praise when you've no chance of blaming? It doesn't mean a thing.

CULLY : What happens to your reciprocating opposites, Mr Bolfry, if we can't be anything but a lot of sanctified Yes Men?

COHEN : Hallelujah all the time. Not much encouragement to the Creator to stick to His job.

JEAN : That's the stuff to give them, Conk! And I thought you were too much the gentleman to open your head.

25

COHEN : No offence meant, of course.

McCRIMMON : Young man, do you realise that your foolish words are jeopardising your immortal souls ?

COHEN : That's all tinky-tonk with me. We ain't got any immortal souls.

BOLFRY : I begin to believe it. Mr McCrimmon, it seems to me we cannot begin our battle for the souls of these persons until they realise that they have souls to battle for.

McCRIMMON : It is terrible indeed. Our duty is plain. We must wrestle with them. We must admonish and exhort them.

BOLFRY : It is my duty no less than yours.

McCRIMMON : But stop you a minute. I know that this is only a dream, but there must be logic, even in dreams. I understand you to say that you are a devil.

BOLFRY : But I am also, like yourself, a servant of One whom I need not name.

McCRIMMON : I am a very distressed man. You must not quibble with me nor use words with double meanings.

BOLFRY : I am bound by my contract with our young exorcist here to tell nothing but the plain truth. My distinguished relative is in the same position as I. I am the same Instrument of Providence as he who smote Job's body with boils for the good of his soul.

McCRIMMON : That is a way of looking at it. Certainly it is a way of looking at it, whatever.

BOLFRY : More than that, if it is of any interest to you, I am an ordained Minister of the Gospel.

McCRIMMON : Do you tell me that ? Where were you ordained.

BOLFRY : In Geneva in 1570.

McCRIMMON : What did you say ?

BOLFRY : In Geneva, I said.

McCRIMMON : But in what year ?

BOLFRY : The year is immaterial. I can't swear to it within two or three years. But ordained I am. And I have preached, among other places, in the High Kirk at North Berwick, to the no small edification of the lieges.

McCRIMMON : Will you swear to that ?

BOLFRY : Mr McCrimmon, my Yea is Yea and my Nay is Nay.

McCRIMMON : It is a most remarkable thing, but from what I have heard from your lips so far, your doctrine appears to be sound.

BOLFRY : None sounder. And now that you are satisfied, I have a proposal to make.

McCRIMMON : What is your proposal ?

BOLFRY : I propose that we adjourn to the adjoining sacred edifice and there admonish and exhort our brothers and sister in a place suitable for these exercises.

McCRIMMON : You mean my kirk ?

BOLFRY : Where else ? Is it not the place most suitable for a conversation ?

McCRIMMON : It is suitable. But all this is very strange.

BOLFRY : All life is very strange. Shall we go ?

McCRIMMON : I cannot enter the kirk in my nightshirt ; though it is true that I have dreamed that same more times than once.

BOLFRY : Go upstairs then and change. I shall wait for you.

McCRIMMON : Well, well. Come with me, Marget. . . . And in case I wake up before I come down again, Mr Bolfry, let me assure you that it has been, upon the whole, a pleasure to meet you. I hope I have not passed the stage of learning . . . even from a—a Being of your—your Nature.

BOLFRY : Sir, you are most polite. I hope to be able to reciprocate the compliment.

[*Exeunt* MR *and* MRS MCCRIMMON, BOLFRY *holding the door open for them*]

JEAN : I never heard the like of that !

BOLFRY [*mildly*] : Of what, my dear ?

JEAN : You're on his *side* !

BOLFRY : What did you expect ?

JEAN : I don't know. I certainly didn't expect such a pious Devil !

BOLFRY : My dear young lady, you don't know everything, as you are very shortly to find out.

JEAN : If you want to know my opinion, I think you're drunk.

BOLFRY : Drunk ? Dear me ! Tut tut, tut tut !

[*He helps himself*]

CULLY : Well, I don't know what you chaps feel, but I'd feel the better of a drink myself.

MORAG : No !

CULLY : What do you mean by No ?

MORAG : Don't leave the circle. He'll get you if you leave the circle.

BOLFRY : She's quite right. Quite right. Quite right. You are a percipient little slut, my darling.

JEAN : But . . . I mean, it's all nonsense . . . but what happens on the way to church ?

BOLFRY : Nothing. Nothing. The Holy Man will protect you. They have their uses, Holy Men. Not that I am really dangerous. But we are mischievous a little, and fond of experiments. Eve and the apple was the first great step in experimental science. But sit down, Mister Gunner Cully. There is plenty of time. Let us continue our delightful conversation. Let me see. Where were we ?

JEAN : Does it matter very much ? You're the most inconsequent character I ever met.

BOLFRY : Oh, no, no. I follow the pattern. If there is

28

one. Perhaps that's what's wrong with you young people. You don't seem to have any pattern. The woof, as it were, is flying loosely about in space. There is no drama about your associations. Now, I am very fond of the Drama. I have done a little bit in that way myself. To my mind the really interesting life is that which moves from situation to situation, with character developing naturally in step with that orderly progress. Now what is the matter with the four of you is that you haven't a situation among you. You are a quartette that has forgotten its music. We must do something about it. Let me see, Mr Cully.

CULLY : Well ?

BOLFRY : Here we have a common soldier who——

CULLY : I'm not a common soldier. I'm in the Royal Artillery.

BOLFRY : Here we have a young intellectual——

CULLY : There's no need to use foul language. Call me what you like, but not that.

BOLFRY : Very well, then. Here we have a product of our universities and public schools. I know I am correct there.

CULLY : How do you know ?

BOLFRY : Because you can't listen patiently and because you have no manners. Here we have this delicately nurtured youth cheerfully bearing the rigours of the barrack and the bivouac. Why ? Has he a secret sorrow ?

CULLY : No, I haven't. And I'm bearing the rigours because I've blooming well got to. I was stuck for a commission on my eyesight, but I'll be in the Pay Corps within a month with any luck. And then goodbye rigours of the barrack and bivouac.

BOLFRY : None the less, an interesting character. A

philosopher. An observer of Life. Obviously the juvenile lead for want of a better.

CULLY : Thank you.

BOLFRY : Don't mention it. There is about him a certain air of mystery which we shall presently resolve. The leading woman, on the other hand, is cast along more stereotyped lines. She is what happens in the third generation after one of the many thousand movements for the emancipation of women. So is Mr Cully, by the way.

JEAN : What in the world do you mean by that ?

BOLFRY : You are only faintly feminine and he only slightly masculine. All these women's movements tend to have a neutralising effect on the human race. Never mind. It will make our little drama interesting to the psychologist, and we are all psychologists nowadays. We come now to what used to be called comic relief.

COHEN : That wouldn't be me, I don't suppose ?

BOLFRY : Yes. There is nothing dramatic about the poor unless they are very funny or very tragic.

COHEN : Wotjer mean by the poor ? I ain't never had a bob I haven't worked for.

BOLFRY : That is what I mean by the poor. As for the extremely charming little person on my right, I haven't decided whether she is funny or not. As she is an unsophisticated savage, she is probably significant of something which will no doubt emerge.

CULLY : What about the minister ?

BOLFRY : He will provide personality. The drama will revolve about him and . . . ah, yes . . . his lady wife. As I had nearly forgotten all about her, she is probably the key to the whole business. There, my dear friends, are the Dramatis Personae. We have now——

COHEN : Where do you come in ?

30

BOLFRY : I am the Devil from the Machine. Here we have our persons in the play. We know very little about them, because, so far, there is nothing much to know. We cannot imitate the old dramatists and describe them as Cully in love with Jean, Conk in love with Morag, Jean in love with Cully, Morag——

MORAG : Now, I am not, Mr Bolfry, no indeed at all. And you needn't be saying it.

JEAN : Nobody's in love with anybody else. Not here, anyhow. Why should they be ?

BOLFRY : The animals went in two by two for a very particular reason. And when a drama has no other especial interest it would be unkind to deny it a love interest. I think the least you can do is to fall in love as quickly as possible. You are wasting time.

JEAN : Except Conk and Morag.

MORAG : Now, Miss Jean ! . . .

COHEN : We told you before we was only talking about budgerigars.

BOLFRY : Budgerigars ! Love birds ! Brilliant images of tenderness and desire with every delicate feather-frond alive with passion ! We taught them speech that they might teach us their mystery. And what did they say : ' Cocky's clever. Cocky's clever. Chirrup, chirrup. Good morning, good evening.' That's all. And yet how much better do you express the primeval urgencies within you ? ' Cully's clever. Jean's clever. Chirrup. Good evening.' I must teach you how to express yourselves better, young enemies of Death. Come then. Why don't you tell Miss Jean what you think of her, Cully? She would be extremely flattered.

JEAN : No, I wouldn't. He told me already what he thinks of me, and I've slapped his face. You're a silly old ass. If you've come here to talk about repressions and inhibited personalities I wish you'd stayed in Hell.

You know perfectly well that if it weren't for inhibitions every living thing on this earth would run down in a few minutes.

BOLFRY : Of course it would. And how shockingly you misunderstand me. I love repression. You repress your passion to intensify it ; to have it more abundantly ; to joy in its abundance. The prisoner cannot leap to lose his chains unless he has been chained.

JEAN : Then what *are* you talking about ?

BOLFRY : About you. Come. I'll marry you.

JEAN : But I don't want to marry you.

BOLFRY : No, no. I mean, I'll marry Cully and you. I'll bind you by the strongest and most solemn contract ever forged in heaven. Think of the agonising fun and excitement you'll have in breaking it.

JEAN : No. Thank you very much.

BOLFRY : But why don't you do something ? Why is the blood galloping through your not unsightly limbs ? Why are the nerve cells snapping and flashing in your head if you are to wrap this gift of life in a napkin and bury it in a back garden ?

JEAN : We are doing something.

BOLFRY : Indeed ?

JEAN : We're fighting Hitler.

BOLFRY : And who is Hitler ?

COHEN : Blind me, I'd 've thought if anybody knew the old basket it 'd be you.

CULLY : Do you mean to tell me that we've all gone to the trouble of fetching a damned medieval hypothesis out of Hell to tell us what life is all about, and now we have to tell *him* ?

JEAN : Mr Bolfry, dearest, Hitler is the man who started the War.

BOLFRY : Is he ? I thought I had done that. How is the War getting on ? . . . No. Don't tell me. I'll try to

32

guess. [BOLFRY *helps himself to another drink*] I should think some lunatic has been able to persuade his country that it is possible to regiment mankind. I should think the people he has persuaded are my old friends the Germans. They are sufficiently orderly and sufficiently stupid so to be persuaded. I should conjecture that mankind has risen in an intense state of indignation at the bare possibility of being regimented. I should think that the regimenters will succeed in hammering their enemies into some sort of cohesion. Mankind will then roll them in mud for a bit and then pull them out and forget all about them. They will have much more interesting things to attend to—such as making money and making love. . . .

Plays for Plain People (*Mr Bolfry*)

SYDNEY GOODSIR SMITH

Hallowe'en 1943

RIN and rout, rin and rout,
Mahoun gars us birl about,
He skirls his pipes, he stamps his heel,
The globe spins wud in a haliket reel.

There, the statesman's silken cheats,
Here, the bairnless mither greits ;
There, a tyrant turns the screw,
Here, twa luvers' broken vous.

Enemies out, enemies in,
Truth a hure wi the pox gane blind,
Nou luvers' lips deny luve's name
And get for breid a chuckie-stane.

We kenna hert, we kenna heid,
The deevil's thirled baith quick and deid,
Jehovah snores and Christ himsel
Lowps in the airms o Jezebel.

The sweit that rins frae his thornit brou
Is black as the standan teats o his cou,
In the waltz o tears, and daith and lies
Juliet's fyled wi harlotries.

Ay, luve itsel at Hornie's lauch
Skeers like a candle in the draucht,
The dance is on, the waltz o hell,
 - The wind frae its fleean skirts is snell.

gar, cause to *birl*, spin *wud*, mad *haliket*, giddy, wild *greit*, weep
thirled, enslaved, enthralled *Skeers*, shies *snell*, bitterly cold

It whips black storm frae lochan's calm,
Sets banshees in the house o dwaum,
Gars black bluid spate the hert o me
—And waters guid sirs' barley bree !

A wheen damned feckless fanatics
Wad halt the borneheid dance o Styx,
Their cry o truth the whirlwind reaps—
For pity's drunk and mercy sleeps.

Orpheus alane dow sauve frae deid
His ravished Bride gin but she'd heed—
Ay, truth and luve like Albyn's life
Hing wi a threid, kissed by a knife.

Nichtlie, owre some huddered toun
The pipes and fiddles screich and boom—
The chaudron's steered by Maestro Nick
Wi a sanct's hoch-bane for parritch-stick.

He lauchs his lauch, the angels greit
Wi joy as they dine on carrion meat ;
Ablow, bumbazed dumfounered cods,
We seek the sternes in dubs and bogs.

Our ingyne's deaved, our mous are shut,
Our saul contract like a runkled nut,
Een canna see the trees for the wuid
And hert's gane dreich for want o bluid.

For want o luve we live on hate,
For want o hevin praise the State,
For want o richts we worship rules,
For want o gods the glibbest fules.

dwaum, dream *barley bree*, whisky *wheen*, few *borneheid*, headlong
dow, can *huddered*, huddled *hoch-bane*, thigh-bone *bumbazed*, bewildered
cods, fellows *sternes*, stars *dubs*, gutters *ingyne*, mind, intelligence
deaved, deafened

Obey, obey ! Ye maunna spier !
(Libertie's forjeskit lear !)
While Cloutie pipes it's crime to think,
—It's taxed e'en hiecher nor the drink !

O rin and rout, we birl about
Til the rhythm o the Deil's jack-boot,
Black as auld widdie-fruit, Mahoun
Bestrides a kenless mapamound.

The Deevil's Waltz

spier, inquire, ask   *forjeskit*, broken down, jaded   *lear*, custom, knowledge
widdie, gallows

Spleen

STEIR bogle, squat bogle,
Bogle o sweirness and stuporie ;
Wersh bogle, wae bogle,
Bogle o drumlie apathie ;
Thae twa haud this fule in duress—
Malancolie, Idleness.

In duress vile, ye muckle fule,
Cock o your midden o sloth and stour,
Geck o the yill and a restless saul
I dwaum like a convict, dowf and dour
As the runt o a riven aik
Whar ghouls can sit or their hurdies ache.

Steir, fat *sweirness*, tediousness, laziness *wersh*, insipid *stour*, dust
Geck, fool, victim of trick *yill*, ale *dowf*, listless, torpid *aik*, oak
hurdies, backside

The westlins sun, reid owre The Gowf,
Fluids aa the Links wi glamorie,
I sit wi my bogles dour and dowf,
Idleness and Malancolie ;
Like a braw new pennie Sol dwynes doun
Fou like my hert—but the saul tuim.

The Deevil's Waltz

dwyne, waste away   *Fou*, full   *tuim*, empty

BRUCE MARSHALL

A Day with Mr Migou

Migou would have preferred to go alone with his wife to Odette's first communion, but Mademoiselle Turbigo and her mother insisted on coming too because first communions were so pretty, so they said. Madame Migou wore her best black satin dress and the fox fur for which she had been inveigled by the advertisements in the underground into paying twelve monthly instalments of seventy-five francs, and Migou wore his new black suit, or at least it had been new ten years ago. Madame Turbigo was wearing her best clothes too, and Mademoiselle Turbigo herself was dressed up to the nines as usual, but of course she wasn't wearing her best clothes because all her clothes were best clothes nowadays now that Monsieur Frimandière of the Société Anonyme Frimandière was her lover.

Maco and Lalus waved them off, and Maco said that they must be sure and look in at the café and have a snifter when the ceremony was over. It was a fine day, and above their heads the sky stretched, blue and silken, like Mary's girdle. The pavements were full of little girls in white going to their first communion at the chapel of Sainte-Geneviève. The flutter of their veils smeared the world with new hints of Christ, and even those who had lost their faith looked at them with a tender smile. Migou walked with a self-conscious air and wished that Marie's new shoes wouldn't squeak so much, but he soon grew accustomed to his new feeling of importance because there were plenty other self-conscious looking men about with wives and squeaking shoes. Odette walked with her prayer-book firmly in her hand and with her head demurely lowered.

There was a terrific jam in the church because all the front seats had been reserved for the communicants, and the parents and friends had to hugger-mugger together at the back. A mincing cleric in surplice and cassock ushered Madame Migou and Migou and Mademoiselle Turbigo and her mother all into a row together, and smiled at them with sickly insistence as though to say, ' I'm not really as holy as you think I am, and I know you're not really as worldly as you pretend you are.' Migou knelt and tried to pray when he saw that Marie and Mademoiselle Turbigo and her mother were also kneeling and trying to pray, but a woman came side-stepping along the kneeling cushion and jabbed him in the stomach with the ferrule of her umbrella, so he had to begin all over again. It was a long time since he had prayed and he started off on the first prayer he could remember, ' Hail, Holy Queen, Mother of Mercy, hail,' but when he got a little way he found that he had for-gotten the words so he prayed instead, ' Make Odette a good girl, not too religious, but make her a good girl ; make Marie well again ; and make me soon earn more money.' Then he sat upright and saw that, although Madame Turbigo was sitting upright too and was gazing at the rest of the congregation with beady, birdy curiosity, Marie and Mademoiselle Turbigo were still praying, with their faces jammed right down on top of their arms almost as though they were weeping. Migou wondered if Marie was praying that she wouldn't die, but of course she wasn't going to die because she had been looking so much better of late, and had been able to get through the week's washing in a single day instead of two days like this time last year ; but he couldn't understand what Mademoiselle Turbigo had to pray about, because she couldn't very well wish for a richer lover than she had.

The lame priest who lived above the bakery limped

in to say the mass in stiff white shining vestments. The children in front all knelt down for the *Judica me, Deus* and the *Confiteor*, but most of the parents stood up because they didn't wish to look too pious in front of their friends. When the celebrant had read the gospel the abbé Pécher entered the pulpit to preach the sermon. He was a tall, thin, emaciated, ill-looking priest who loved God a lot. Migou knew him well by sight, because he was always scurrying about the district in his cassock, taking off his hat as politely to those who didn't go to mass as to those who did.

This was a great day in the life of those children who were going to receive the Body of Christ for the first time, the priest said, turning his sore, lighted eyes on the parents as though trying to make them love God too. It was a great miracle which God wrought each time that a priest consecrated the Host at mass, because He poured Himself Body, Soul and Divinity into the species of bread and wine, and was as truly present on the altar as He had been on Calvary. If men and women could only realise this beautiful truth, was it too much to hope that social unrest and wars might one day cease ? In Germany Hitler had given a wrong creed to youth, and youth had lapped it up and become strong and purposeful. If the children of France would only besiege the altar rails it was certain that French youth would become stronger and more purposeful than German youth, because God was very much more powerful than Hitler. We must also remember that in the Eucharist God slaked his thirst for us as well as we our love for God. The priest preached on with enthusiasm for a little, and then began to repeat himself wearily as though despairing of making the people understand. Then he stopped and held his lined sad face over the boys and girls as though praying that Christ would cool them. Then he made the sign of the

Cross high over the congregation and vanished into the sacristy.

The mass went on. The priest who lived above the bakery prayed with Peter and Paul, with Clement, Xystus, Cornelius, Cyprian and Lawrence. God smote Himself down into the Host, and His precious blood welled up in the chalice, and the sacring bell rang out and the hen choir in the organ loft bleated, ' *Benedictus qui venit in nomine Domini.*' At the *Agnus Dei* Migou had to bury his face in his hands so as to hide the tears. He remembered his own first communion and how he had sworn that no matter how much his friends laughed at him he would serve God for ever, and he remembered how he had failed. By the time the sacring bell rang out again for the *Domine, non sum dignus,* he was blubbering away in ecstasy, and swearing that he would never lie, cheat or look lewdly at women again. ' *Corpus Domini Nostri Jesu Christi custodiat animam tuam in vitam aeternam* ' he heard the priest say over and over again as he passed and repassed along the altar rails laying the frail flake of God on the tongues of the kneeling children, but he was unable to look up in case people would see that he had been weeping. When at last he raised his head the communion was over, and the priest was back at the altar and the candle flames had blurred to shafts of gold through the haze of his tears.

He still felt humble and good and pious as he stood in the street afterwards and kissed Odette because she had just made her first communion, and he was surprised to see that his wife and Mademoiselle Turbigo and her mother had been weeping too. Perhaps down in themselves everybody wanted to love God and be pure and brave and kind, and were deterred only because they were silly and afraid that other people might think them silly if they tried. After all, it was just as likely that the

world was ' about ' loving God and being pure and brave
and kind as ' about ' aeroplanes and cinemas and wireless
sets and book-keeping and central-heating systems.

They were all rather subdued as they walked back down
to the Boulevard Exelmans towards Maco's café, but
Maco's red face was as unconverted as ever above his
waistcoat as he stood behind his counter arguing the toss
with Lalus, who had just dropped in for a quick one in
between diddling customers. ' So everything went off
all right ? ' he shouted at them through the doorway, and
came out on to the terrace to serve them with drinks. A
cluster of concierges gathered round Odette and began to
congratulate her on her first communion. Odette stood
gravely and showed them her new prayer-book and
communion card. The concierges made a great clatter
about how beautiful Odette was and about how beautiful
the Blessèd Virgin was, and then went back to their
kitchens to peel potatoes.

Migou and his wife had intended asking only Mademoiselle Turbigo and her mother back to lunch, but Maco
was so generous with the drinks that they felt they had
to ask him too, and then Lalus kept hanging about so
they had to ask him as well. And then as they were
about to leave the café Verneuil, who had just finished an
early shift on his bus, came along with Piquemelle, who
had been too badly smashed up in the war to work at all,
and of course they had to ask them also. Madame Migou
said that she was afraid that she mightn't have enough for
them all to eat, but Maco said that that wouldn't matter
at all, and Verneuil said that as long as there was plenty
to drink that was all that mattered to him. Migou felt
rather proud being seen crossing the avenue with Maco
and Lalus, because they were so much wealthier than he
was and had motor cars in which they drove their fat
hams of wives out to Fontainebleau on Sundays, but he

was also pleased that he had the grace of God back, golden
and bubbly within him, and wasn't ever going to want to
commit adultery again, and he knew that it wasn't just
drink but because he had seen his own daughter, flesh of
his flesh, make her first communion. Madame Lacordaire
and Lacordaire, who was home for his lunch from his
morning sail down the city's sewers, were standing about
in the entrance and looked as though they wanted to be
invited too, but Madame Migou pretended not to notice
because she knew she wouldn't have enough plates to go
round.

Maco and Lalus were already pretty well stewed, and
they put their arms round one another's necks and sang
as they took a good look at the legs of the yellow tart
who was going up the stairs in front of them.

Quand un pompier rencontre un autre pompier ça fait deux pompiers,

Maco sang.

*Quand deux pompiers rencontrent un autre pompier ça fait trois
pompiers,*

Lalus sang.

> *Quand un vicomt-e*
> *Rencontre un autre vicomt-e*
> *Ils se racont-ent*
> *Des histoires de vicomt-e,*

Maco sang.

But behind them again Piquemelle, climbing the stair
on Verneuil's arm, was prophetic and serious.

' One of these fine days France is going to pay for the
selfishness of Frenchmen and for her unwillingness to
think logically,' he said.

Migou, bringing up the rear with Odette, wondered
what the child, who had just received the Body of Christ
for the first time, must make of Maco's and Lalus'

43

hilarity. His soul still shining with zeal, he wanted to shout at them to shut up and to tell them that this was a holy day because Odette had just made a vow to love God and to keep His commandments, but he knew that he couldn't do so without being guilty of the solecism of asserting that religion was true outside church as well as inside.

They all crowded into the tiny flat and stood about, making it seem tinier. While Marie was hunting out extra plates Migou poured vermouth for his guests. Odette moved among them in her white dress, gravely showing her prayer-book and her communion card. Some nodded at her absent-mindedly, and some came back from their potations to be little again and to walk for a flicker with Christ. Migou could not read from her eyes whether the child was loving Jesus because she had a sacrament in her soul or because she was wearing a pretty dress. On the communion card Our Lady looked like Lilian Gish, and had round her head a printed hoop which said that she was the Immaculate Conception.

Before they sat down to eat the gentlemen asked if they might put themselves at their ease, which meant that they took off their jackets and put on their caps. There weren't enough chairs to go round so Migou sat on the bed. Maco said he would sit on the bed if Mademoiselle Turbigo sat on the bed with him, but the yellow tart said that she would be afraid to risk her virtue, at which there was general laughter. The first course was hors-d'œuvres variés, and all the guests heaped their plates with slodging great helpings of sardines, anchovies, shrimps, olives, potato salad, herrings, Russian salad, beetroot, meat paste and œufs durs mayonnaise. Napkins were tucked under collars and bodices, and knives seized half-way down the handles as though they were entrenching tools. Migou was sad at the thought of the money the feast was costing him, but he soon worried no longer when he caught sight of Marie's friendly face.

'It's funny, this God business,' Verneuil said. 'Everything evolved from mud so there's no God.' Odette looked sadly up from her plate.

'I'd like there to be Our Lady all the same,' she said.

Migou was so shocked that he dared to be angry. 'Of course there's a God,' he said, stretching across to the table and patting the child's hand. 'Don't you worry about that. You've only to look at the stars at night to understand.'

'Our friend Migou's becoming a parson,' Maco mocked.

'There are parsons and parsons,' Migou declared with a courage which was not due wholly to the wine he had drunk. 'And the abbé Pécher's as good a parson as any in France, and what's more he preached a very good sermon this morning. And after all what the priests say about loving your neighbour is only common sense. If we all loved our neighbours there'd be no wars. Just think of how we all try to do our landlords down, for example, leaving the light on in the stairs so that they have to pay more money. Now if we were as careful of our landlord's property as our own our landlords might be kinder to us and reduce the rent. And then if we were to try the same thing on an international scale . . .' Conscious that he had never made such a long speech in front of Maco and Lalus before, Migou broke off unhappily.

'There'll always be wars,' Piquemelle said out of his sore sightless eyes. 'There'll always be wars for the same reason as we never learned the truth about Stavisky : human nature. And one of these four mornings there's going to be a very big war indeed.'

'There's the Maginot Line all the same,' Maco said,

sloodging a great gush of wine over a mouthful of food. 'We're as safe as houses behind that.'

'There are twice as many German babies born every year as there are French babies,' Piquemelle said.

'There's the Maginot Line, I tell you, and then there's always England,' Maco said.

'I fought in one war and I'm not going to fight in another,' Verneuil said. 'The next time the strafing begins I'm doing a bunk.'

'Oh, no you won't,' Migou said. 'You'll " march, child of the fatherland, that no impure race may feed on the furrows of our fields." '

'All that's stupid,' Lalus said. 'For one thing Hitler hasn't got the mass of the German people behind him, although of course they've got to pretend that they're behind him. And there are too many Germans alive who know what war is.'

'I think war's terrible,' Madame Turbigo said.

'There oughtn't really to be any wars after what Jesus said, ought there ? ' Odette said.

'What France needs more than anything else is discipline,' Piquemelle said.

But this was a hard saying and nobody could bear it, so they all scowled a little at Piquemelle even although he had been so terribly wounded for France, and shook their heads in commiseration.

> *Si demain tu vois ma tant-e*
> *Compliment-e-*
> *La de ma part.*

Maco sang to change the subject.

The next course was roast mutton plugged with garlic. Everybody began to smell like acetylene lamps, although as they all smelt together nobody smelt anybody else.

Maco ate more noisily than anybody else, pronging great slices of meat on to his fork and ramming them into his mouth with a flourish, and washing them down with gigantic gulps of wine. Everybody talked with their mouths full and nobody listened. Odette alone was silent, picking her meat with grave endeavour. Migou wondered if she were wondering what this bibbing and gluttony had to do with loving Him Whose kingdom was not of this world, but when the coffee and the liqueurs were served and she slid silently from the room he was too imbecilically drunk himself to wonder about anything at all.

Maco ripped open his waistcoat. Through a gap in his shirt his distended belly bulged out like the inside of a football.

' Life's lovely all the same,' he said.

' There's only one thing I need and that's to win the big prize in the lottery,' Verneuil said.

' If I won I'd buy a yacht,' Maco said.

' There's no two ways about it,' Lalus said. ' When one wins one must be discreet. One mustn't be like Bonhoure and run off with one's ticket to the Pavillon de Flore the day the result of the draw's announced. When I win I'll get the bank to cash my ticket for me. Like that I won't have a lot of camels queueing up outside the shop to cadge on me.'

' If I win I'll say " *merde* " to the managing director of the Société des Transports en Commun de la Région Parisienne,' Verneuil said. ' And I'll never do another stroke of work as long as I live.'

' And if I won I'd send you to Switzerland,' Migou said, smiling at the familiar tender face of his wife.

' And if I win I'll buy a new wireless set,' Madame Turbigo said. ' Something that makes a noise.'

' That's another thing that's ruining France,' Piquemelle

said. ' The philosophy of facility. And then to be sure of winning you'd have to live for thirty-six thousand six hundred and sixty-six years and take a ticket in every draw.'

' That's nonsense,' Maco said. ' Monsieur Bonhoure won the first time he took a ticket.'

Piquemelle didn't answer, but everybody could see that he was annoyed. Migou began to feel sorry that he had invited him, because although he respected him for his wounds he really was a gloomy fellow with all his talk of another war. Lalus started boasting that he could still make love to three girls one after another provided they were pretty enough. With the remnants of his new zeal Migou tried not to listen, but the wine he had drunk was stronger and he was soon laughing as loudly as the rest. Down on the terrace of Maco's café he could hear the guffaws of other parents celebrating their children's union with God. He emptied his liqueur glass and tipped himself our some more brandy. All was for the best in the best of worlds ; it was the month of May, the month of Mary.

Yellow Tapers for Paris

ANDREW YOUNG

The Paps of Jura

BEFORE I crossed the sound
    I saw how from the sea
These breasts rise soft and round,
    Not two but three ;

Now, climbing, I clasp rocks
    Storm-shattered and sharp-edged,
Grey ptarmigan their flocks,
    With starved moss wedged ;

And mist like hair hangs over
    One barren breast and me,
Who climb, a desperate lover,
    With hand and knee.

The White Blackbird

Hard Frost

FROST called to water ' Halt ! '
And crusted the moist snow with sparkling salt ;
Brooks, their own bridges, stop,
And icicles in long stalactites drop,
And tench in water-holes
Lurk under gluey glass like fish in bowls.

In the hard-rutted lane
At every footstep breaks a brittle pane,
And tinkling trees ice-bound,
Changed into weeping willows, sweep the ground ;
Dead boughs take root in ponds
And ferns on windows shoot their ghostly fronds.

But vainly the fierce frost
Interns poor fish, ranks trees in an armed host,
Hangs daggers from house-eaves
And on the windows ferny ambush weaves ;
In the long war grown warmer
The sun will strike him dead and strip his armour.

The Green Man

The Fear

How often I turn round
To face the beast that bound by bound
Leaps on me from behind,
Only to see a bough that heaves
With sudden gust of wind
Or blackbird raking withered leaves.

A dog may find me out
Or badger toss a white-lined snout ;
And one day as I softly trod
Looking for nothing stranger than
A fox or stoat I met a man
And even that seemed not too odd.

And yet in any place I go
I watch and listen as all creatures do
For what I cannot see or hear,
For something warns me everywhere
That even in my land of birth
I trespass on the earth.

The White Blackbird

F FRASER DARLING

The Atlantic Seal

THE Atlantic seal feeds largely on rock fish such as saithe, pollack or lythe, and on some crustaceans. Therefore it is a coastal species, though not of the inner sheltered coasts as is *Phoca vitulina*. Wherever there are skerries round which the rock fishes live, there a seal takes his place for the summer, fishing diligently and eating far more fish than is needed to provide the energy he is using. This is the time when the animals are laying on fat underneath the skin, probably a hundredweight and a half of soft fat. Lighthousemen report them from the Flannans, Dhu Artach and Skerryvore, from Cape Wrath, Stoer and Rudh' Re, from the Butt of Lewis and Barra Head, and all remark on the fact that they normally disappear in August.

If the observer is at a breeding station, say Rona or Treshnish, in June, he will not find the place deserted. Some seals, both young and adult, will be found feeding round the islands. My own estimate is that about 10 per cent of the population remains to harvest the fish of the immediate neighbourhood of the breeding ground. There is, perhaps, a disproportionate number of yearlings, but it cannot be said at all that yearlings do not migrate, for the appearance of these about West Highland coasts farther inshore and in more sheltered waters than the adults is a noticeable phenomenon in late spring. Their faded coats are yellowy-fawn in colour and they are not unlike the common seal in size and appearance. Their habits nearly approach these of the common seal at this time, and it is mostly these yearlings (eight to nine months old) which cause the trouble in the salmon bag nets.

51

Some or possibly all of these migrant yearlings do not come back to the breeding ground in the first season, a habit comparable with that of some birds that take more than one year to come to maturity. Different colonies vary in the number of yearlings to be seen in the breeding season. There were a few on Rona, none at Lunga of the Treshnish and many at Oronsay. It would appear that at each nursery there are conditions or traditions influencing movements and age-groupings to be seen during the autumn breeding season. These influences are not yet known. Exactly the same state of affairs may be observed at Britain's gannetries, and the parallelism between the sea birds and seals in this and other respects is a matter for the naturalist's wonder.

The observer on the nursery islands from July onwards sees the number of seals gradually increasing. They begin to spend more time out of the water in August, but not on the main mass of the island as yet. Both at the Treshnish Isles and at North Rona there are certain skerries favoured by the immigrant seals, and it is on these they gather, lying hauled out in close groups. The adult bulls tend to have a rock of their own where they almost overlap each other in their slumbers—and still there is no quarrelling. There are many bulls to be seen as well among the increasing numbers of cows on these resting rocks. Cows are more quarrelsome and more vocal than the bulls, but they pack close all the same. A certain number of yellow yearlings haul out on some rocks, but other skerries are frequented wholly by adults, and it is at these latter places that it is possible to make accurate counts of the increase of numbers through late summer. Here is a typical example from Rona, the counts being made during the afternoon each day, at which time lying-out is common :

On 14th August—56 ; 15th—72 ; 16th—103 ; spell of

52

rough weather during which the rocks were untenable ; 26th—170.

The annual association of the seals with the land is their time of greatest danger. There is possible danger of predatory animals, including man, to an animal whose activity is much curtailed by being ashore ; there is the danger of the licking surf and the equinoctial spring tides to the young calves, and the very massing of the beasts produces quarrelsome behaviour which may bring casualties. The social system of the seals, as well as their metabolism, has become finely adapted to lessening this danger—and the preliminary resting period on the outlying skerries observed at two widely differing nurseries is in line with this axiom. The animals certainly quarrel on these rocks, but not seriously, and as no territorial behaviour is shown they are able to mass close together.

This resting period finishes at the end of August and now the adult bulls begin to come ashore to the breeding grounds. It is amazing to see the climbing power of these 9-foot and 6–7-cwt. animals. There is great gripping strength in their hands, which hold on while their belly muscles contract and expand as they heave themselves upward and forward. The bulls take up their chosen places and lie quiet there. Preferably they lie by a shallow pool of water, which becomes more or less the centre of their territory and is the place where coition occurs later. Now the Treshnish Isles are volcanic in origin, with sheer cliffs falling to erosion platforms at approximately sea level. These shelves of lava are the breeding ground of the seals. The animals cannot get far away from the sea and we find the territories of the bulls set in linear fashion along the coast. Rona is cliff-bound, and an immense swell makes the sea's edge a dangerous place. The seals of Rona come farther inland and stay there without frequent return to the sea. The bulls come as far as 300–400 yards from the water and as high as 300 feet above it. The plan of the territories, therefore, is not linear as on the Treshnish, but like a honeycomb or draught-board.

Cows come into the territories from the sea two to five days before calving, and the number of seals ashore increases throughout September. On one strip of shore on the Treshnish Isles where the first bull took up his territory on 28th August, numbers grew from two on that date to seventy-eight on 15th September. The cows leave first for the sea as the breeding season declines, and once more the seals are found on the resting rocks, lying in close masses. There they lie like empty bags during late November and December, changing their coats, and it is not until this is completed that the seals return to the sea and leave the breeding island for the feeding areas once more.

Let us look closer at the life of the seals on the breeding territories and nursery grounds. There are many more adult bulls on Rona than can immediately take up territories. These animals lie on the rocks at a place where there is most traffic up to the territories, and this traffic tends to be up accepted tracks which give easiest access. This bull rock may be called the reservoir, for five hundred bulls can be seen there, and the cows stay among them a short time before going up to calve. No challenging behaviour is to be seen at the reservoir, which is strictly neutral ground.

The bulls inland in possession of territories will not trouble each other much either. Challenge comes from fresh bulls emerging from the sea and working their way up from the reservoir. Sometimes the sight of the possessor is enough to deter the new bull, but if not the two will indulge in a primary display of weapons, comparable with the challenging display of stags. The bull rolls over from side to side, turning his head sideways in the direction of the roll, opening his mouth and raising his hand. The canine teeth on each side and the powerful claws are thus shown to the opponent. An Atlantic bull seal has such a large development of muscle and foreface that the canines cannot be seen head-on. The limit of challenging behaviour is when the bulls come muzzle to muzzle, heads raised. If that does not suffice there is a fight with teeth and claws. Great rips may be made in the hide, and once started the fight goes on for some minutes until both appear seriously wounded. As mentioned in the chapter on the red deer, such biological wastage is unusual. Sabre-rattling is cheaper. Defeated bulls or spent ones return to the reservoir and there all challenging behaviour is set aside. Here again the comparison with the stags is close.

When a bull comes ashore for the breeding season he is very fat, extraordinarily fat, yet he looks what he is, as fit as a fiddle. He has now had his last meal for a month or two, and I would not be surprised to find after further observation that he may go three months without a square meal, for he will not go to sea again permanently until he has changed his coat on the resting rocks. He now begins to live on his blubber and gradually loses condition. This is the position on Rona, but on the Treshnish where the animals are nearer the sea the bull will spend many hours in the water opposite his territory, gently patrolling the length of it. All the same, I do not think the Treshnish bulls feed though they are in the water. The inland territories of Rona are not kept by the same bull from beginning to end of the breeding season ; there is always the traffic up of fresh bulls and down of spent ones, and it is probable that each territory has a succession of three of four bulls, between 28th August and 15th October, though there is little change in the first fortnight. I cannot be certain that some of these spent bulls do not return to the territories again, just as a stag will come down from the resting neutral corrie, but I do not think they do.

Atlantic seals are polygamous, each bull having four or five cows. If the sex ratio is near equality at birth and there is a slightly heavier mortality in the males thereafter, the adult stock of a polygamous species still appears to have a large excess of males. But assuming a succession of three of four bulls in the territories and the normal harem as being four or five cows, almost all of the adult bull population will be in service some time or other during the season, and the apparent excess of males at any one time is no true indicator of the situation for the season as a whole.

The cows are free to go wherever they like. Sexually they belong to the bull in whose territory they may happen to be at any one moment. This is unlike the social system of the Alaskan fur seal and of the elephant seal (*Macrorhinus angustirostris*), each of which species collects a harem of up to sixty cows, and the harems are herded by the bulls. I am told that although quarrelsomeness is not common between the cows the actual crowding and dynamic activity of the bulls are responsible for casualties among the young, and two ardent bulls have been known to pull a cow in two. This type of rutting behaviour which makes for a large surplus of bulls hanging about on the outskirts of the breeding ground, and is associated with great disparity in size between bulls and cows, is biologically wasteful, especially so when the eager bulls reach the extreme of injuring cows. Bertram (1940) has drawn attention to this correlation between the size of bull and size of harem. In the Atlantic seal the harem number is low and the difference in size between sexes, though marked, is not extraordinary. A big bull may measure nine feet and an adult cow is very generally six feet long. A cow weighs between three and four hundredweight.

The Atlantic bull seal within his territory is not extraordinarily active among his few cows. They are within an area possibly ten yards square and the cows are jealous and quarrelsome. Were they crowded closer than this injury to the calves might be serious and much commoner. The matings take place eleven to fourteen days after the birth of the calf. Coition usually occurs ashore, preferably in a shallow pool, but the bare rock or the open sea may be used. The bull, then, has been ashore at least three weeks without any cow having been in season. During all this time he has been ready to fight for his territory in which sexual satisfaction has not been obtainable. The north end of Rona is by this time—the latter end of September, completely invaded by the seals, and some have climbed a very steep hillside to the top of the ridge. I once saw a cow seal heavy in calf half-way up the west cliffs of Rona, where they were about 150 feet high and at an angle of 45 degrees. Had it not been bare, rough, stable rock she could never have finished her climb. Another calf was successfully reared at the edge of the 300-foot sheer column of the western cliff. Professor D'Arcy Thompson has told me that he once came on an Alaskan fur seal bull at the summit of a hill about 2,000 feet high.

All these cows ashore in the territories of Rona were ones with a calf or about to calve, and all the bulls were adults with territories or seeking them. Now it was indicated a little earlier in this chapter that the social system of the seals was finely adapted for lessening the danger from their association with the land. In 1937, on the Treshnish Isles, I had been surprised to find that no maiden cows came ashore for breeding on the island where we were encamped, and there were no immature animals to be seen either. It was a puzzle circumstances did not allow me to solve at that time. But on Rona there is no maze of little islets and skerries ; the observer can see almost everything to do with the seals from the island itself. I found that the maiden cows collected on the large flat skerry, Loba Sgeir,[1] at the south-west corner of the island, and a few were to be seen among the reservoir of bulls on Leac Mor Fianuis. There was a large number of bulls on Loba Sgeir, mostly young adults, and that was where the mating of the maiden and the barren cows took place. This flat skerry is practically always safe for the seals because it is ringed by a very bad surf, but it would not serve as a place for the calf to be born on, for the sea washed right over it in really bad gales. It was observed that no breeding territories were apparent on Loba Sgeir. Bulls and cows lay cheek by jowl and mating occurred with comparatively little quarrelling. In fact two- to three-year-old seals are far more playful than those in any other age class. I saw frequent mock battles taking place on Loba Sgeir between young bulls, sometimes between a cow and a bull, but only rarely between young cows. Like their older sisters they were too apt to become seriously quarrelsome.

It is not desired to draw a teleological conclusion, but one must point, all the same, to the value which the fully adult territorial behaviour has for the survival of the calves. It makes for sufficient room for each cow and calf during that fevered fortnight of maternal jealousy after the calf is born. At the same time, I do not wish to imply that unlimited room or solitariness is a good thing for cow and calf. The point will be mentioned again below.

There remains to be described the behaviour of mother and calf and to note the interesting metabolic processes

[1] Note the name Loba Sgeir and the Portuguese name for seal, *Lobito*.

which fit them for a period of life outside their chosen element. Birth is usually very rapid and the afterbirth is shed within half an hour. The calf when born is clad in a thick coat of fluffy hair, cream or ashen in colour. The head appears large and discrete from the body, and the limbs look relatively long, for as yet the calf is thin. If a still-born calf is skinned a dense loofah-like layer of connective tissue is found immediately below the skin. This tissue opens up to accommodate fat in the same way as a new loofah opens up to take water. The new-born calf is about thirty inches long and weighs about thirty pounds.

The mother takes very little notice of the calf for the first quarter of an hour after birth ; then she offers it her two teats and within half an hour the calf is taking its first meal of milk which is ten times as rich in fat as cow's milk ; she does not lick it at all though she will smell it. The first two days of its life the seal calf is more active than it is for the next month. It is possible to tell a new calf at a glance because its two hind flippers tend to spread to the side and it half-uses them in scrambling about those journeys of a few yards hither and thither. After two days the flippers remain longitudinal and are not used. Here, presumably, is some measure of evolutional recapitulation, a half-successful use of the hind feet for a few hours. These small adventures of the calf are responsible for much trouble between the cows, and any calf is liable to be severely bitten by a cow not its mother. If a bull finds a calf in his way he will pick it up and shake it (thirty pounds is nothing to him) and put it down again unhurt.

The over-anxiousness and jealousy of the cows over their calves mean that the bull of a harem is sometimes attacked with great ferocity. The bull backs away quickly from the cow behaving in this fashion and makes as if to defend himself only when the cow is upon him and then he does her but little harm.

I have asked myself why, if the cows are so jealous, they should be so closely gregarious ? The limited number of suitable nursery sites might impose a density of population causing extreme quarrelsomeness, but after seeing two different nurseries, I think the seals could spread out more if they wished. There is a probable biological advantage, but again it is not suggested that the closely gregarious habit and constant fussiness are followed *because* of any end they may serve. I found that in places where the cows could get to and from the water easily— as on the Treshnish Isles—they spend much more time out of the water with their calves when they are closely gregarious than when they are isolated. If predatory animals were present there would be an obvious advantage in the cows remaining with the calves.

Immediately after the first feed the cow begins to show maternal affection, which increases in intensity during the following three or four days. She shuffles round in order to touch the calf with her muzzle and then to scratch it lightly with her fore-paw. This scratching is a habit almost invariably practised after feeding has taken place, and after the first feed the calf comes itself towards the mother's head and is scratched from head to tail down the back.

The seals of Rona have their calves well up from the sea, so the danger from swell and spring tides is small. But on the Treshnish Isles the calves are never more than a few yards from the water's edge. One is accustomed to seeing carnivorous animals carrying their young in their mouths in the face of danger, but the Atlantic seal cannot do this. She has but one young, weighing 30 lb. at birth, and the closeness of her head to the ground makes it almost impossible for her to carry the calf.

What the cow can do for her calf, then, is limited, but that little she does well. I have seen a cow move her newly born calf twenty to thirty yards by shuffling it along between her paws. Where there is a heavy surf with ground swell at high tide, the cow lies below her calf at the water's edge and breaks the force of the waves to the calf. She curls herself almost half round it, and the calf is caught against her instead of being sucked back by the swell into the sea. If the calf is perverse, its mother will make as if to snap, and these threats are successful in helping to get the calf above the reach of the surf. I saw a cow on Rona holding her calf against the cliff with her paws at a place where it could climb on to a ledge. This type of behaviour is often conducted with perseverance, and I have seen a cow maintain it for the six tides of a three-day onshore gale at the time of a spring tide.

Young grey seal calves will play happily in the pools of an erosion platform or in the sea if it is quiet and there is an easy beach for them to climb ashore. But their long white coats are unsuitable for much swimming exercise and a calf would not seek escape into the sea. If they get there by accident such as by the lick of the swell at high spring tides, young calves will swim vigorously and make valiant efforts to get ashore. Sometimes, when they have been unsuccessful, I have examined the bodies. The claws have been worn away ; the chin and palms of the hands have been raw. At these times the calf cries pitifully with almost exactly the sound of a human child.

The calf is fed at about two-hourly intervals during the first few days and then at rather longer periods. Each meal appears to be a good one, for suckling takes from ten minutes to half an hour. The growth rate is very rapid, for it reaches about eighty-four pounds weight at a fortnight old, i.e. an average of four pounds a day. This increase has been made on milk alone and wholly at the expense of the mother's body, for when she comes up from the sea before calving she starves until she returns after weaning the calf. An observer is soon able to tell to a day how long any cow has been out of the sea by her degree of fatness. Similarly, the age of a calf can be judged accurately by its increasing degree of fatness. A cow loses about two hundred pounds weight between calving time and her return to the sea after changing her coat, and a bull loses three hundred pounds or more in the same time.

The calf begins to shed the fluffy white coat at thirteen days, beginning on the muzzle, the paws and a patch on the belly ; it assumes a very beautiful blue coat within the next fortnight. This is a time when the calf moves very little at all. It is common to see an almost-blue calf lying in the middle of the old hair which it has been several days in casting and rubbing off its back by rolling this way and that.

The time when the white coat is shed is synchronous with weaning. In this species, as in many other mammals and birds, the birth coat of fluffy hair or down appears to have a highly valent quality for the mother. Once hard fur or feathers are showing, maternal care rapidly declines. There is variation in maternal care. Most calves are weaned at precisely a fortnight old, but a few are suckled to three weeks, and I once saw one in full-blue coat being fed by its mother. At weaning they are left absolutely by their mothers and have to find their own way to the sea—the same process as in the gannet, the puffin and the petrels and shearwaters.

The calves have but a little way to go on the Treshnish Isles, and they already have some experience of going in and out of the water in playful fashion ; but on North Rona where many are born high on the island or on the edges of the cliffs the journey is fraught with danger.

Many make sheer drops of fifty to seventy-five feet into the sea. These calves, which have fed and prospered so richly on nothing but mother's milk, face a period of complete starvation from a fortnight old. They may get to the sea in a week, but some take a month to do it and even then do not appear in an urgent hurry. From a telescoped infancy they enter a protracted childhood, for their live-weight increase from then to one year old is small. The calves of the season can be easily recognized by their extreme buoyancy. When they rise to the surface a good half of them comes into view like a bobbing cork. Conversely, if the adult animals are frightened into the sea when changing their coats, their lack of buoyancy is apparent.

I have been struck by the solitary nature of month-old calves which have newly taken to the sea. They find little crabs and molluscs and may sometimes be seen on the sea-bottom from a cliff above turning over stones with their little hands. Gregariousness has to be re-established, and at a year old, or rather nine months, it is obvious how they have formed a group of their own with favoured rocks for lying out.

The complex social system, the specialized metabolic processes, and the protracted gestation period of eleven and a half months which allows calving and mating within a short period ashore, all combine to lessen the whole time of association with the land. One thing remains for us to remember—the flocking of these seals to a very few breeding stations, and their comparative helplessness ashore at that time, lay them open to particular danger from exploiting mankind seeking commercial gain. It is for us all to protect the seals adequately, for of few other species have we such a rich heritage.

Natural History in the Highlands and Islands

HUGH MACDIARMID

Wheesht, Wheesht

WHEESHT, wheesht, my foolish hert,
For weel ye ken
I widna ha'e ye stert
Auld ploys again.

It's guid to see her lie
Sae snod an' cool,
A' lust o' lovin' by—
Wheesht, wheesht, ye fule !

Penny Wheep

snod, tidy

Blind Man's Luck

HE just sits oolin' owre the fire
And gin' a body speak t' him, fegs,
Turns up the whites o's een
Like twa oon eggs.

' I've riped the bike o' Heaven,' quo' he,
' And whaur ma sicht s'ud be I've stuck
The toom doups o' the sun
And mune, for luck ! '

Penny Wheep

oolin', crouching *fegs*, faith ! *oon*, shell-less, addle *ripe*, pillage
bike, nest *toom*, empty *doups*, ends

Somersault

I LO'E the stishie
O' earth in space
Breengin' by
At a haliket pace.

stishie, rumpus, hullabaloo *Breengin'*, bursting, hurtling *haliket*, headlong

64

A wecht o' hills
Gangs wallopin' owre,
Syne a whummlin' sea
Wi' a gallus glower.

The West whuds doon
Like the pigs at Gadara,
But the East's aye there
Like a sow at the farrow.

Penny Wheep

wecht, weight   *whummlin'*, overturning   *gallus*, callous
whuds, dashes, thuds by

Sabine

A LASS cam' to oor gairden-yett
An' ringle-e'ed was she,
And sair she spiered me for a leaf,
A leaf o' savin-tree.

An' white as a loan-soup was she,
The lass wha'd tint her snood,
But oot my gudewife cam' an' straucht
To rate the slut begood.

The lassie looked at her an' leuch,
' Och, plaise yersel',' said she,
' Ye'd better gi'e me what I seek
Than learn what I've to gi'e.'

Penny Wheep

yett, gate   *ringle-e'ed*, showing whites of eyes   *spiered*, besought
savin'-tree, sabine, said to kill fœtus in womb
white (*as a loan-soup*), pallid (as thin and weak as charity soup)
tint her snood, dishonoured herself   *begood*, began

NORMAN DOUGLAS

The Werewolf

DEPRIVED of converse I relapsed into a doze, but soon woke up with a start. The carriage had stopped ; it was nearly midnight ; we were at Terranova di Sibari, whose houses were lit up by the silvery beams of the moon.

Thurii—death-place of Herodotus ! How one would like to see this place by daylight. On the ancient site, which lies at a considerable distance, they have excavated antiquities, a large number of which are in the possession of the Marchese Galli at Castrovillari. I endeavoured to see his museum, but found it inaccessible for ' family reasons.' The same answer was given me in regard to a valuable private library at Rossano, and, annoying as it may be, one cannot severely blame such local gentlemen for keeping their collections to themselves. What have they to gain from the visits of inquisitive travellers ?

During these meditations on my part the old man hobbled busily to and fro with a bucket, bearing water from a fountain near at hand wherewith to splash the carriage wheels. He persisted in this singular occupation for an unreasonably long time. Water was good for the wheels, he explained ; it kept them cool.

At last we started, and I began to slumber once more. The carriage seemed to be going down a steep incline ; endlessly it descended, with a pleasant swaying motion. . . . Then an icy shiver roused me from my dreams. It was the Crati whose rapid waves, fraught with unhealthy chills, rippled brightly in the moonlight. We crossed the malarious valley, and once more touched the hills.

From those treeless slopes there streamed forth deliciously warm emanations stored up during the scorching hours of noon ; the short scrub that clothed them was

66

redolent of that peculiar Calabrian odour which haunts one like a melody—an odour of dried cistus and other aromatic plants, balsamic by day, almost overpowering at this hour. To aid and diversify the symphony of perfume I lit a cigar, and then gave myself up to contemplation of the heavenly bodies. We passed a solitary man, walking swiftly with bowed head. What was he doing there ?

'Lupomanaro,' said the driver.

A werewolf. . . .

Old Calabria

The Peasant

I REMEMBER watching an old man stubbornly digging a field by himself. He toiled through the flaming hours, and what he lacked in strength was made up in the craftiness, *malizia*, born of long love of the soil. The ground was baked hard ; but there was still a chance of rain, and the peasants were anxious not to miss it. Knowing this kind of labour, I looked on from my vine-wreathed arbour with admiration, but without envy.

I asked whether he had not children to work for him.

'All dead—and health to you !' he replied, shaking his white head dolefully.

And no grandchildren ?

'All Americans [emigrants].'

He spoke in a dreamy fashion of years long ago when he too had travelled, sailing to Africa for corals, to Holland and France ; yes, and to England also. But our dockyards and cities had faded from his mind ; he remembered only our men.

'*Che bella gioventù—che bella gioventù !* ' [a sturdy brood], he kept on repeating. 'And lately,' he added,

67

' America has been discovered.' He toiled fourteen hours a day, and he was eighty-three years old.

Apart from that creature of fiction, the peasant *in fabula* whom we all know, I can find little to admire in this whole class of men, whose talk and dreams are of the things of the soil, and who know of nothing save the regular interchange of summer and winter with their unvarying tasks and rewards. None save a Cincinnatus or Garibaldi can be ennobled by the spade. In spleenful moments, it seems to me that the most depraved of city dwellers has flashes of enthusiasm and self-abnegation never experienced by this shifty, retrogressive and ungenerous brood, which lives like the beasts of the field and has learnt all too much of their logic. But they have a beast-virtue hereabouts which compels respect—contentment in adversity. In this point they resemble the Russian peasantry. And yet, who can pity the moujik ? His cheeks are altogether too round, and his morals too superbly bestial ; he has clearly been created to sing and starve by turns. But the Italian peasant who speaks in the tongue of Homer and Virgil and Boccaccio is easily invested with a halo of martyrdom ; it is delightful to sympathise with men who combine the manners of Louis Quatorze with the profiles of Augustus or Plato, and who still recall, in many of their traits, the pristine life of Odyssean days. Thus, they wear today the identical ' clouted leggings of oxhide, against the scratches of the thorns ' which old Laertes bound about his legs on the upland farm in Ithaka. They call them *galandrine*.

Old Calabria

The Dragon

WHAT is a dragon? An animal, one might say, which looks or regards (Greek *drakon*); so called, presumably, from its terrible eyes. Homer has passages which bear out this interpretation:

$$\Sigma\mu\epsilon\rho\delta\alpha\lambda\acute{\epsilon}o\nu \ \delta\grave{\epsilon} \ \delta\acute{\epsilon}\delta o\rho\kappa\epsilon\nu, \ \text{etc.}$$

Now the Greeks were certainly sensitive to the expression of animal eyes—witness ' cow-eyed' Hera, or the opprobrious epithet ' dog-eyed'; altogether, the more we study what is left of their zoological researches, the more we realise what close observers they were in natural history. Aristotle, for instance, points out sexual differences in the feet of the crawfish which were overlooked up to a short time ago. And Hesiod also insists upon the dragon's eyes. Yet it is significant that *ophis*, the snake, is derived, like *drakon*, from a root meaning nothing more than to perceive or regard. There is no connotation of ferocity in either of the words. Gesner long ago suspected that the dragon was so called simply from its keen or rapid perception.

One likes to search for some existing animal prototype of a fabled creature like this, seeing that to invent such things out of sheer nothing is a feat beyond human ingenuity—or, at least, beyond what the history of others of their kind leads us to expect. It may well be that the Homeric writer was acquainted with the Uromastix lizard that occurs in Asia Minor, and whoever has watched this beast, as I have done, cannot fail to have been impressed by its contemplative gestures, as if it were gazing intently (*drakon*) at something. It is, moreover, a ' dweller in rocky places,' and more than this, a vegetarian —an ' eater of poisonous herbs,' as Homer somewhere calls his dragon. So Aristotle says : ' When the dragon has eaten much fruit, he seeks the juice of the bitter lettuce ; he has been seen to do this.'

Are we tracking the dragon to his lair ? Is this the aboriginal beast ? Not at all, I should say. On the contrary, this is a mere side-issue, to follow which would lead us astray. The reptile-dragon was invented when men had begun to forget what the arch-dragon was ; it is the product of a later stage—the materialising stage ; that stage when humanity sought to explain, in naturalistic fashion, the obscure traditions of the past. We must delve still deeper. . . .

My own dragon theory is far-fetched—perhaps necessarily so, dragons being somewhat remote animals. The dragon, I hold, is the personification of the life within the earth—of that life which, being unknown and uncontrollable, is *eo ipso* hostile to man. Let me explain how this point is reached.

The animal which *looks or regards.* . . . Why—why an animal ? Why not *drakon* = that which looks ?

Now, what looks ?

The eye.

This is the key to the understanding of the problem, the key to the subterranean dragon-world.

The conceit of fountains or sources of water being things that see (*drakon*)—that is, eyes—or bearing some resemblance to eyes, is common to many races. In Italy, for example, two springs in the inland sea near Taranto are called ' Occhi '—eyes ; Arabs speak of a watery fountain as an eye ; the notion exists in England too—in the ' Blentarn ' of Cumberland, the blind tarn (tarn = a trickling of tears), which is ' blind ' because dry and waterless, and therefore lacking the bright lustre of the open eye.

There is an eye, then, in the fountain : an eye which looks or regards. And inasmuch as an eye presupposes a head, and a head without body is hard to conceive, a material existence was presently imputed to that which looked upwards out of the liquid depths. This, I think, is the primordial dragon, the archetype. He is of animistic descent and survives all over the earth ; and it is precisely this universality of the dragon idea which induces me to discard all theories of local origin and to seek for some common cause. Fountains are ubiquitous, and so are dragons. There are fountain dragons in Japan, in the superstitions of Keltic races, in the Mediterranean basin. The dragon of Wantley lived in a well ; the Lambton Worm began life in fresh water, and only took to dry land later on. I have elsewhere spoken of the Manfredonia legend of Saint Lorenzo and the dragon, an indigenous fable connected, I suspect, with the fountain near the harbour of that town, and quite independent of the newly imported legend of Saint Michael. Various springs in Greece and Italy are called Dragoneria ; there is a cave-fountain Dragonara on Malta, and another of the same name near Cape Misenum—all are sources of apposite lore. The water-drac . . .

Old Calabria

Mr Heywood

MR JAMES HEYWOOD, of 26 Kensington Palace Gardens, was a sort of cousin ; he had a noble paunch and a rosy, clean-shaven countenance, softly beaming. His house, and the lawn at the back of it on which I used to disport myself, were my earliest impressions of London, dating from 1876 or 1877. It was Heywood who gave me the first English book I read by myself, *Erling the Bold.* He

was a kindly old fellow; one never went there from school
without receiving half a sovereign or a sovereign as tip
(' boys need money more than we do,' he used to say);
he took you to the Lyceum to see *Romeo and Juliet* with
Irving and Ellen Terry, or to the Westminster Aquarium
where you could admire Pongo, the first gorilla, and a
lady called Zaza who was shot out of a cannon; he built
a public drinking fountain in the wall just outside the
north entrance of Kensington Palace Gardens; and,
among other things of that kind, he had also brought out
an English version of Heer's important work on *Die
Urwelt der Schweiz*. I think he was a Fellow of the
Royal Society.

So far good; but meanwhile he was growing madder
from day to day—a bundle of innocent eccentricities.
He wore wigs of different colours, white, brown, grey
and black, as the fancy moved him; he carried a supply
of ginger-breads in his pocket because ' you never know
when you may be hungry '; worse still, he took to
mixing up one person with another, which was awkward,
especially at dinner-parties; for he was obstinate about
it, and stuck to his mistake.

Albeit he had become decidedly peculiar, I kept up my
friendship with him, partly because I liked him (he was
one of those who were kind to me as a boy—spontane-
ously kind, I mean, and not out of a Victorian sense of
duty), and partly, I confess, because I liked also his
succulent, long-drawn-out luncheons, and the exquisite
bottle of port which followed. Those were luncheons of
the old school, when men were neither afraid of paying
for good things, nor yet of eating them. Now we have
calories and vitamins—sheer funk—and, even among the
rich, a cheeseparing spirit which is a disgrace to civilisation.
The things they expect you to eat!

I called on old Heywood for the last time one afternoon

in 1890. The butler, as usual, showed me into his study, which was on the right-hand side of the hall. He was alone in there. He greeted me with urbanity, but without affection. We discussed the prevailing epidemic of influenza ; then, after a pause in which neither of us seemed to have anything to say, he observed :

' You're not asking me much about my symptoms, are you ? Shall I keep up the treatment ? '

' My God,' I thought, ' he is taking me for Sir Francis Laking. And he'll be furious if I try to undeceive him. What's to be done ? Clear out. . . . '

' I must see you later, Mr Heywood, about that. I only thought I would drop in for a moment . . . it was on my way . . . to an important consultation ' (pulling out my watch) ' . . . good gracious ! nearly four o'clock. . . . Let me just feel your pulse . . . good ; very good. Steadier than last time. Yes, do keep up the treatment. And now please forgive me for running away ' . . . and with some such excuse, I made to depart. He caught me by the sleeve and said :

' Ah, but you're not going away without this,' and took a weighty little envelope out of a drawer and gave it me.

When opened in the street it yielded five sovereigns and five shillings—my fee for professional attendance.

It occurred to me afterwards that an appointment may have been made for the real Laking to call on that same afternoon ; if so, what about *his* fee ?

Looking Back

Miss Wilberforce and Mr Keith

HE quite understood. Miss Wilberforce must be protected against herself. And he disagreed heartily. Nobody must be protected against himself. The attitude of a man towards his fellows should be that of non-intervention, of benevolent egotism. Every person of healthy digestion was aware of that cardinal truth. Unfortunately persons of healthy digestions were not as common as they might be. That was why straight thinking, on these and other subjects, was at a discount. Nobody had a right to call himself well disposed towards society until he had grasped the elementary fact that the only way to improve the universe was to improve oneself, and to leave one's neighbour alone. The best way to begin improving oneself was to keep one's own bowels open, and not trouble about those of anybody else. Turkey rhubarb, in fact. The serenity of outlook thereby attained would enable a man to perceive the futility of interfering with the operation of natural selection.

The speaker, he went on, had dropped the word charity. Had the tribe of Israel cultivated a smattering of respect for psychology or any other useful science instead of fussing about supernatural pedigrees, they would have been more cautious as to their diet. Had they been careful in the matter of dietary, their sacred writing would never have seen the light of day. Those writings, a monument of malnutrition and faulty digestive processes, were responsible for three-quarters of what was called charity. Charity was responsible for the greater part of human mischief and misery. The revenues of the private charities of London alone exceeded five million sterling annually. What were these revenues expended upon ? On keeping alive an incredible number of persons who ought to be dead. What was the result of keeping these people alive ? A deterioration of the whole race. Charity consisted in setting a premium on bodily ill-health and mental inefficiency. Charity was an oriental nightmare ; an endeavour to raise the weak to the level of the strong ; an incitement to improvidence. Charity disturbed the national equilibrium; it lowered the standard of mankind instead of raising it. Charity was an unmitigated nuisance which had increased, was increasing and ought to be diminished.

By way of varying the phraseology, but not the thing, they had called themselves philanthropists. The meaning of that venerable word had decayed of late in characteristic fashion. Prometheus, the archetype, brought fire from heaven to comfort certain people who had the wit to appreciate its uses. He did not waste his time wetnursing the unfit, like a modern philanthropist. What was a modern philanthropist? He was a fellow who was always bothering you to do something for somebody else. He appealed to your purse for the supposed welfare of some pet degenerate. Prometheus appealed to your intelligence for the real welfare of rational beings. A rich man found it extremely simple, no doubt, to sign a cheque. But an act was not necessarily sensible because it happened to be simple. People ought to dominate their reflexes. Prometheus did not choose the simplest course —he chose the wisest, and found it a pretty tough job, too. That alone proved him to have been a man of sound digestion and robust health. Had it been otherwise, indeed, he would never have endured that vulture business for so long.

The deputation exchanged glances, puzzled by this pompous and peevish exordium. It did not promise well; it sounded quite unlike Mr Keith's usually bland address. Perhaps he had not yet breakfasted. 'We ought to have waited,' they thought. One of the listeners was so annoyed that he began :

' A paradox, Mr Keith, is not necessarily sensible, because it happens to be simple '—but was overborne by that gentleman, who proceeded calmly :

' So much for generalities. Now Miss Wilberforce is

75

a lady of independent means and of a certain age. She is not an infant, to be protected against herself or against others; she has reached years of indiscretion. Like a good many sensible persons she lives in this country. Of course a residence here has its drawbacks—very grave drawbacks, some of them. But the drawbacks are counterbalanced by certain advantages. In short, what applies to one country does not always apply to the other. Yet you propose to treat her exactly as if she were living in England. That strikes me as somewhat unreasonable.'

' Mr van Koppen has promised us. . . .'

' He may do what he likes with his money. But I don't see why I should become the pivot for making my good friend do what strikes me as a foolish action. I am too fond of him for that. Mr van Koppen and myself have many points in common; among other things this feature, that neither of us is of aristocratic birth. I suspect that this is what made you count on me for a subscription. You thought that I, having a little money of my own, might be tempted by certain sycophantic instincts to emulate his misplaced generosity. But I am not a snob. From the social point of view I don't care a tuppenny damn for anyone. On the other hand, my origin has given me something of Dr Samuel Johnson's respect for what he calls his betters. I like the upper classes, especially when they behave according to their old traditions. That is why I like Miss Wilberforce. She conducts herself, if report be true, with all the shamelessness of a born lady. Born ladies are not so common that we should hide them away in nursing homes. All forceful seclusion is dishonouring. Every little insect, drunk or sober, enjoys its freedom; and if you gentlemen were not philanthropists I would try to point out how galling your proposal must be, how humiliating to a high-spirited woman, to be placed under lock and key, in charge

of some callous attendant. But to what purpose?
Turkey rhubarb——'

'I am afraid, Mr Keith, that we have come at an
inopportune moment.'

'It is quite possible. But I won't keep you much longer
—you must be dying to attend that funeral! In fact, I
would not detain you at all if I did not feel that you
expected some kind of explanation from me. What were
we saying?'

'Turkey rhubarb.'

'Ah, yes! I was trying to be fair-minded which, by
the way, is generally a mistake. It struck me that perhaps
I over-emphasized its advantages just now. Because, of
course, there is something to be said against the use of such
drugs. In fact, now I come to think of it, there is a good
deal to be said in favour of constipation. It is the cause
of our English spleenfulness, and this spleenfulness,
properly directed, has its uses. It engenders a certain
energetic intolerance of mind. I think the success of our
nation is largely due to this particular quality. If I were
an historian I would amuse myself with proving that we
owe not only Magna Carta but our whole Empire—
Canada, Australia and all the rest of them—to our costive
habits of body. What befits a nation, however, does not
always befit a man. To crush, in a fit of chronic bilious-
ness, the resistance of Bengal and add its land to the
British Empire, may be a racial virtue. To crush, in a fit
of any kind, the resistance of our next-door neighbour,
Mr Robinson, and add his purse to our own, is an individual vice. No! I fail to discover any personal
advantage to be gained from excess of bile. The bilious
eye sees intensely, no doubt, but in a distorted and narrow
fashion; it is incapable of a generous outlook. Cloudy,
unserene! A closing-up, instead of a widening-out. The
bowels of compassion; what a wonderful old phrase!

77

They ought to be kept open. I look around me, and see extraordinary little goodwill among my fellow-creatures. Here is Miss Wilberforce. What she yearns for is the milk of human kindness—gentle words, gentle dealing, from all of us. Instead of that, every one is ready to cast stones at her. She is treated like a pariah. For my part I do not pass her by ; I am not ashamed to consort with sinners, if such they be ; I would like, if I could, to make her free and happy instead of imprisoning her in a place of self-reproach. A healthy man is naturally well-disposed, not on principle or from any divine inspiration, but because his bodily organs are performing their proper functions. His judgment is not warped by the black humours of indigestion. He perceives that natural laws, however harsh they seem, are never so harsh as our amateurish attempts to circumvent them. Modern philanthropy is an attempt of this nature. It is crass emotionalism. Regarded from the point of view of the race, your philanthropy is a disguised form of brutality.'

' Mr Keith ! '

' All sentimentalists are criminals.'

South Wind

Chocolate

CHOCOLATE once stood in so high repute for the excitation of desire that its employment was fiercely condemned by the puritanical sort ; vanilla likewise ; from our Shakespeare and others of his day we learn that potatoes, having but recently arrived in the Eastern world, were taken to be potent for increasing the geniture. It was even so with tomatoes. And so it was with truffles, upon their re-discovery in France.

Here are the quackeries which demonstrate how the

wish will grow to be father to the thought. For see what happens : the potato, now common, has ceased to be an aphrodisiac, likewise the tomato ; truffles, costly as before, are still esteemed as such.

Regarding chocolate, I judge it to be of neutral effect ; a cloying product fit for serving-maids ; yet possessed of value as an endearment, an incentive working not upon body but upon mind ; it generates, in those who relish it, a complacent and yielding disposition. Deprived of chocolate, your lover of serving-maids is deprived of a persuasive helpmate.

As for vanilla, all meats flavoured with it are sickening to the palate of grown men, though not of youth ; I had sooner dispense with love than purchase it through the ministration of so noisome a condiment. Inasmuch, nevertheless, as curiosity in experiment is the mark of every scholar ; and inasmuch as a Frenchman of today, a Monsieur Richard, in full seriousness declares vanilla to engender *an erotical excitation which cannot be doubted*, I essayed with equal seriousness this drug in various combinations ; experiencing, at the end, no more than some slight desire to vomit.

Paneros

Idiots

A REALLY fine morning at last ; glorious sunshine.

' Now for those idiots,' says Mr R., and so do I. We have found out about them from the inn people.

It appears that two, a man and a woman, come from the Walserthal, which has always been famous for its crop of imbeciles ; the third was born at Raggal, likewise fertile mother of idiots, because everybody marries into his own family there. These Raggalers are such passionate agriculturalists and so busy, all the year round, with their fields and cattle, that they refuse to waste time scouring the province for so trivial an object as a wife with fresh blood, when you can get a colourable substitute at home. Our particular idiots live, all three of them, on the road to St Anne Church, in that workhouse which, so far as I know, has sheltered from time immemorial the poor of the district, the aged, the infirm of mind or body. There is always a fine assortment of wrecks on view here. Sisters of Charity look after them.

Sure enough, the first thing we saw was one of the man idiots hacking wood out-of-doors. He was of the deaf and dumb variety, with misshapen skull ; he took no notice of us, but continued at his task with curious deliberation, as if each stroke of the axe necessitated the profoundest thought. Weak in the head, obviously ; but not what I call an idiot. If he could have spoken, he would doubtless have uttered as many witticisms as one hears in an English public-house after closing time. The woman was also there, sitting on the bench beside a Sister of Charity. Undersized, stupid looking, with mouth agape ; nothing more ; I have seen society ladies not unlike her in appearance. She can sew and knit stockings and even talk, they had told us. Mediocre specimens, both of them. And how about the third one, we inquired ? He was working in the fields, said the Sister. Working in the fields. . . .

These things call themselves idiots. Even idiots, it seems, have degenerated nowadays. Mr R. was dreadfully disappointed ; and so was I. He vowed I had led him to expect something on quite another scale ; and so I had. He extracted a promise, then and there, that I should show him over Valduna, the provincial lunatic asylum near Rankweil, in the hope of unearthing a few idiots worthy of the name.

Now of course you cannot have everything in this

world. You cannot ask, in a district otherwise so richly endowed by Nature as this one, for the *fine fleur* of imbecility—for *crétins*. To see these marvels you must go farther afield, to places like the Valtellina or Val d'Aosta (and even there, I understand, the race is losing some of its best characteristics. These doctors !). But one might at least have kept alive a specimen or two of the old school, just for memory's sake ; idiots such as my sister and myself used to see, while rambling as children about these streets with the *Alte Anna*, our nurse. On that very bench where the modish lady was reclining today, or its predecessor, there used to sit two skinny old mad women side by side, with their backs to the wall. There they sat, always in the same place. They were as mad as could be, and older than the hills. A terrifying spectacle—these two blank creatures, staring into vacuity out of pale blue eyes, with white hair tumbling all about their shoulders. One of them disappeared—died, no doubt ; the survivor went on sitting and staring, in her old place. There was another idiot whom we liked far better ; in fact we loved him. He was of the joyful and jabbering kind, and he lived near the factory. His facial contortions used to make us shriek with laughter. Sometimes he dribbled at the mouth. When he dribbled copiously, which was not every day, it was our crowning joy.

Together

G S FRASER

The Black Cherub

Per la contradizione che nol consente
DANTE

BECAUSE the contradiction does not allow
Us to be happy and also to know how
I will give a penny to anyone who begs
And say my prayers at night to a girl's legs,

Because the contradiction does not consent
That what we say resemble what we meant
My sonnets perish in a burning shower,
My prose preserves the balance of the power,

Because the contradiction thinks it well
That casuists on the whole should go to hell
I shall balance revolution against heaven
And die a bourgeois still, and still unshriven,

Because the contradiction does not permit
Hegels to find a resolution for it
Hitlers who seek to unify the world
Shall be in the southernmost flames of hell curled,

With all the other fraudulent counsellors
Who tell the wicked how to cast down towers,
Who sell for gold the city or the girl,
And for whom now hell's horrid bagpipes skirl,

For they all go down to the teeth and the claws and the ice
Where Judas and Brutus realise they are not nice,
And the great poets wander and sniff from high
At the smell of hell's ineffable *canaille*,

And the only lucky are like Uberto who
Thought that they knew more than they really knew,
And who swell up erect from their bed of night,
' As if they held the Inferno in great despite,'

Or the scholarly old homosexual who still
Retains a pride in his grammatical skill
And though he must dodge the column, and cannot choose,
' Runs like the sprinters who win, and not who lose.'

Since our pride is not from God, by our own will
We can keep ourselves from the filthiest pouches still :
From the lake of pitch where the devils bite like curs
Or the sea of filth that engulfs the flatterers,

But at night we may go down on our cold knees :
' To-morrow, God, make me not a drunkard, please :
But let me have the pleasure of being drunk,'
And contradiction has us, and we are sunk,

Or, ' Let my love be pure and gentle at last :
And let it be cleansed from the stains and the pains of the past :
And let the girl come easily to my bed,'
And the black cherub holds the hairs of our head.

But worse than us the hypocrites who cry,
' Let the world have peace, and let the starving die :
Let the rich lie in an easy bed at nights :
Let the fat dog sleep whom the wicked flea bites,

' O, let us have peace and let the heart be still :
The cold and the empty of heart will never kill :
Let the poor know how strong are the bars of the cage
That they may not shake them in their futile rage ! '

For from love alone, and not from the cold grease
Of your rich tables, will you build peace,
Nor with your poverty constrain God's plenty :
Per la contradizione che nol consente !

The Traveller has Regrets

NAOMI MITCHISON

Sämund's Daughter

ABOUT harvest-tide there was fighting at the Ford, and
there men killed Sämund Bigmouth, and with him the
Easterling Bodvar, who was betrothed to his daughter
Gersemi. Now at the end of the day Gersemi found them
both and wailed for them, and they were brought home
to Sämund's new steading. Bodvar had a great iron
sword with a hilt of sea ivory ; when he died it was
fast in his hand and the blade through a man's throat.
Gersemi took it for her own, and all winter she had it
laid beside her in bed ; but Sämund's sword went to her
eldest brother, Kol.

She was a big, light-haired girl, with a deep voice and
old enough to have her own mind about things ; she
was red-cheeked, and her hands were rough from hay-
making and tending of beasts ; she was quick at learning
any new craft and clever with words ; Sämund had given
her land and gear of her own. Kol and the rest of the
brothers would have had her marry some friend of theirs
now Bodvar was dead, but she would have none of it.
Wooers came cold over ice and snow to the steading,
but she sent them away with no comfort, and soon enough
it was spring and Gersemi set out across the wet pastures.

She combed and tied her hair back like a man ; she
put on breeches of grey stuff; her shoes were of strong
ox-hide, and her gloves were sealskin, well sewn ; her
coat was woollen and thick ; over it she had ring-mail,
good against sword or axe. Her cloak was made of a
great white bear pelt from the north, a fairy bear that
once had strange dealings with the Finn wizards ; its
claws met over her breast, the head fell behind, and on
the under-side were written runes of great power. This

cloak had been part of her mother's dower, and never did the fur wear thin. Her little horse was shag-haired and straight-backed like the wild horses, but he answered well enough to the bridle. She made fast a pack to the saddle ; in it were strings of polished amber and some few coloured stones and beads of coral, things that have their price all the world over. She carried a little bow and hunting arrows ; but her strength was in her axe and Bodvar's sword ; this way she looked as good a fighter as any man south of the Ford. So she set out.

Now at first she went east, riding along by the sea coast, because she feared to turn south and inland among the strange forests. She swam her horse across two great rivers, near the mouth, and came at last to a salt marsh, very wide and full of small willows ; the people, too, were not friendly, so then she must needs face south, following up small valleys in a country for the most part low lying and full of lakes and swamps, with but few men in it from one week's end to the next. As it got to be summer she found the bear pelt hot and heavy, but she would not leave it off because of the runes on it. Sometimes she bathed and washed her clothes, but she was afraid of being a naked woman alone, with the chance of wild men or wandering gods and devils seeing her. She shot deer and hares and birds, or what she could, and ate them with roots and the uncoiling fern ends, and when she came on a hut or a wagon she got milk and often bread ; the folk hereabouts were mostly small and ugly, and feared her ; she could not speak their tongue, and she was very far from home.

One night she and her horse rested among low trees by the edge of a stream ; a mist rose up round them and she slept ill, seeming to hear voices from across the stream speaking words that were near to her own. The horse, too, started, as more than once a mare whinnied to him, close by yet out of sight or smell. In the morning the mist was still high, so she waited till it cleared, but with the mist the voices died away, and call or search as she might, there was no-one at either side of the river.

Towards midsummer she came to a great wall of mountains, pine and rock going right up into the sky ; skirting about them for days, and following up a river, she came to a pass still under light snow, where the wind cut through her bearskin and the little horse stumbled and shivered. Each side of her great peaks jagged high and harsh towards the bright, cold sun, and she prayed aloud to whatever gods lived there, and to her own gods, Odin and Thor and Vidar, and to Skade, goddess of the snow mountains in the north. So in the end she came over the pass and down into a great tangle of valleys. More than once men passed her, traders with mules for the most part, and often she stayed the night in a hut and got food and fodder there. Not once was she taken for anything but a young man, and she was ever thought well of for the sake of her sword and her gold bracelets. The people here were beginning to be different ; many were tall and fair and handsome like her own brothers, and their tongue was near enough to hers for her to learn it quickly and gladly.

When the pinewoods came to an end and the southward-facing ridges flattened out to a warm green plain, she saw a walled town before her and rode very cautiously ; yet she had heard tell of cities, and how in strange countries many men would build their steadings together and live, as it were, all in one huge hall that no enemy could break into. Slower and slower she went as she came near, but it seemed all man-made, and there were children playing by the gates of the wall, so she took courage. She watched others riding in, and at last rode in herself, over the boat bridge and between the towers of the gate, a little pale, and breathing quickly as she looked from side to side. At first the noise was terrible—all those voices : her little horse shied at them, and so did she. Every moment she would think they were speaking to her, and it all went too quick for her to make out the words. But soon she found she was only one among many and no-one noticed her. At this she suddenly felt it was all wrong, that here was she, daughter of Sämund Bigmouth, who had owned all the land from the Ford to Vig's Bay, but none of the Southerlings knew ! She wanted to shout, to draw that sword of hers, to make the shaggy horse plunge and scatter the sweet-sellers and ride them down ! Oh, then they'd look at her ! But there were walls all round and a narrow gate behind : so she did nothing.

By and by she came to a shop at the corner of a street ; the floor of it was on a level with her foot, and all over it —piles and rolls and shining coils—there was stuff she had never seen before, gleaming, soft, all coloured like hill-sides in May. She stopped and stared : there was a little man sitting inside the shop, a brown, black-bearded man with rings on his fingers. He spoke—he spoke to her ! She shook her head, not understanding, and gave him greeting in the Goth tongue. At once he changed his speech and went on in words she knew. He took up a piece of the stuff and passed it through his fingers.

' You must have strange sheep down here ! ' said Gersemi.

' Sheep ! ' cried the little dark man, waving his arms, ' never a sheep went near this ! '

Gersemi settled herself to listen while he explained ; she nodded ' Yes, yes,' but as to believing this fine, wonderful cloth was made by little worms that lived on leaves—not she !

She dismounted, looking at piece after piece ; it felt as tender as it looked : such webs must Freya weave on her golden loom. There were beautiful dresses, the same stuff, but embroidered with stiff gold : she must remember she was a man. But there were coats of it too, short-sleeved and long-sleeved, scarlet and green and blue : oh, she had to ! But surely they were worth a queen's ransom ! She daren't. She backed a step towards the saddle again ; the merchant brought out still more. After all, this could only be one town of many ; what was its name ?—Vindobona. Not even Rome-burg, where the great king Caesar lived ! There was one coat she liked best of all : bright, bright red, with little pieces of shining hard stuff round the neck and hem. She picked it up.

'What will you take for this ? '

The merchant named a price, but she looked blank at it.

'What is an aureus ? '

He fumbled in a box at the back of the booth and showed her the funny little gold piece, not much more than a finger's width, with the long, narrow head looking half scornfully down its nose on the one side, and on the other the proud trampling little man, stick in one hand, victory in the other.

She had seen stamped gold before, but only as ear-rings or brooches ; she had no idea what it was worth. She took off one of her amber necklaces and held it out ; the merchant rubbed one of the beads and peered at it.

'Another string of these and the coat is yours.'

She loosened the second necklace ; it was a big price to pay, but the coat—oh, the coat brighter than coral !

Suddenly there was a hand on her arm and she jumped round, feeling for her dagger. But it was a friendly hand and a friendly, bearded face.

'You are a stranger here ? '

She hesitated a moment, but this was a fair, blue-eyed man, he might have the truth.

'I have never seen a walled city before.'

He laughed.

'You look it! Now, what do you want? This? Very well.'

He picked up the necklace, glared at the merchant, and began shouting abuse at him; the poor little brown man was bowing, trembling, flourishing his hands, appealing to Gersemi! But she let her new friend have his way. In the end she got her necklace back with less than half of the beads gone, and the silk coat as well. Oh, Gersemi was happy!

She went on beside the man, answering his questions.

'Yes, I have come across the pass, right over from the other side.'

'And before that?'

'I came from the north, far and far, forests and rivers and plains and swamps between here and there; I've been riding south since before the spring sowing.'

'Are you Goth?'

'No, not Goth.'

'What, then?'

'The gods of Asgard are my gods; Sämund Bigmouth was my father; I am called Gersemi.'

'You are not very old to have come so far; you have not even the beginnings of a beard yet.'

'No. What do they call you, friend?'

'I am Avilf; I am going off to the Assembly now, with my men. Will you come?'

'Where? What Assembly?'

'In Illyricum, up among the hills. We are going to make Alaric king.'

'Is he a great chief?'

'You've never heard of Alaric! Come with me, and

you shall have fighting and gold and women and anything else you choose out of the Greek cities ! Will you
be my battle friend ? '

' Yes ! ' cried Gersemi, thinking of nothing but adventures, and they shook hands on it. Then Avilf took
off his middle-finger ring which was of silver, set cross-
wise with garnets and blue glass, and gave it to Gersemi.
She gave him in exchange one of her bracelets of soft,
twisted gold ; they looked well at one another's faces,
and they were friends.

Avilf had a cousin of some sort in Vindobona ; he and
Gersemi stayed in the house, and his men lived casually
among the outbuildings. One day Gersemi was telling
them about her riding, and of the night when she heard
the voices in the mist. Avilf and his cousin nodded at
each other, and told her how long and long ago the Goths
had journeyed from one land to another, pressed by
hunger for new homes and more sunshine, and how at a
certain river the bridge had broken under the feet of the
great host, and half of them with their horses and cattle
had been left behind ; and still they were there, man or
spirit or echo, and more than once travellers had come
on their voices at night. Avilf ended, ' That was a lucky
sign for you ; we will tell Alaric, and you shall have
honour for it.' And he taught Gersemi much swordcraft
that she did not know, and she showed him the battle
strokes of the northern axe. She got herself a silk cloak
too, red like the coat, with gold cords and a heavy silver
buckle, and only used the bearskin for her bed ; it was
far too hot now, and here she felt safe enough without
the runes.

Avilf showed her all the sights of the town, and by and
by she stopped looking surprised at everything. He
explained the church with some pride, saying, ' You
ought to be baptised.'

Gersemi looked cautiously round at the bright-coloured ikons.

' Do your gods ask it of strangers ? '

' Of course,' said Avilf cheerfully. ' If you are not baptised you'll die and be burnt in hell.'

' Isn't there a sacrifice I can make instead, Avilf ? '

So he began explaining all over again. But Gersemi was still very much puzzled about everything except that among the followers of these same gods of his some were bad men who had been led astray by a rival godling, one Athanasius, and some were good men and followers of Ulphilas : you could tell them because they said the Son (and he, thought Gersemi, was Balder the Beautiful who died and went to Hel, but will come back after Ragnarok) was ' like the Father in such manner as the Holy Scriptures declare.' What were the Holy Scriptures ? A book of runes ? Then Avilf could read ! It was all very wonderful, but one way and another she put off being baptised, and then the time came for them to start for the plains of Illyricum and the Assembly of the Goths.

They left Vindobona and its swarming lanes behind, their horsehoofs echoed under the gate arch, they were past the crops, they were on the sandy forest road, Avilf and Gersemi, and a hundred armed men behind them, with slaves and pack-horses and light carts full of food and wine skins. For a little they went east, then almost due south on the flat monotonous plain, burning in the sun, breathless under the trees. Then eastwards again, passing the end of a long lake, blue and level, with dried beds of rushes stretching far out from it at every side. Still it was flat and dull, with only a grey shadow of mountains far away to the south ; the road led them through a low forest, grass, crops and small huddled towns—a fort, a market and a jumble of wooden houses inside a wall and a ditch. By now they had begun to meet others on the same errand, and all the talk was of Alaric, Alaric—Alaric the Balt, the all-ruler, who feared neither Hun nor Roman, Alaric who had fought under Theodosius in the days when there was still an emperor worth serving, Alaric whom they loved and trusted, Alaric the King !

Gersemi listened and wondered ; it was all so big, more than she could understand at first. She remembered that she had thought it a great army when her father and Bodvar went out with the men from south of the Ford, but this—she had seen more folk in a month than in all her life before ! She had to be careful, to bathe or change her clothes hastily and in the dark, to sleep alone if she could ; she might not let herself be challenged to swim or wrestle, nor would she willingly go among other women, where a sudden look, wrongly answered, might pierce all her disguise. But anything strange she did was put down to her being a northerner, and she was too solid and straight-faced for any old fighter to make love to her as a boy.

One evening at dusk they saw distant, tiny fires starring the horizon ; the next day they rode into the great ring of wagons and chose themselves a place. Avilf seemed to have hundreds of friends here ; he was hardly a moment alone, and always he and Gersemi were feasting or being feasted. Torches and bonfires flared, men shouted and sang, and danced in linked swaying circles, horses whinnied, oxen bellowed, women and children screamed across the camping grounds ; there were horns and trumpets and a thud of drums, all the armour was polished, all the cloaks were new and coloured, all the jewels were flashing, the tents were scarlet and white, the wagons were striped with fresh paint, and either the sky was blue at noon, or streaky orange at sunset, or at night soft black, swarming with thousands of stars. Here, when all had come, they held the Assembly with shouting and clashing, and they lifted high on the shield Alaric, the yellow-haired King !

Gersemi was there with the others : why not ? She was Avilf's friend, so she was the friend of any Goth ; she would fight for them, so she was one of them. Dim and far was the Ford and the windy steading of Sämund ; long ago it was she had watched the grey waves beating on the reef across Vig's Bay ; longer ago still when she had walked in blue, trailing robes and given kiss for kiss to Bodvar the Easterling. Now she was Alaric's man, she was making ready to follow him south for a sacking of cities and a vengeance on the emperors who had despised him !

She found it all very simple. But it was not so simple to Alaric and his nobles, who knew somehow that they had the light and the hope now, when Rome was sinking down into the pit she had digged, when Arcadius was no more than a name behind Rufinus, and the child Honorius almost less than a name behind Stilicho who was himself a Vandal.

When they moved, they moved quickly, a long glittering line of shields and lances. Again Gersemi rode beside Avilf, her scarlet coat and cloak a little stained perhaps, but bright enough yet ; the bearskin and her sewn-up pack of beads and jewels were safe in a wagon behind. She sang songs to herself and laughed at the scattering peasants and taught her little horse to do tricks like the Goth horses. Almost at once they got into hills, splashing and clattering up old water-courses, stumbling and slipping on stones and dry grass. It was up one cliff and down another to get into Thessaly, passes where they could scarcely go two abreast, a hot, strong scent of mountain herbs, and on the knotted wild vines the first grapes Gersemi had ever tasted. In the middle of the mountains were great fertile tablelands where they raided cattle and horses or burst in on the middle of the harvesting ; then up and up again and over and down, and below to the left a blue glitter of sea. Between the waves and the cliffs they filled the narrow strip of plain with their army ; here they had gone cautiously, but none had barred the way. Gersemi, riding on the sand and looking up across the spears at the towering hillside, asked where they were.

' Thermopylæ,' said Avilf, ' a good place for an attack if these Greeks had been men enough to face us.'

For a time they went on by the sea, and then it was inland and climbing again, the green plain of a river, a great bright lake and the shut gates of Thebes seen from a mile away. But soon they came out on to a city, a bigger city than they had come to yet, a city light and strong, and facing them ; and all that day they prepared for the attack.

It meant nothing to Gersemi when Avilf told her, a little awed himself even, that this was Athens. She lay down on the bearskin and slept soundly, not afraid of tomorrow ; but she woke a little before dawn when the stars were paling but still bright in the west. There was a cold wind, so she took the skin to wrap about her when she got up ; she could just see the black rune marks on the inside, and ran her finger up and down them, wondering what they meant and what the fairy bear had really done and whether it spoke their own language to the Finns. She went to the top of a mound so as to see the whole city ; every moment it got clearer, till high up she could see the outline of a great temple and a statue beside it. She left her mound and went quietly nearer and nearer : Athens—what did Avilf mean by saying it like that ?

There was someone moving on the walls. Very likely.

Someone—tall. She rubbed her eyes ; was it this grow-
ing light that seemed to make the someone grow with it ?
Now there were two of them, a man and a woman ; and
big, and shining ! Who were they ? She called low to
Avilf, who started up and ran to her with :
' What is it ? What have you seen ? Why are you
looking like that ? '
She pointed. ' Avilf, can't you see them ? '
He shook his head.
' But can't you ? Oh, you must ! Look—straight
ahead, standing on the wall ! '
' Who ? What are they like ? '
She hesitated.
' I thought just now they were a man and a woman.
But they're not ; they're Gods. She—she's a Valkyr :
or more than that. Her hair's like a flame under her
helmet. She's holding a long spear, and her armour's all
gold. And there's a great snake—Oh, Avilf, she's pointing
down at us ! There. She's gone on ; she's like a statue
moving. And he—angry ! He's like a Roman soldier,
only so tall, so strong : a god, but not one of my gods.
Oh, his face ! '
Avilf was shivering too, and staring where she pointed :
' I see nothing. You must be dreaming still. They'll
go with the light.'
' But it was with the light they came.'
Avilf looked from Gersemi to the city, frowning :
' Athens—she'd have guardians if any city has. Oh,
I'm cold ! '
Gersemi threw half her cloak round him—she wasn't
thinking of cold now. He pulled the white bearskin
across his back, then suddenly gave a sharp cry :
' Oh, Christ, I see them too ! '
' Who are they, Avilf ? '
' I don't know. Gods. Come back, Gersemi. They're

looking at us ! ' He pulled at her arm. ' Come back, lad, we must warn the others ! '

So back to the sleepy camp they ran, looking fearfully over their shoulders at those two great figures with the dawn now gold on their spear tips. They told the guards, they woke the nobles, everyone crowded and whispered and looked. Some saw at once, others only when they touched the rune-marked bearskin. Alaric the King, he saw. But when the sun was fully risen, that armed Athene and that fierce and guardian Achilles were vanished into the wind. Nevertheless, Alaric made a treaty with Athens and there was no fighting there.

But after that they went to the Peloponnese, over the old hills where fennel and wild parsley yet grew ; but Pan fled before them. And when they came to the cliff-walled plain of Sparta neither Castor nor Pollux came to stay the sacking of their city. Corinth, Argos, Sparta, all flames, all in ruins, and everywhere the barbarian Goths.

It was all over long ago ; the flame is less than ash, the walls are dust, and would still be dust if all that had never happened ; death has been over the same ground many times since then : nobody cares. But in that winter it was real enough : all the breaking in of savagery —men half-beasts again—on the old poised wonder of Greece : terror and death, men flying and stabbed in the back as they ran, the yells of the Goth spearmen across the breaking walls, women and boys from gentle homes, flowers and books and music, torn screaming away to serve barbarian masters, and never again, not once, to see the old peace and happiness, their old, sweet houses again.

There was seldom any standing-out against the Goths ; few were killed and not many even wounded. Avilf had his helmet broken in and his scalp cut by a tile thrown off a roof, but Gersemi was unhurt. She had started wearing the bearskin again when the cold days came, and that had been a good protection ; let alone that her mail shirt would turn most blows. She had plenty of confidence, and she loved the rushing and yelling and all the things they did together in a great blood-mad crowd. It was splendid to feel that these white god-built cities were nothing against their strength, they, the masters of the world ! She loved to handle the spoil afterwards, heavy gold of the gem-set cup, bright gold topping the ivory of the statues of goddesses, and most of all the women's things, necklaces and ear-rings, hair-pins, bracelets, girdles and all the marvellous frail tissues, silk enough to pull and trample and tear to pieces with hands and teeth if that was the mood ! Many times the scarlet cloak had been replaced already, and the little horse had gold and silver bells on his bridle and tassels of cut crystal plaited into his mane.

When it was her turn for the other loot—the black-haired, dark-eyed Greek maidens —she would always say she had sworn on oath to touch no women until she was twenty ; and this seemed reasonable enough to the others, who wondered sometimes to find such a boy so fierce. She had very little fellow-feeling for these poor women, they seemed another kind from herself, and besides—what else had ever happened to women in war ? She thanked all her gods that she herself had got away from it and was almost the equal of a man. She could do anything else—anything ! Oh, it was a good life.

When the Bough Breaks

DOUGLAS YOUNG

Ice-flumes Owregie their Lades

GANGAN my lane amang the caulkstane alps
that glower abune the Oetztal in Tirol
   I wan awa heich up amang the scalps
o snawy mountains whaur the wind blew cauld
   owre the reoch scarnoch and sparse jenepere,
wi soldanellas smoort aneath the snaw,
   and purpie crocus whaur the grund was clear,
rinnan tae fleur in their brief simmer thaw,
   and auntran gairs o reid alproses, sweir tae blaw.

And syne I cam up til a braid ice-flume,
spelderan doun frae aff the Wildspitz shouther,
   a frozen sea, crustit wi rigid spume,
owredichtit whiles wi sherp and skinklan pouther
   frae a licht yowden-drift o snaw or hail,
clortit by avalanche debris, gaigit deep
   wi oorie reoch crevasses, whaur the pale
draps o sun-heatit ice ooze doun and dreep
   intil the friction-bed, whaur drumlie horrors sleep.

They say ice-flumes maun aa owregie their lades,
and corps o men win out ae day tae licht.
   Warsslan remorseless doun reluctant grades
the canny flumes hain their cauld victims ticht.

---

ice-flumes, glaciers   *owregie*, give up   *lades*, loads   *caulkstane*, limestone
   reoch, rough   *scarnoch*, scree   *auntran gairs*, occasional patches
   sweir, unwilling   *spelderan*, sprawling   *owredichtit*, wiped over
skinklan, glittering   *yowden-drift*, down-driving storm   *gaigit*, fissured
     oorie, dank   *drumlie*, turbidly filthy

But no for aye.   Thretty or fowrty year
a corse may ligg afore his weirdit tide
    and yet keep tryst.   Whiles they re-appear
gey carnwath-like the wey the glaciers glide,
    whiles an intact young man confronts a crineit bride.

A Lausanne pastor wi's Greek lexicon
vanished awa amang the Diablerets,
    syne eftir twenty year the Zanfleuron
owregya the baith o them til the licht o day,
    still at the Greekin o't.   Twa Tirolese,
faaen doun a gaig, ate what they had til eat,
    scryveit their fowk at hame, and syne at ease
stertit piquet.   Baith had the self-same seat
    saxteen year eftir, but their game was nae complete.

In Norroway in Seeventeen Ninety Twa
frae fifty year liggin aneath the ice
    a herd appeared and syne beguid tae thaw
and gaed about as souple, swack, and wyce
    as when he fell frae sicht i thon crevasse.
Sae sall it be wi Scotland.   She was free,
    throu aa the warld weel kent, a sonsy lass,
whill whummlet in Historie's flume.   But sune we'll see
    her livan bouk back i the licht.   Juist byde a wee.

                                                    A Braird o Thristles

corse, animated corpse   *weirdit*, fated   *gey carnwath-like*, exceedingly distorted
            beguid, began   *swack*, strong   *wyce*, intelligent
    sonsy, well-conditioned, thriving   *whill*, until   *bouk*, bulk, body

SIR ALEXANDER GRAY

A Father of Socialism

CHARLES FOURIER occupies a singular position among the fathers of socialism ; indeed, viewed from any angle, he is a unique and enigmatical phenomenon. He was born in Besançon in 1772, the son of a linen-draper in reasonably easy circumstances. On leaving school he travelled for a time, somewhat extensively, for various firms, visiting Belgium, Germany and Holland. On his father's death he inherited sufficient to enable him to start business in Lyons. In the troubles of 1793 Lyons, revolting against the Convention, was bombarded. Fourier narrowly escaped being shot, and he did lose his entire fortune. Thereafter for two years he served, an unwilling soldier, in the army. During the remainder of his life nothing happened to Fourier, not even marriage. He travelled for various firms ; he was a clerk ; he served commerce intermittently, but always on the lowest rung of the ladder. On the strength of an exiguous legacy, at times he did nothing ; and he wrote a number of extraordinary books in which he said the same things over and over again. He floated about between modest private hotels and furnished apartments, and in this depressing environment he died in 1837, being then sixty-five years of age.

Such is the outline. Yet two reasonably authenticated incidents deserve mention for their influence on the development of his mind. When a boy in his father's shop—indeed at the age of five, it is said—he received correction from his father for revealing to a customer some petty trick in the retail business ; and the infant Fourier, realising that commerce was built on deceit, swore, like the infant Hannibal, that he would destroy the great enemy, which in this case was commerce. He complained that he was taught to tell the truth in church, and to tell lies in his father's shop. References to this 'Hannibal oath' occur throughout the literature of Fourier. Later, having attained man's estate and being at Marseilles, it was his duty to assist at dead of night in discharging into the harbour a cargo of rice, which the owners had allowed to spoil in expectation of a rise in price. Fourier, observing the stealthy destruction of what had once been food, and thinking of the hungry men sleeping uneasily all around, realised anew the shortcomings of civilisation and of commerce alike, and found occasion to renew his 'Hannibal oath.' Fourier did not succeed in destroying commerce ; on the contrary, he spent a large part of his life as one of the least of its bondsmen. But the two legends are none the less significant.

As to the man himself, Fourier is almost the perfect example of furtive insignificance. Indeed he is worse than that. His was the insignificance, the timidity, the absurdity which inevitably provoke a smile even in recollection. An apostle of chaotic liberty, he nevertheless had a mania for orderliness, and was never happy unless things could be docketed and arranged in series. Even when he gained disciples, he never could be prevailed upon to speak, and throughout life had a great gift of silence. Old-maidish in his habits, he had two passions, one for cats and the other for flowers. Perhaps music should be added as a third : he never could resist the impulse to march behind the band. Only very moderately educated in his youth, he belongs to the race of authors who have no desire to know what others have thought or said. Despite his modesty, he has accordingly no hesitation in proclaiming himself the first person for two thousand years to illumine the world's darkness. In a phrase which should give comfort to all, Emile Faguet has said of him that he has the disadvantages of ignorance which are great, and the advantages of ignorance which are enormous. 'Moi seul' and 'moi le premier' are recurrent motives in the writings of this unheroic commercial traveller who was cast for the part of Timorous rather than of Great-Heart. Take, as an example at random, one resonant blast of his goose-quill :

Moi seul j'aurai confondu vingt siècles d'imbécilité politique ; et c'est à moi seul que les générations présentes et futures devront l'initiative de leur immense bonheur. Avant moi l'humanité a perdu plusieurs mille ans à lutter follement contre la nature ; moi le premier. . . .

and so on, rising to one of his few recurrent tags : ' Exegi monumentum aere perennius.'

Fourier, moreover, had a childish, rather than a childlike, faith in God and the goodness of God. Indeed, in some respects, Fourier's ' theology,' to give it a somewhat pretentious name, provides the foundation stone of all his theories, and will require to be noticed in somewhat greater detail presently. Lastly, and it is the point which distinguishes him from the rest of mankind, Fourier was blessed or cursed with a most riotous and unpruned imagination, so unrestrained indeed that it is doubtful how far he could have passed any of the ordinary tests of sanity. There is nothing which his disordered imagination cannot vividly conceive, either at the foundation of the world or in the days of Harmony yet to be realised, and he writes it all down in the minutest detail, with the calm assurance of a perpetual private secretary to Providence from whom nothing has been concealed. It would perhaps be unjust to suggest that no writer, living or dead, has ever produced a larger volume of outrageous nonsense than has Fourier. A much subtler diagnosis is required.

In him the form is always much more grotesque than the substance ; but undeniably he clothes all he has to say in a fantasy and an imagery which are so charged with the ludicrous that Fourier is scarcely to be read without, intermittently, loud guffaws of uproarious and irreverent laughter. Moreover, everything about Fourier is bizarre. A reader not accustomed to such things may be surprised to find a ' Postface ' at the end of a volume, or to be confronted with an ' extroduction,' a ' postienne ' or a ' citerlogue.' The diatonic scale turns up in unexpected places ; there are strange symbols, K's, X's and Y's, now lying on their back, now standing upside down. In at least one case (*La Fausse Industrie*) the pagination would defy an army of detectives to unravel. Fourier may at times be a hilarious farce : at times he is also an impenetrable mystification. Let no-one, approaching Fourier, imagine that he is taking up a volume marked by the decorum, the austerity and the conventionality of John Stuart Mill.

Before attempting to give a more or less orderly account of that chaos that is Charles Fourier, it may be permissible to state briefly wherein lies his significance, and what is his place in the unfolding of socialist doctrine. Stated somewhat summarily, the importance of Fourier lies in the fact that, like Saint-Simon, he is a link, and a very interesting link, between the eighteenth and the nineteenth centuries. They are indeed very different links, though they have this in common, that these two fathers of socialism are not in essence particularly socialistic ; they are disfigured by strangely conservative features which do not appear in the child. They both cling to property ; they are alike devotees of inequality. The essence of Fourier is that, as he looked round the world, he saw that everything was wrong, not merely a few things here and there, but the whole scheme of things. It was in a sense civilisation itself that was wrong—civilisation with all its attendant conventions and consequences. In this respect he is an echo, perhaps a caricaturing echo, of that greater voice from the eighteenth century, of Jean Jacques Rousseau, who also found that somehow the human race had taken the wrong turning. And if both found that our civilisation was a poor thing, a whited sepulchre, there is this to be said for the insignificant Fourier, as against his mightier predecessor, that he was at least constructive. Rousseau is after all little more than a wail of despair, an ineffective wringing of hands. But Fourier knew, with the utmost precision and definiteness he knew, what he wanted and what had to be done, and how in short the world could be put right in the brief space of two years. It is only necessary to abandon Morality, that evil legacy of civilisation, and to listen to our natural impulses, and we should straightway overcome all the trickery, the deceits, the hypocrisy, the divided interests, the parasitism which is what civilisation is. We shall in fact have established Harmony, and Harmony is the co-operation of men who sing at their work. Nothing could be simpler. It only requires a capitalist, and not even a very big one, to give the thing a start, and the rest is as easy as falling off a house.

In a sense Fourier's religion provides the starting-point of all his observations and of all his criticisms. It pervades all his thoughts, and it will constantly recur in almost every paragraph of this chapter ; for this reason it may be as well to seek at the outset the dominant *idées mères* of Fourier on this subject. The old truth that man created God in his own image, that ' thou thoughtest I was altogether such an one as thyself,' is nowhere more startlingly illustrated than in the case of Fourier. That God is good, that God has done well in all that he has done, that he has done nothing without a meaning and a purpose, sum up in general terms the essence of Fourier's religion ; but with the acute logic of a somewhat unbalanced mind, he pushes this body of doctrine to conclusions which are much less orthodox than are usually drawn from these premises. He is severe on those who ' half believe ' in God. Belief in the goodness of God implies belief in the goodness of all that God has done ; it is therefore inconsistent with a belief that a good God could make man with evil impulses and passions against which men have to wage incessant war. This, which is the line of the moralist and the theologian, is to establish war between God and man ; indeed it is to set God at war with himself. We should seek for the laws of God in the impulses that come from God ; he foresaw, for example, that we should wish to eat three times a day. Those who write facetiously about *la galanterie et la gourmandise* are ignorant of the importance which God attaches to our pleasures ; for it is by ' Attraction '—by pleasure—and not by constraint, that God governs the universe. It is thus that he governs planets and insects ; it is thus that he intended to govern Man.

Moreover, in creating this unhappy world of ours, God was not engaged, as Burns would have put it, in trying out his ' prentice hand.' He has created milliards of globes before ours, and has thus acquired vast experience *pendant l'Eternité passée*. Elsewhere, even more patronisingly, he explains that God has had ample time to learn by experience in creating men in milliards of other worlds. In short, he knew what he was doing when he made men as they are ; and instead of correcting the work of God we should endeavour to find out how he meant his works to be used.

And, primarily, God's intentions were that we should enjoy ourselves. Not only so, it would be an insult to

God to expect him to provide merely mediocre pleasures. To ask merely for our daily bread—*le misérable pain*, says Fourier, who never could abide bread—is to misconceive the magnanimity of God. In a phrase which comes with a certain shock by reason of its reversal of Christian ideas, ' Dieu nous doit beaucoup, puisqu'il peut beaucoup ' ; he owes us infinite happiness in this life and in the life to come. It is God who is *our* debtor. He hath made us, and not we ourselves ; in fact (though Fourier does not stress the point) we were not consulted. He gave us a yearning for happiness; and as (by definition) his power is infinite, he owes us happiness pressed down and running over, a perpetual and unconditional pouring out of a blessing from the windows of heaven, so that there shall not be room enough to receive it.

Fourier, as has been hinted above, presents his criticisms of life and his social theories in a fantastic and indeed grotesque framework. It would be easy, by appropriate selections, to present him as a figure of farce and low comedy ; but it would probably be equally wrong, again by appropriately different selections, to present him as a sober-minded and austere critic, adding his ponderous brick of thought to the construction of the socialist edifice. Many writers in their references to Fourier give the reader no hint, or but the merest hint, that Fourier was most emphatically not as other men : indeed in some respects he is a unique phenomenon in the world's literature. This designedly tactful drawing of a veil over Fourier's peculiarities is mistaken, if only because it gives a wrong and one-sided view of the man he was. After all, there is nothing to be ashamed of in being slightly deranged. For all we know, it may be the condition of the bulk of humanity : it all depends on the standards we choose to apply. But in the case of Fourier, there is this further most decisive reason against suppressing any acknowledgment of his eccentricities that his sanity and his apparent deviations from normal sanity are strangely intermingled. Indeed his whole criticism of civilisation to a certain extent postulates as a background his fantastic cosmogony and his views regarding the stages through which humanity must pass.

With this semi-apology for an apparent departure from accustomed austerity, we may endeavour to illustrate some of the more unexpected ideas which may surprise a reader embarking, unwarned, upon the turbulent waters of Fourier. Most intimately interwoven with the essence of his thought are his theories regarding the Cosmos. This world has been granted a life of 80,000 years ; there are 40,000 of ascending vibrations and 40,000 of descending vibrations. The arithmetic may seem weak, since there is also a period of 8,000 years of complete happiness, the *Apogée du Bonheur*. Doubtless this minor discrepancy is covered by Fourier's general reservation that everything he says is subject to an exception of an eighth or a ninth. In all there are thirty-two periods, sixteen in the upward and sixteen in the downward ladder. We are at present in the fifth of the first eight stages, having passed through what Fourier calls the *Sectes Confuses, Sauvagerie, Patriarchat* and *Barbarie*. Ahead of us lies *Garantisme*, a stage in which human rights will be effectively guaranteed to us ; at times, however, it is rather suggested that we may by-pass *Garantisme*. These eight stages take up 5,000 years, and we shall then find ourselves in Harmony— indeed more and more delirious grades of Harmony, for 35,000 years. Thereafter for 8,000 years we shall have that lofty tableland of perfect bliss, after which the world will go downhill again through precisely the same stages in the inverse order ; and at the end, if any of us are left, we shall be transported to another planet.

It is when we approach Harmony that things will begin

to hum. A Northern Crown (after the manner of Saturn's rings) will encircle the Pole, shedding a beneficent aromatic dew on the earth. The sea will cease to be briny, and, greatest of delights, will be transformed into lemonade, for which unsatisfying beverage Fourier seems to have had a marked partiality. Six moons of a new and superior quality will replace our present inefficient satellite. A new race of animals will emerge. In place of the lion, there will be the anti-lion, all that a lion is not, docile and serviceable ; there will be anti-wolves and anti-bears, and a whole race of really nice beasts. If things are only taken in hand at once, telescoping various stages, the anti-bug may be looked for in 1829, along with the anti-rat. This is indeed good news for *le beau Paris*, *si richement meublé de punaises*, of which incidentally there are forty-two varieties. Our argosies, knitting land to land, will be drawn by anti-whales. After these marvels, it is perhaps rather a disappointment to know that we shall then live only 144 years, of which, however, 120 will be spent in the active exercise of love.

It is perhaps a corollary to this lively interest in the history of the globe that Fourier is also so much concerned with the stars and the planets, which in so many ways influence our lives now and hereafter. The stars and planets are animated beings like ourselves, only perhaps more so. They also have their passions, and from their passions spring other stars and planets, but also plants and animals. The planets seem to be androgynous, like plants self-contained for purposes of reproduction ; but they also have intercourse with other planets. Unless Fourier is more confused than usual, the Aurora Borealis merely betokens that the Earth is holding out lonely hands of love to Venus. Fourier tabulates at considerable length the various animals and plants we owe to Jupiter, the Sun, Venus and so on. The death of Phoebe (otherwise known as the Moon) plays a large part in this astronomical fantasy. Phoebe, whom he rather rudely calls a *cadavre blafard*, died of a putrid fever, contracted from the Earth fifty years before the Flood : it was indeed the death of Phoebe that caused the Flood. The absence of her contribution to the last creation caused some strange omissions in the animals and plants we ought to have had. In particular, the world has been the poorer by the absence of a very special gooseberry, of which it was robbed by the untimely decease of Phoebe. The discriminating reader will have begun to discern dimly how the anti-lion and the anti-bug are to be generated : another creation, under more favourable conditions and therefore consisting predominantly of good beasts, is pending, and will mark the transition to Harmony.

Fourier's concern for human happiness is not limited to what happens in this transitory life. He believes not merely in immortality ; he believes also in metempsychosis. We shall return again and again, and keep on returning ; and that is one reason why we should be so intensely interested in what is going to happen. It is important that this should be a world worth returning to. On all this, Fourier is as extensively and as exactly informed as he is regarding the death of Phoebe. He knows exactly how long we shall be away, when and how we shall return. He knows how what we do now influences the lives of those waiting to come back, and again it is all told with a wealth of ludicrous detail which may not be so exciting as his account of the passionate drama of the love affairs of the planets, but is equally full of information which, as the reviewers say, is not readily available elsewhere.

Enough perhaps of the fantastic side of Fourier ; yet perhaps so much is necessary, firstly because these extravagances may not be dismissed as idle weeds that grow in the sustaining corn ; they are, as has been suggested above, an integral part of Fourier ; and secondly, because it is as well that the reader should know in advance that there are moments of wild surprise in the perusal of our author.

The Socialist Tradition

ALEXANDER SCOTT

The Gowk in Lear

It wasna the King, it wasna Heich-Degree
    That sang fornent the levin—
Reivit o micht and dwyned in majestie,
    He hurled a challance at heaven.

Nor Fairheid sang at the drumlie yett o death
    Whar shade and sunlicht grapple—
Deep in a dungeon's dark she tint her breath,
    A raip aroun her thrapple.

And Lealtie happit his truth in a ragment o lees,
    A babble o Bedlamish blether—
Wud as the wind he skirled at the levin's bleeze,
    His tongue gane wersh as the weather.

Nane o them, Lealtie, Fairheid, Heich-Degree,
    Cud sing whan the thunder duntit—
Wae had stown their sangs frae aa the three,
    And dule had left them runtit.

For wha cud sing whan the lift was a fiery lowe
    Whar muin and starns were burnan ?—
Nane but a Gowk wi naething but dreams in's pow
    Cud mak at a time o murnin.

Nane but a Gowk wi nae mair wits nor a burd
    Cud sing lik the marlit mavis—
Whit man that's wyce sae luves the livan word
    As sing i the howe whar the grave is ?

fornent, against   *levin*, lightning   *Reivit*, robbed   *Fairheid*, beauty
drumlie, shadowy   *wersh*, bitter   *runtit*, cleaned out   *lift*, sky
lowe, flame   *marlit*, speckled   *wyce*, sane

Nane but a Gowk cud sing whan the warld was hell
  And Christ dung doun bi the Deevil—
Nane but a Gowk ower glaikit tae fash for himsel
  Cud lauch i the lour o evil.

Nane but a Gowk cud sing—whan wyce men's sangs
  Were stown, and saunts were quaet—
The weird o the warld, sae wyvit o richts and wrangs
  That nane but a Gowk cud spey it.

The Latest in Elegies

glaikit, daft   *weird*, fate   *wyvit*, woven

NEIL M GUNN

Up from the Sea

THE boy's eyes opened in wonder at the quantity of sea-
tangle, at the breadth of the swath which curved with the
curving beach on either hand. The tide was at low ebb
and the sea quiet except for a restless seeking among the
dark boulders. But though it was the sea after a storm
it was still sullen and inclined to smooth and lick itself,
like a black dog bent over its paws ; as many black dogs
as there were boulders ; black sea-animals, their heads
bent and hidden, licking their paws in the dying evening
light down by the secret water's edge. When he stepped
on the ware, it slithered under him like a living hide.
He was fascinated by the brown tangled bed, the eel-like
forms, the gauzy webs. There had been no sun to congeal
what was still glistening and fresh.

A faint excitement touched his breast, his lips parted,
his eyes shot hither and thither. He began rooting at the
bed with his boots, stooping every now and again to
examine the head of a tangle. At length he found one
with a small delicate limpet stuck in the cup of its head ;
a young one because its round stem was slim and not two
feet in length. As he snicked it free its leathery tail-
frond flicked sea-mist to his face. His teeth began to
water. He cut the brown stem two inches from the shell
with his pocket-knife, which had one strong sharp blade.
As he pared off the claw-roots that curled round the
hollow where the shell was, he was very careful not to
remove the shell. The shell was the jewel in its head,
importing tenderness and sweetness. It was also something to ' show off.' He put the tangle head in his pocket
and lifted the folded sack that had slipped from under
his arm. Then he went on rooting amongst the bed

until he had found two more tangles with shells. But
neither was so delicate, so thin skinned, as the first. The
first was a beauty ! When he had dressed them and
stuffed them in his pocket, he gave an involuntary shiver ;
his teeth clicked and he brought the back of his hand to
his wet nose. His nose was colder than his hand. His
body twisted and wriggled inside his clothes searching for
warmth. But his round dark eyes were on the boulders
down by the hidden sea-edge. It was time he got his
' baiting.'

Below the high-tidal sweep of tangleweed the beach
sloped in clean grey-blue stones rounded and smooth,
some no bigger than his fist, but some larger than his head.
As he stepped on them they slithered and rolled with a
sea noise. The noise rose up and roared upon the dusk
like a wave. All around no life was to be seen, there was
no movement but the sea's. It was too lonely a place to
make a noise. He was relieved to come on firmer ground
where the boulders began. He went out amongst the
boulders quietly until he came to the mussel bed. Then
he folded back the bag and squatted down, and began
tearing the clusters of mussels from the ground.

Sometimes stones stuck to the roots, but these he caught
and tore off easily. Many of the mussels were very small,
and a small mussel made an insufficient bait. Big fat
mussels were what were needed. It took the same labour
to shell a big mussel as a small one. Indeed it was easier,
because the two sides of the small mussel were so close-
shut and delicate that the knife-blade would not go in
between them, and so was inclined to slip and cut the
ball of the thumb. It was very vexing to cut a thumb
when working in salt water. Besides, the salt water was
great for making the cut keep on bleeding. And then,
as everyone said, it was a difficult thing to get an open
wound to heal readily in cold or wintry weather.

. . . His hands were now bitterly cold. He could not feel his fingers. There was a drip of water to his nose which he brushed slowly away with the back of his hand, at the same time pressing the hand hard against his nose as though to warm the point, pressing it harder still, till his whole body quivered with the sustained effort to draw heat from inside him. But no heat came, and as he straightened himself his teeth chittered. Then he began smartly slapping his arms across his breast, as his father did and the other fishermen. But the clip of his finger-tips against the curves of his back was painful.

He kept up the manly exercise for a little to satisfy appearances, but he knew he wasn't really letting his hands slap properly. It was too sore. The cold had now chilled them to the bone and the fingers were growing painful. He put them under his blue jersey and knuckled them against his stomach. He drew them forth again, closed them into squirming fists, cupped and blew on them, pressed them against each other. In a sudden frenzy he began slapping them round his sides again, but now in real earnest, not caring for the pain.

Gradually the heat began to come. The tingling of it grew. The arrowy stabbing in the numbed fingers became unbearable. They began to burn in agony. He looked at the reddened swollen tips, holding them claw-upwards in an utterly helpless gesture. His body writhed and little dry sobbing sounds came from his throat.

But he would not cry. He only pretended to cry in order to ease the anguish. He could have cried readily enough. His body twisted and doubled up, but he daren't touch anything with his fingers now. Something inside was trying to force its way through them. The tingling flesh was swollen and wouldn't let the thing pass. Then suddenly the pain reached a point from which it had to recede or he would have cried.

With the throb of the pain dying down, the relief was exquisite. He even pressed the thumbs hard against the finger-tips to make the pain sting a little, as though he were catching it up and hurting it before it slipped away altogether. Now his hands were in a glow. He felt exhilarated. From his pocket he drew forth the young tender tangle, and scraping the transparent skin off its end with white even teeth, he bit on it exactly as a dog bites on a bone. The tangle was not so hard as a bone, but very nearly. Saliva flowed into his mouth, and with wet red lips and sharp teeth he sucked and gnawed, moving the tangle-end this way and that until his stretched mouth ached in the effort to give the crunching molars a real chance. But the bit he broke off was sweet and tender to his palate, and its salty flavour excited a greater flow of spittle than ever, so that his mouth moved richly and he swallowed many times. A tangle was always a little disappointing in the first minute, as though the memory of it contained more food. But once you started gnawing you could not stop.

With a final look at the shredded end, he stowed the tangle in his pocket. If he didn't hurry it would soon be dark. And his father would be waiting for the bait. And, anyway, he would pick up another young tangle with a shell on his way back. He would keep it whole to show off, because the other boys were playing football. He himself liked playing football better than anything. First of all he had said to his mother that he wouldn't go to the ebb. The mood had come on him to be dour and stubborn. It was a shame that he should have to go to the ebb, with the other boys playing football. The injustice of it had hit him strongly. His father had said nothing. But if he didn't go then his father would have had to. And by two or three in the morning his father would have to be aboard. It must be terribly cold in the

dark out on that sea ; out on that sea in the small hours
of a sleety morning, or on a morning of hard frost, with
a grey haar coming off the water like ghosts' breath.

The loneliness of the bouldered beach suddenly caught
him in an odd way. A small shiver went over his back.
The dark undulating water rose from him to a horizon
so far away that it was vague and lost. What a size it
was ! It could heave up and drown the whole world.
Its waters would go rushing and drowning. He glimpsed
the rushing waters as a turbulent whiteness released out
of thunderous sluices. 'But you can't,' he half-smiled,
a little fearfully, glancing about him. A short distance
away, right on the sea's edge, he saw one of the boulders
move. His heart came into his throat. Yet half his mind
knew that it could only be some other lonely human in
the ebb. And presently he saw the back bob up for a
moment again.

Yes, it was a man. Seeking among the boulders there
like some queer animal ! He looked about him carefully.
There was no-one else. There were just the two of them
in the ebb. Here they were on this dark beach, with
nobody else. A strange air of remoteness touched him.
It was as though they shared this gloomy shore, beyond
the world's rim, between them. There was a secret
importance in it. He stooped and began filling his bag
with mussels, picking big ones in a manly way. The
water was now merely cool to his burning hands. He
worked with great energy, a red sea-anemone stopping
him for less than a minute. This one had feelers out that
quietly retracted to his touch. Whereupon he squeezed
the red jelly with a knack that sent a little spirt of water
out of it. As he swished some bloated weed away below
the red anemone, he disclosed, however, a pocket of dulse.
This had the unexpectedness of a pleasant find. He had
quite forgotten about dulse. He ate some of the tender

fronds, and shaking the water from the rest of the bunch, stowed it in his pocket on top of the tangles until his pocket bulged and overflowed.

When he thought he had gathered sufficient mussels, he stood up and tested the weight of the bag. Then he said he would gather twenty more to make sure. He gathered twenty-five and then three more for luck, and then made it thirty, adding one after that to make dead certain.

As he came erect, the man who was also gathering mussels in the ebb straightened himself and put his hand in the small of his back. His back curved inward. So it was Sandy Sutherland. Swinging his bag on to a boulder, the boy got under his burden and started off towards Sandy, but yet slanting away from him to make his approach not too deliberate.

' Is it yourself, Hugh, that's in it ? ' The note of surprise in Sandy's voice was pleasant and warm. His face was whiskered, his ways quiet, his eyes dark-shining and kind.

' Yes,' said Hugh, pausing, and tingling a little with shy pleasure.

' Getting your father's baiting, I see.'

' Yes.'

' Aren't you cold ? '

' Oh no.'

' Well, you're plucky,' said Sandy. ' And it's your father that's lucky. Here I have to be down myself.' He said this with no grudge in his voice. It was half a joke. ' And my back has got the cramp in it, sure as death.' Though he was over sixty, his whiskers were black with a very white hair here and there. He took out his pipe. ' Was your father at the line when you left ? '

' Yes. He had just cleaned it.'

' It would be fair stinking, I suppose ? '

'Yes, the bait was rotten. You could smell it all over the house,' said Hugh, smiling, a faint flush on his face.

'I'm sure,' nodded Sandy. 'It's hard enough work baiting the line. And then to have to take all the bait off again without using it is—is enough to try the patience.'

'It is that,' said Hugh. 'It's been a big storm.'

'It was blowing as hard the night before last as it blew this winter. Indeed there was one gust that woke me up I thought the roof was going.'

'The roof of Dan Ross's barn was torn off, and a screw of Totaig's hay was blown into the burn.'

'So I heard. Totaig wouldn't be pleased at that !'

'No.'

'I could see him spreading it out yonder all day.'

'Yes !' Hugh gave a small laugh. Totaig was cross in the grain and mean. Sandy gave a chuckle also.

'Well, I'll be coming with you, if you wait till I gather one or two more. What sort of baiting have you yourself ?'

'Oh, I think I have plenty.' Hugh dropped his bag on a boulder and caught Sandy's eyes measuring the quantity in a secret glance.

'Perhaps you have, then.'

'Oh, I think so,' murmured Hugh.

But there was a faint reserve in Sandy's voice, as though he didn't like to suggest that the boy might not have gathered a full baiting.

It was a delicate point. Hugh saw that if Sandy could find a hidden or off-hand way of adding a few, he would do so.

'Perhaps you have, then,' Sandy repeated. 'Though you could gather one or two more for luck if you like while I'm finishing off. It would save you tomorrow night maybe.'

'Father isn't wanting a full baiting,' Hugh explained 'There's not much short of half one at home.'

'Oh, that makes a difference ! To gather more would be waste. Indeed, I'm thinking you have a full baiting there as it is, if not more.' The voice was amused rather than relieved. But Hugh understood perfectly.

'I think there's plenty,' he considered, as if now a trifle doubtful.

'Plenty ? I should say so ! Do you think I have as many as you myself ? '' He measured both bags with an eye. 'I should say nearly.'

'You have more, I think,' judged Hugh politely.

'Well, if you say so. But remember it's you I'll blame if I'm short ! It's a cold place this, anyway.' He lit his pipe, sending great clouds of blue smoke about his head. 'We'll chance it. So let us be going.' He shouldered his bag cheerfully and they both set off.

Besides the sea's breath, there was no wind, and the only sound was the wash among the boulders, with a deeper note from the rocks beyond the beach where the quietening water swayed sullenly in a murmurous boom-oom.

The light was now more than half gone, and the figures of the man and the boy, bent a little under their burdens, gathered as it seemed all the eyes of the place upon them as they walked away. Heads stooping forward, backs slightly arched, dark stumbling figures, moving up from the sea. Sparks of fire suddenly came from the old man's head. Each spark shone distinct and round, sprightly and mocking, gleaming wayward moments of an intenser life. The defeated water choked among the boulders. Through a rocky fissure a lean tongue thrust a hissing tip—that curled back on itself in cold froth.

They won clear of the weeded boulders. They approached the foreshore. Their fists gripped across

their breasts upon the ends of their sacks. The twist of
canvas bit into their shoulders, bit the boy's neck, as they
stumbled up the slope of grey-blue stones. The stones
rumbled and roared, carrying each foot back to the sea.
But foot went before foot, and soon they were on the
high-tidal bed of weed. Treacherously it slithered under
them, and when the boy stumbled the man cried to him
to take care. Soon they were over that, first their legs
disappearing beyond the crest of the beach, then their
bodies, and finally their heads. An eddy of darkness like
a defeated wind swirled in among the boulders. There
was nothing left for the watching eyes to see beyond that
crest but the first pale stars in heaven.

Morning Tide

The Little Red Cow

THE red cow had come back to the gate and now let out
a prolonged broken bellow at their backs, ending with a
choking gust.

'Gode, she'll roar her guts out,' said the ploughman,
taking his haunch from the wall, and turning round.

The cattleman laughed. 'For the size of her, she fair
beats the band !'

'I think she hurt her throat that time,' said the shepherd
interestedly.

They all looked at her. She was small, a shaggy dark-
red, and getting on in years, but her brown eyes were
deeply glittering, youthful, full of wild mad fires. A tuft
of hair on her brow let drop a few coarse strands over the
left eyebrow, giving her a ferocious look. One could
fancy that what was troubling her might drive her insane.

'What do you think is really wrong with her ?' asked
the ploughman.

122

'She's just strange,' said the cattleman. 'She's finding everything strange. That's all.'

'I think she's hurt herself,' said the shepherd, watching her.

'Not she!' said the cattleman.

The red cow opened her mouth and bellowed lustily five times in succession. They thought she was never going to stop, and even the shepherd, who was a quiet man, laughed.

'No, her throat seems all right,' he said.

'What do you think is wrong with her, Donul?' asked the cattleman. 'You should know, seeing you come from the same country.'

'Och, she'll just be finding herself strange,' answered Donul, looking over the dyke at the cow, and smiling in an awkward grown-up way, pretending he hadn't seen the cattleman's wink.

'Gode, she doesn't believe in keeping her breath to cool her porridge,' said the ploughman.

This gusty humour made them feel friendly to one another, and for the moment almost tender to the little red cow.

'She's for the butcher, I suppose?' said the shepherd.

'Where else?' answered the cattleman. 'Did you think she was for Kinrossie's prize herd?'

'You never know,' said the shepherd dryly. Regarding Donul with his considering eyes, he added: 'You wouldn't care for a trip out to the Argentine with her, would you, Donul?'

'I might do worse,' said Donul.

They were drawing the lees from the fun of this new thought when the red cow bellowed until the steading echoed. 'Aw, shut up!' said the ploughman. Stooping, he picked up a muddy stone and threw it at the cow. It hit her in the flank and she turned her wild eyes on them, but did not move. ' Man, ye're dour ! ' said the plough-man. ' Get off ! Whish ! Get out ! ' But though he raised his arms in a threatening jerk, the cow did not move. ' Ye for a stupid bitch,' said the ploughman, summing her up without heat as he rubbed his fingers against his hip.

' She does look dour, does she not ? ' said the cattleman. ' They're like that, them that come from the West.'

' It's in the breed,' said the shepherd, not thinking of Donul. ' Actually they're mild and gentle brutes, though they look wild.'

'I've known them very treacherous,' said the cattleman.

' Ay, but only when they've young calves following them,' answered the shepherd.

They discussed this until the bellowing distress of the brute forcibly claimed their attention again. ' Put the dog at her,' said the ploughman.

' Here, Toss ! ' called the cattleman. The old collie with the grey mouth got up from the dry spot by the cart-shed door and came across. ' Hits ! Drive her off ! Get into her ! ' The dog leapt on to the wall, saw the bellowing beast, and knew what he had to do. As he barked, the cow swung her head, but he easily avoided it, and in a very short time had her careering madly before him. When he thought he had driven her far enough, he stopped, without any shout from his master, and came slowly back.

' He's a wise old brute, that,' said the shepherd. They straightened themselves, and the shepherd said he must be getting home. The others went along towards the farm cottages for their food. Their day's work was over and they had enjoyed the talk by the wall.

In the darkening, Donul slipped away from the bothy where he lived with three other men, wearied of the look of their bodies and the sound of their talk. The red cow was still bellowing, but now with longer intervals between each outbreak. The other beasts in the field paid no attention to her, had paid no attention from the beginning. They were of a group that had travelled together for tomorrow's sale. The little red cow was all alone.

Donul knew quite well why she bellowed, knew it as though she were kin to him and were moved by the same emotions. She was of the breed of Old Hector's cow and of their own. He could see her moving about her home croft, tethered here, enclosed there, or herded by someone like Art or Neonain. A girl like Morag had milked her, after first clapping her, then speaking to her, and finally helping her to let down her milk by humming an old Gaelic air. The crofter who owned her had probably decided to sell in a hurry, because the young cow was coming up, and the problem of wintering was difficult. Or perhaps he was of the kind who thought he would get a better price by taking a chance in the market, for it was being said that Mr Nicolson was making a pile of money by not giving anything like the right price for the cattle he bought on the spot. And certainly, to Donul's knowledge, he had made a large profit off the beasts they had brought from Clachdrum. But it was another matter to call the man 'a robber.'

Or was it? The irruption of the bellowing red cow into his new difficult life had disturbed him deeply, had irritated him, and at times during the day had maddened him. In a moment of involuntary listening, he had heard the sound of her in the distance give out a curious echo, as though the field were encompassed by high prison walls. Actually he had had to turn and look at her to dissipate the fancy, and when he did, there she went, padding the ground, restless, wandering, seeking a way out.

Now in the deep dusk falling into night, the fantasy came back upon him; the prison walls grew higher and darker than ever, and echoed the sound into a distance remote and forlorn and terrible. The only way he could bear this was by shutting his heart in anger against the cow. He knew what the beast was shouting for. He knew only too well, damn her. He knew all right. Shut up! Oh, shut up!

Then a thought came to him. If he opened the gate and quietly drove her out, she would go straight home. He felt this with perfect certainty. She would go down glens and cross rivers and swim lochs and climb mountain ranges, day and night. That she had come part of the way by train made no difference. Certain beasts had the instinct that found the way home from any place. Men had told him of dogs and cattle that had done it, and even sheep. This beast was one of that kind. He now realized for the first time the nature of the instinct itself. It stirred in his own breast. He stopped, turned half round, and knew with a profound inner conviction that he was facing directly home. He sniffed the air and got the faint but distinct home smell of peat. Nostalgia went crinkling over his skin in a shiver. He had a swift blinding dislike of the cattleman and the other strange people. In a bitter spite he decided it would serve them right if he let the cow out. He was full of spite. He spat. And suddenly in an involuntary but clear vision, he saw the cow nearing home, stumbling a little on her weak legs because she was now in such a hurry, mooing softly through her nostrils, her wide eyes shining, a slaver at her mouth.

His body was trembling, his forehead cold. Those on the croft did not want the cow back. They needed the money. Dismay stood in their staring faces.

The little red cow bellowed far over on the other side of the field. Beyond the dark wall the sound went into the night, into regions of fear and terror. The primeval forces of fear and terror lurked and convoluted there, formless but imminent, and the little red cow went baying them like a beast of sacrifice.

Donul turned and made back for the bothy, holding himself with all his strength against running, his chest choked, his legs trembling. At the gable-end he paused, took off his bonnet, and wiped his forehead and his damp hair. He faced the horrific black formlessness as long as he could ; then he went into the bothy.

In the morning he was sent into the field to round the cattle up and take them to the market in the county town. It was a very busy day, for the farmer had many beasts of his own for sale in another field. The cattleman was shouting. The dogs were barking. As Donul drew near the red cow, the brute looked at him with her shining eyes, her head lowered, waiting, dumb. And intense anger swept over Donul. ' What way was yon to behave, you bloody fool ! ' he said harshly and drew his stick with all his force across her buttocks. He was ashamed of her, the fool that she was, and tried to hit her again ; but with a sudden snorting, a queer sound, not of pain, she started running, like a cow in heat, towards the gate. ' Canny with them ! ' shouted the cattleman as he opened the gate and let them through. Donul controlled the dark emotion that assailed him, by gripping his stick hard and not looking at the cattleman.

He had great difficulty driving the red cow along the main street. The other beasts grouped together and let vehicles past, but the little red cow hadn't even the sense to get out of the way. With splayed forelegs and head down, she waited. Once when Donul gave her a re-sounding whack, a fur-clad townswoman winced, her face suggesting that surely there was no need for such brutality—beasts were best handled by kindness. The cow went up a side lane and knocked over an empty perambulator and a message-boy's bicycle with a full load of groceries. Out of this pandemonium, after a final savage ' Shut up ! ' to the message-boy, Donul got her back to the main street. She went into a shop. The rest of the beasts had meantime overshot the right-hand turn to the auction mart.

By the time he had them penned, Donul was blown and red in the face.

As the sale proceeded, the cattleman and others he knew came round the ring. The incident of the cow in the shop provided a subject for amusing talk under the high urgent voice of the auctioneer.

' Did she offer to buy anything, Donul ? '

' No, man,' said Donul, trying to make a joke of the question by taking it seriously, but his smile was awkward, his face congested.

' Leave you Donul alone.'

' I'm not caring whether I'm left alone or not,' replied Donul.

They laughed, throwing a wink or two, and as one man mimicked his voice, his heart went black. But he did not walk away from them, and presently they scattered, each to get his own lot into the ring. ' I'll leave the red cow to you,' called the cattleman.

He heard them laugh as they went and knew they were laughing at him.

What should he do now ? The cattle were being sold a few at a time. He saw dealers marking their catalogues. Was the red cow a ' lot ' in herself, or what ? He went out and began to ask one of the mart men how he would know when the red cow was due to appear. The man gave him an abrupt look, shouted at someone, and hurried off. They were very busy. Donul decided he would go and wait by the pen, where he was astonished to find the red cow now all alone. She mooed at him, her eyes shining, a slaver at her mouth. But the moo was one of distrust, though in it, too, there was an incredible something that spoke to his flesh and bones. The half-pedigree heavy stock were new to him, with a certain strange indifference about them, and he was not dismayed by this ; but the crofter's cow was intimate to him as his inner self.

After a discreet glance around, he spoke to her. ' Ah, you fool, what was the sense in behaving like yon, with everyone looking at you ? ' He spoke to her in Gaelic, and she answered him at once through her nostrils, her mouth shut. The sound of understanding, of longing, gave his heart a turn. ' Be quiet ! ' he ordered, turning his back on her.

He leaned against the wooden rail of the pen, his elbows resting on it. Men came and emptied pen after pen, with shouts, and the whacking of sticks on hides. He felt the red cow's head between his shoulders, pushing him. ' What the devil are you up to ? ' he demanded in English as he swung round.

Time passed. He suddenly saw the cattleman and two others at the other entrance to the mart. The cattleman raised his stick, pointing Donul out, and they laughed. A great voice roared ' Hurry up, there ! ' from the near entrance.

' Are you wanting her now ? ' called Donul.

' What the hell ! '

Swiftly Donul opened the gate of the pen, but now the little red cow was dour and would not move. ' Get out ! ' yelled Donul, pushing her fiercely.

' Damn it, do you think we can wait for you all day ? ' bellowed the man at his back. But the little red cow took an astonishing amount of punishment from the man before she went along the passage-way, hit into the open gateway of the ring, and had to be shoved bodily through it, followed by Donul.

'She's not so tough as she looks, gentlemen,' cried the gentlemanly auctioneer. There was a laugh. 'Well, who'll start me at ten pounds ? . . . eight ? . . . seven ? Come along, gentlemen. Well cared for, plump crofter's cow.' He made a gesture to Donul, 'Show her round.'

Donul tried to get her to move, but she had her fore-legs splayed again and her head lowered. By sheer force he heaved her hindquarters round three inches, but that was all. He felt red and hot ; sweat broke out on his forehead. He became intently conscious of the tiers of faces surrounding him under the roof of the mart. The sting of the watching faces maddened him as he struggled in the ring with the little red cow. There was a tittering laugh from one corner. He knew that laugh. Soft snorts broke out here and there from the amphitheatre.

Smiling, the auctioneer swung round, lifted a glass of water from the clerk's table behind him and drank in a gentlemanly way. He generally had to provide his own humour, and humour at any time was a godsend ; it lightened the proceedings and brought bids more readily.

Donul lost his head. 'My curse on you, get round !' The Gaelic words tore harshly through his straining muscles and produced at once a general laugh. The unexpected Gaelic fitted the scene so precisely ! Donul drew back and hit the little red cow a wild wallop with his stick. His fierce earnestness was something to behold. Push and hit, push and hit, but she would not be ordered about. No fear ! The audience chuckled. They knew her type. One of the ring men entered and, with impor-tant impatience, shouldered Donul backward. In a blinding flash of anger Donul half swung his stick with the intention of knocking out the brains of the ring man, but recovered in an awkward stagger. This byplay of emotion was not lost on the audience, and when the little red cow held her own against the ring man they felt that the score was even. Then the ring man caught her tail, but the auctioneer, in his Olympian way, raised his hand. 'I think,' he said, 'you can all see her, and she's good stuff! Who'll bid me seven pounds? . . . six? . . . Five pounds, thank you, five pounds I am bid, I am bid five pounds, five—five guineas—I am bid five guineas, ten, five-ten, thank you, I am bid five-ten . . .' At six pounds the auctioneer took half-crowns, and at six pounds five shillings the little red cow was knocked down to the local butcher who had a small farm. 'Will you take her in the same pen, Mr Grant?' asked the auctioneer politely, leaning from his dais. The butcher nodded. 'Pen sixty-nine,' called the auctioneer. The clerk made an entry in his ledger. The iron swivel was swung back with a clack, the gate opened, and Donul exerted his force. In a half-blind staggering run the little red cow charged from the arena, Donul on her heels—a dramatic exit that left a grin on the air.

'God, don't you know how to handle a beast yet?' shouted a mart man at him when at last the gate of pen 69 was shut. As the man hurried away Donul gripped the top of the rail until his hands were white. Emotion was swirling in his head, black drowning whirls of it, but he held against it, until up through it came his blind will, his voice, cursing them, cursing them all. Curse them, but I'll hold my ground! shouted his thought with such intense bitterness that his eyes suddenly stung. From deep down in her the little red cow mooed.

Young Art and Old Hector

Rumbelow

Said Rumbelow : I sail the sea
With three-and-thirty wishes,
And if the Lord is good to me
Mayhap He'll grant the nether Three
Before I feed the fishes.

I WANT to see the Southern Isles
And brown girls, naked, dancing there
With moon-white blossom in their hair.
I want to see the River Nile
Slide like a fat green snake between
The dusty pyramids, and dream
Of Israel sweating there—
How unctuously the Hebrews sweat !
I've seen black Jews of Cochin drip
Like *mussucks* full of running jet. . . .
O Indian beaches ! I must ship
Aboard an Indiaman again
For Mangalore and Calicut,
And Eastward yet, where tropic rain
Falls like a cataract to shut
The green-and-opal world away
Behind a curtain of glass-grey.
Green parrots in the trees—I want
To ride upon an elephant
Down sombre paths through silent teak,
Echo-less, wet, and endless aisles
Where only parrots speak.
I want to see gnarled crocodiles
Slumbrous and scaly in the mud ;
I want the jewel in a Moghul's ear,

A ruby red as the spirting blood
Of a stumbling, sword-stuck mutineer ;
Pretty grass-green emerauds ;
And whiter pearls than a shark's belly
Turning in the Indian sea—
Nay, but not for vanity,
Not for simple pride, I tell 'ee,
Covet I such dainty gauds. . . .
But once I saw
A Ranee and her women walk,
Laughing, into a lotos-pool.
They were more beautiful
Than thought or memory can draw.
As fair as moonlight !   When they did talk
It seemed small birds flashed to and fro,
And they were lithe and delicate,
With little pouting breasts, backs straight,
And eyebrows like a taut thin bow,
Bright beetle-black ; and they alone
Of all the women I have known
Were perfect—well, a perfect stone
Might buy perfection ; for pearls
Out of their stinking oysters peer,
Like Nature's unoffending bawds,
To argue prettily with girls
And stop a wife's uneasy fear. . . .
Lord, but how quickly angry dust
Whirls like a desert storm to lust !
Salt water breeds this lechery.
But I have simple wishes, too,
For innocenter things to do—
I want to kill before I die,
Two Frenchmen and three Portuguese,
A Hollander, and after these
The man who slept with Susie Pye

A year ago come Lady Day,
An Isle of Pines mulatto—*foh* !
Such appetites in women grow,
To lie with black men, and in Lent !
But we're not born to find content
In homeward things, and we must go
About the waste of waters till
Our timbers settle
On tidal mud or Noah's hill,
Where there's leave to rest or play
For a season or a day ;
Then it's up again and haul,
Head to sea and next land-fall,
Ararat will vanish fast,
Look on it and look your last,
We're for Popocatapetl. . . .
About the waste of waters, Lord,
With this unruly crew aboard
Of wishes wilful as a boy
And hunger huge as Horse of Troy !
But here are sober wishes, three
That live together quietly :
I want to read the Bible through,
From Earth's beginning in the Void
To Jesus flowering out of Jew
And Babylon destroyed.
I want to buy a Cashmere shawl
That Mother may be comforted,
Who nearly perished, so she said,
Of cold last Fall.
I want to find a girl who's true,
And I to be as true as she—
There are three, Lord, let me win,
Bible, Shawl, and Constancy,
And Constancy a twin !

So Rumbelow went back to sea
  Counting up his wishes.
The Thirty came to hand or knee,
  Rumbelow ! Rumbelow !
But ere he got the nether Three
The greenest wave of all the sea,
  Rumbelow !
Came aboard for him and he
  Went to feed the fishes.

A Dragon Laughed

IVOR BROWN

Good Words

Braxy

Braxy is a strange and ugly matter, splenetic apoplexy in sheep. So braxy mutton is the flesh of sheep that have fallen dead and then, less accurately, of sheep that have been killed by accident. So the hungry shepherd might not always despise a bit of ' braxy,' and in war-time, on the hills where there were no restaurants or canteens and only the pressure of keen air upon hard-working hungry bodies, there were sometimes, I fancy, more sheep that had accidents than might have been expected from the peace-time figures. Much of this war-time braxy would be good feeding, coveted and well earned. I was reminded of braxy by coming across some lines, still well known in a phrase or two, but rarely remembered in full. Written in 1901, they referred to the vast possessions of the Marquis of Breadalbane.

> From Kenmore
> To Ben Mohr
> The land is a' the Markiss's ;
> The mossy howes,
> The heathery knowes,
> An' ilka bonnie park is his.
> The bearded goats,
> The toozie stots,
> An' a' the braxy carcases ;
> Ilk crofter's rent,
> Ilk tinkler's tent,
> An' ilka collie's bark is his ;
> The muir-cock's craw,
> The piper's blaw,

The gillie's hard day's wark is his ;
From Kenmore
To Ben Mohr
The warld is a' the Markiss's !

The author was James Mactavish of Waterside, Doune, a renowned breeder of black-faced sheep. He and his father were tenants of Waterside for close on a century.

Toozie is tousy or tousled, a nice, curly sort of word. A toozy lass is often to be seen beside a tinkler's tent. The Scottish tinklers, a type of native gipsies, are now often called tinkers. The brief 'tink' does for both forms. Stots are not, as the rhyme suggests, stoats. They are usually steers and sometimes heifers.

Say the Word

Cateran

The Highland cateran, an aptly sounding word for the tough yokel, is the same as the Irish and Shakespearean kern or kerne. This latter marches across our stages and dramatic texts in frequent association with a gallow-glass, the couple sharing a line not only of *Macbeth* but of *Henry VI*, Part II. Shakespeare has a particularly lively set of epithets for kerns. They are crafty and they skip : they are uncivil, shag-haired and rug-headed. The double allusion to the towsled curls of a cateran or kern suggests the spectacle of Irish prisoners brought to London or that journey to Scotland which some believe Shakespeare must have made. (Some of his craft and period certainly made 'a stroll of players' as far as Aberdeen.) Both cateran and gallow-glass are Gaelic words. The former comes from Caithairne, meaning peasantry. Its application to the roving cattle thief came later. Rob Roy and his men lowered the once unblemished name of cateran. Indeed I was reminded of the cateran by reacquaintance with Bailie Nicol Jarvie, who said of Rob :

And then he's sic an auld-farran lang-headed chield as never took up the trade o' cateran in our time ; mony a daft reik he has played—mair than wad fill a book, and a queer ane it would be—as gude as Robin Hood, or William Wallace—a' fu' o' venturesome deeds and escapes, sic as folks tell ower at a winter-ingle in the daft days.

Presumably Caithness is Caithairne-ness, the headland of the caterans—in the original and reputable sense of the word. But I shall be reminded of the Catti or Clan Chattan and refuse to be embroiled in this argument.

Just Another Word

Claret

Not a striking word, yet obviously it has its appeal. Why otherwise should it have usurped, as far as Britain is concerned, the red wines of Bordeaux ? It signifies clear wine, but claret is not markedly clear. The victory is an odd one. Dr Johnson's absurdly crude view that claret is a wine for boys, with port allotted to men, was never shared in Scotland. I like the lines of Allan Ramsay after he has surveyed the snow on ' Pentland's tow'ring tap ' and called for the ' tappit hen,' which is a Scots vessel with top or crest holding about three quarts.

> Good Claret best keeps out the Cauld
> And rives away the Winter soon,
> It makes a Man baith gash and bauld,
> And heaves his Saul beyond the Moon.

This proper attribution to claret of brave, spirit-lifting and translunar powers preceded Johnson's nonsense in time and answered it before it was spoken.

Gash is sagacious. A man with a long chin the Scots

used to call ' gash gabbet.' I must remember that when next I have the pleasure of reviewing a Jack Hulbert show. Has Hulbert ever, when delighting Glasgow or Edinburgh, found himself described as gash gabbet in the *Glasgow Herald* or *The Scotsman*? Probably not. Scots journalists are proud of their English (justly) and their readers have mainly ceased to understand Scots. I read that gash has now become a naval term for anything free or ' scrounged.'

But we are wandering from the pleasures of claret, a term adjectively applied by Herrick to the cheeks of a charmer. Most of the clarets we drank of late (and hope to drink again) are not of a colour with which ladies would like to be much imbued. Andrew Young, on the other hand, writes of the ' claret-coloured birches ' when describing a Highland glen in winter. He thus gives support to my previous contention that wine-dark, seemingly wrong for the Aegean seas on whose surface Greek epic spawned it, will do very well for the bloom coming off our native woods in winter. I certainly know combes, denes and bottoms in the English shires where a vapour, hanging over the leafless twigs upon a sun-shot winter afternoon, is fairly to be described in terms of the Bordeaux vintages. The sight of it is so exquisite as to heave one's soul, if not beyond the moon, at least slightly over one's shoulders.

It is queer that the British should call two such important wines as Bordeaux and Rhenish by names strange to the growers. Claret was a word used in Elizabeth's England. It occurs once in Shakespeare, if you permit *Henry VI*, Part II to be Shakespeare's own. Jack Cade, when enjoying his brief triumph in rebellion, proclaims claret now to be everyman's tipple, though he puts it more grossly. Hock began to edge its way in early in the following century. Hamlet speaks of Rhenish, and

Shakespeare uses the term several times. The victory of Hock is surprising ; it is an abbreviation of Hockamore, an Anglicisation of Hochheimer. Hochheim is on the Main, not the Rhine. But it was important enough to give a general name in England to the Rhine wines as well as to its own.

I Give You My Word

Daze

It is right that the North should have the best terms for cold. The South has lost the use of daze for numb, narrowing its usage to strong effects on eye and brain, just as it has limited ' starve ' to matters of appetite. The Yorkshire child who, when settled in an air-raid shelter of the dank and draughty kind, cried out to his mother, ' Ee Moom, ba goom, ma boom is noom,' might have called his posterior dazed had he lived a little earlier. In Scotland the use of daze does, I believe, linger. How well it sits in Gavin Douglas's sharp, clear and tingling description of a Scottish winter.

> In this congealit season sharp and chill,
> The caller air penetrative and pure,
> Dazing the blude in every creature,
> Made seek warm stovis and bene fyris hot.
> In double garment cled and wyliecoat,
> With michty drink, and meatis confortive. . . .

The last robust and reassuring word surely amplifies and justifies my earlier note on the original implication of confort or comforts.

A Word in Your Ear

Geck, Girn and Gowl

The fate of James Hogg's ' Bonnie Kilmeny ' does not greatly stir me. Hogg, whether being fey or Jacobite, seems to me to have had less gumption than is to be expected in Ettrick Shepherds. However, he had the vocabulary of his time and place, and it is a good one. The singer of Birniebouzle and Balmaquhapple was certain to have a lingo with the Border wind in it and the smell of neeps after rain. (Surely that exquisite aroma is essential Scotland : it has the sharp tang of so many Scottish things, of whisky especially, and smoked fish, of pine-woods and peat.)

Hogg in the aforesaid ' Bonnie Kilmeny' has one passage containing the three words geck, girn and gowl, which makes a sombre and striking trinity.

> He gowled at the carle and chased him away
> To feed with the deer on the mountain gray.
> He gowled at the carle and he gecked at Heaven.

Previously the carle had ' girned amain.'

If a carle (or churl) girned amain at me I should certainly deem it fair to geck and gowl, as well as girn, back at him. Taking them in order, geck, either as a verb for ' to mock ' or as a noun for a person mocked, is by no means Scottish only. Cries Malvolio,

> Why have you suffered me to be imprisoned,
> Kept in a dark house, visited by the priest,
> And made the most notorious geck and gull
> That e'er invention played on ?

The phrase ' geck and scorn' also appears in *Cymbeline*. Girn is supposed to be a mistaken form of grin. It means to show the teeth at, snarl and generally grizzle and rail. Gowl is more vociferous and is a picturesque form of howl. One might put it this way : if you unfairly geck a fellow-creature, he first girns at you and then, if nothing happens, gowls.

I Give You My Word

Meteor

Colonel Walter Elliot, writing an article with a title drawn from Thomas Campbell's phrase 'The meteor flag of England,' once pointed out that England is still regarded as a terrible and consuming force by some Scots and Welsh, as well as by many others farther off ; he also reminded us, incidentally, that Campbell could flash into poetry as well as perform like an apt rhetorician in the more belligerent types of verse. Meteors splutter and blaze across the skies of art as well as of reality, but Campbell's success was in making meteor an adjective.

> The meteor flag of England
> Shall yet terrific burn,
> Till danger's troubled night depart
> And the star of peace return.

The second couplet is ordinary enough, but the first does powerfully strike a light. The idea of the English or British flag as a fire-ball which creates light and heat wherever it goes has the strength of fancy proper to genuine poetry. The English, as Walter Elliot insisted, have long come to regard themselves as lambs, meek and sparkless, but the outer world, or at least a good deal of it, still imagines British power to be a flambeau, incendiary bomb or even an engine of rocketing conspiracy. (At the time Elliot wrote a prominent American paper was encouraging its readers to believe that the dastardly scheme of Rhodes Scholarships was a vile plot to capture, convert and Anglicise decent, but innocent, young Americans.) That is the mood which sees the Union Jack to be as much a thing of fiery menace as any 'exhalations whizzing in the air.' Campbell was sometimes inspired. His ode on the 'Pleasures of Hope' fell not so far behind Gray in quotability :

Hope for a season bade the world farewell,
And Freedom shrieked—as Kosciusko fell !

It was Campbell, not Gray, who noted,

'Tis distance lends enchantment to the view
And robes the mountain in its azure hue.

The second line slid away, typically, for Campbell was
not a stayer. His poetry came with a meteor flash. And
when he fell, how deep the plunge !

One moment may with bliss repay
Unnumbered hours of pain,

So far, so decently obvious ; but there followed,

Such was the throb and mutual sob
Of the knight embracing Jane.

Here, indeed, was a meteor absurdity.

I Give You My Word

Tosy

Tosy and cosh both mean snug and are very happily used
by John Galt in his *Annals of the Parish*. His Rev.
Mr Balwhidder complains of the tea drinking that has
come unto Ayrshire (1762), but reminds himself that it
does less harm than the ' Conek ' (cognac) with which
previous beverages had been laced.

There is no meeting now in the summer evenings, as I
remember often happened in my younger days, with
decent ladies coming home with red faces, tosy and
cosh, from a posset-masking.

Could there be better adjectives to suggest a modest alcoholic after-glow ? One thinks of the ' decent ladies ' very affable with the minister, and then reduced to tittering and even to less than decent conversation when Mr Balwhidder had passed by.

Cosh, by the way, was the name of one of John Aubrey's sources of information. That glorious gossip, after relating some neat or scandalous episode, would note, ' This I had of old Major Cosh.' The Major suggests one of the ripest of the seventeenth-century talkers. He was doubtless almost always tosy.

A Word in Your Ear

Usky

The Gaels' *Uisge Beatha* (water of life), is familiar to us by the rather mean name of whisky. It first became usquebaugh and by 1770 the English were calling it (and calling for it) by the word we now know. But, for a while, in the early eighteenth century, when Wade's men were exploring and road-building in the Highlands, the term hovered in an intermediate stage as usky, a stage which has its own suitability and attraction. Usky was the spelling used, for example, by Edmund Burt, an officer of engineers who wrote letters from the North of Scotland about 1730, explaining the deeds and pleasures of the natives. They give, he said, to their children of six or seven years as much usky at a nip as would fill a wine-glass. Evidently this strengthened young heads and stomachs for the serious drinking of later years. When some of Burt's fellow-officers audaciously entered upon an usky-drinking match with the locals, the Highlanders were easy victors and left the field without loss, whereas the English casualties were severe. Here is Burt's chronicle of the ruin. ' One of the officers was thrown into a fit of gout, without hopes ; another had a most dangerous fever ; a third lost his skin and hair by the surfeit.' The fourth competitor went ' yellow ' in the slangy modern sense. ' When drunkenness ran high, he took several opportunities to sham it,' and so, presumably, preserved his looks, locks and hide.

It seems to have been a good party on the whole. One has heard of curious effects produced by a carouse, but a case of simultaneous depilation and depellation is new to me, and should stand high among the cautionary tales for the reckless practitioners of absorbency. The standard of consumption in the Highlands, as Burt saw them, was imposing. ' Some of the Highland gentlemen,' observed this Gael-watcher, not denying them the title of gentry, ' are immoderate drinkers of usky, even three or four quarts at a sitting.' Burt himself was an anti-usky man, believing that ' this spirit has in it, by infusion, the seeds of anger, revenge, and murder (this, I confess is a little too poetical), but those who drink of it to any degree of excess behave, for the most part, like barbarians, I think much beyond the effect of any other liquor.' Life in ' the lone shieling of the misty island ' was not, in those days, dry. The collector of customs at Stornoway told Burt that ' one hundred and twenty families drink yearly 4,000 English gallons of this spirit and brandy together, although many of them are so poor that they cannot afford to pay for much of either, which, you know, must increase the quantity drunk by the rest.' Burt did not, however, clinch his argument by relating the statistics of murder to those of usky gallons drunk. It seems a little odd that *uisge beatha*, the spirit of life, should have been the name for a fluid so lethal. In any case, for the kind of skin-destroying, hair-uprooting tipple that Burt describes, usky seems to be an apter, because a rougher, name than whisky.

There were other spellings. A Scottish gentleman, who

visited the Highlands in 1737, was so delighted by the work of Wade, Burt and their men in the civilising of the country that he made his obeisance in a poem of a thousand lines.

> And thee, O Wade, shall coming ages bless
> Whose prudent care did give the scheme success.

At one of the banquets of celebration, given after the building of another Highland bridge, the poet says that the workers

> Then beef and pudding plentifully eat
> With store of cheering husque to their meat.

He also alludes to the ' Houses of Intertainment ' set up for the travellers.

> With corn and grass, enclosures all around,
> Where fitt supplys, for men and horse, are found.
> There various meats and liquors too are got,
> But usqueba must never be forgot.

Those travelling over Wade's roads in 1944, as I had the pleasure of doing, or at least over part of them, were not so lucky with their meats and liquors. Certainly usqueba was not forgot ; but, no less certainly, it was never as much in the glass as it was in the mind.

I Give You My Word

Venust

I have never thought that the Latin word Venus, whether pronounced in the English manner or as Waynoose, was musically adequate to its subject. Yet the old adjective ' venust,' used by the Scots makars, has always pleased me. How did they pronounce it ? ' Venoust,' I suppose, in

146

which case it becomes a pretty addition to the language of love. The Latinism of the Scots poets of the latter part of the sixteenth century, so magnificent in the use of their native words, is sometimes oppressive. Is 'The Day Estivall,' as Hume called it, preferable to 'The Summer Day'? But when a lover woos his tender babe venust, one immediately accepts her as adorable and regrets that the English dictionaries now pass the word by. Alexander Scott's use of it occurs in the lovely as well as alliterative verse :

> My bird, my bonnie ane,
> My tender babe venust,
> My luve, my life alane,
> My liking and my lust.

Certainly this poem is a frank one, but not heavily so. The word lust, now possessing an ugly as well as an adipose tissue, has put on weight with the years, and to Scott was far closer to the German notion of a *lustig* or merry state of mind.

A Word in Your Ear

MAURICE LINDSAY

1   *The Man-in-the-Mune*

THE Man-in-the-Mune's got cleik-i-the-back,
an wullna come oot tae play.
He sits by himsel on a shimmer o Heaven,
an hears whit the starnies say.

But his cheeks gae black, he purls his broo,
an his auld heid shaks wi rage
thru the reengan cloods that jostle the yirth,
whan God's on the rampage !

cleik-i-the-back, rheumatism   *shimmer,* cross-bar

2   *Willie Wabster*

Hae ye seen Willie Wabster,
  Willie Wabster, Willie Wabster ?
He's weil-kennt frae Scrabster
  tae yont the siller Tweed.

He scarts his fingers owre the lift,
  an sets the starns a-shoggin :
when thunner-cloods'll haurdly drift,
  he gies ilk yin a joggin.

An when the mune offends his sicht,
  he coosts it owre his shouther ;
an whiles, tae snuff the sun's gowd licht,
  his winds begin tae fluther.

scarts, scratches   *fluther,* flutter to and fro
148

He gars come dingan on the toun
   the raindraps oot o Heaven,
draps frae his pooch an dangles doun
   in bauns, the colours seven.

Sma wunner that I'm aften scared,
   for I'm no certain whether
he's God Himsel, the warld's ae laird,
   or jist His clerk-o-weather !

3   *Burn Music*

' MURMELL, murmell, murmell,'
   croodles the burn
as heid owre heels
   its watters turn,
puan the blue-gerss
   that hings frae the shair,
an sheinan the stanes
   o its clear cobbl't flair.

' Brattle, brattle, brattle,'
   the wee lynn sings
as tumblan frae craigs
   the burn taks wings ;
a fantice o faem,
   it loups at the air,
an streams lik the mane
   o a white kelpie-mare.

loups, leaps
kelpie, a malignant water-sprite haunting rivers in the form of a horse

' Spitter, spitter, spitter,'
    the drin-draps plash,
runklan the quate pool
    wi gay mountain gash.
' Pwudle, pwudle,'
    the deep pool breathes
as oot tae the river
    it humphs an heaves.

From ' A Suite of Bairnsangs,'
At the Wood's Edge

quate, quiet   *gash*, chatter

EDWIN MUIR

In Orkney

MY mother lived much more in the past than my father, so that when I was a child Deerness became a lively place to me, while Sanday remained blank except for its witches, since the tales my father told me were mainly about the supernatural. One of my mother's stories has stuck in my memory. The family had moved from Haco to Skaill, a farm on the edge of a sandy bay, beside the parish church and the churchyard. She was eighteen at the time. The rest of the family had gone up to the Free Kirk, two miles away, for an evening prayer meeting, a great revival having swept the islands. It was a wild night of wind and sleet, and she was sitting in the kitchen reading, when the door opened and ten tall men, dripping with water, came in and sat round the fire. They spoke to her, but she could not tell what they were saying. She sat on in a corner, dumb with terror, until the family came back two hours later. The men were Danes, and their ship had split on a rock at the end of the bay.

Both her memory and my father's were filled with wrecks, for the Orkney coast is dangerous, and at that time there were few lighthouses. When the wrecks were washed ashore the people in the parish gathered and took their pick. Stories were told of men luring ships on to the rocks by leading, along a steep road, a pony with a green light tied to one side and a red light to the other. It was said, too, that ministers sometimes prayed for a wreck in bad times. A strange tale often told in our family is indirectly connected with all this. One bright moonlight night my father and my cousin Sutherland were standing at the end of the house at the Folly after feeding the cattle, when they saw a great three-masted vessel making straight for the shore. They watched in amazement for a few minutes—there was only a field between them and it—until it melted into a black mist on the water. I was enchanted by the story when I heard it, but as I grew older I naturally began to doubt it. Then when I was seventeen or eighteen I was speaking to a farmer who had lived on the neighbouring farm of the Barns, and he told me the very same story. He had been at the end of his house that night, and he too had seen the three-master standing in for the shore and then disappearing. At the time he was amazed at its behaviour, like my father and my cousin Sutherland, for in the bright moonlight the cliffs must have been clearly visible from the ship ; but they all accepted it, I think, as a magical occurrence.

My father's stories were drawn mostly from an earlier age, and I think must have been handed on to him by his own father. They went back to the Napoleonic wars, the press-gang, and the keelhauling, which still left a memory of terror in Orkney. But in his own time he had known several witches, who had ' taken the profit of the corn,' turned the milk sour and wrecked ships by raising storms. Many of these stories I have heard since in other versions, and these obviously come from the store of legends that gathered when witch-burning was common in Scotland. In one a Sanday farmer, coming back for his dinner, saw the local witch's black cat slinking out of his house. He rushed in, snatched up his gun, and let fly at it. The cat was leaping over a stone dyke when he fired ; it stumbled and gave a great screech, then ran away, dragging one hind leg after it. Next day the witch sent for the doctor to set her leg. My father told this story so well that I could see the farmer with the smoking gun in his hands, and the black cat stumbling over the grey stone wall and running away with a twisted, crab-like glide. When my father told his witch stories we sat up very late ; we were afraid to go to bed.

The Devil himself, as Auld Nick, sometimes came into these tales, and generally in the same way. A farmer would be in the barn threshing his corn with a flail, when he would notice another flail keeping time with him, and looking up would see an enormous, naked, coal-black man with a fine upcurling tail standing opposite him. He fainted at this point, and when he awoke all the corn in the barn would be neatly threshed. But these visits were always followed by bad luck.

My father had also a great number of stories about *The Book of Black Arts*. This book could be bought only for a silver coin, and sold only for a smaller silver coin. It ended in the possession of a foolish servant girl who paid a threepenny-piece for it. It was very valuable, for it gave you all sorts of worldly power ; but it had the drawback that if you could not sell it to someone before you died you were damned. The servant girl of my father's story tried every means to get rid of it. She tore it to pieces and buried it, tied a stone to it and flung it into the sea, burned it ; but after all this it was still at the bottom of her chest when she went to look there. What happened in the end I can't remember ; I fancy the poor girl went off her head. I always thought of the book as a great, black, hasped, leather-bound volume somewhat like a family Bible.

My father also knew the horseman's word—that is, the word which will make a horse do anything you desire if you whisper it into its ear. Some time ago I asked Eric Linklater, who knows Orkney now better than I do, if he had ever heard of the horseman's word up there. He said no, but he told me that when he was a student at Aberdeen University young ploughmen in Buchan were willing to pay anything from ten shillings to a pound out of their small wages to be told the horseman's word. From what my father said I imagine that the word was a shocking one.

The Orkney I was born into was a place where there was no great distinction between the ordinary and the fabulous ; the lives of living men turned into legend. A man I knew once sailed out in a boat to look for a mermaid, and claimed afterwards that he had talked with her. Fantastic feats of strength were commonly reported. Fairies, or ' fairicks,' as they were called, were encountered dancing on the sands on moonlight nights. From people's talk they were small, graceful creatures about the size of leprechauns, but pretty, not grotesque. There was no harm in them. All these things have vanished from Orkney in the last forty years under the pressure of compulsory education.

My father left the Folly for a farm called the Bu in the island of Wyre. There were seven other farms on the island, with names which went back to the Viking times : Russness, Onziebist, Helzigartha, Caivit, Testaquoy, Habreck, the Haa. The Bu was the biggest farm on the island, and close beside a little green knoll called the Castle. In the eleventh century this had been the stronghold of a Viking freebooter called Kolbein Hruga, or Cubby Roo, but we did not know this at the time, nor did any of our neighbours : all that remained was the name and the knoll and a little cairn of big stones. Between the house and the knoll there was a damp green meadow which waved with wild cotton in summer. Then came the dry smooth slope of the Castle, and on the top the round cairn of square grey stones, as high as a man's shoulder and easy for us to climb. My younger sister and I would sit there for hours in the summer evenings, looking across the sound at the dark hilly island of Rousay, which also had its castle, a brand-new one like a polished black-and-white dice, where a retired General lived : our landlord. He was a stylish, very little man with a dapper walk, and the story went that because of his size he had been the first to pass through the breach in the wall of Lucknow when that town was relieved during the Indian Mutiny. He came over to Wyre every spring to shoot the wild birds. I remember one soft spring day when the light seemed to be opening up the world after the dark winter ; I must have been five at the time, for it was before I went to school. I was standing at the end of the house ; I think I had just recovered from some illness, and everything looked clean and new. The General was walking through the field below our house in his little brown jacket with the brown leather tabs on the shoulders, his neat little knickerbockers and elegant little brown boots ; a feather curled on his hat, and his little pointed beard seemed to curl too. Now and then he raised his silver gun, the white smoke curled upward, birds fell, suddenly heavy after seeming so light ; our cattle, who were grazing in the field, rushed away in alarm at the noise, then stopped and looked round in wonder at the strange little man. It was a mere picture ; I did not feel angry with the General or sorry for the birds ; I was entranced with the bright gun, the white smoke and particularly with the soft brown tabs of leather on the shoulders of his jacket. My mother was standing at the end of the house with me ; the General came over and spoke to her, then, calling me to him, gave me a sixpence. My father appeared from somewhere, but replied very distantly to the General's affable words. He was a bad landlord, and in a few years drove my father out of the farm by his exactions.

Between our house and the school there was a small roofless chapel which had once been the chapel of the Castle. In summer it was a jungle of nettles and rank weeds, which on hot days gave out a burning smell that scorched my nostrils. At the school, which stood on a slight rising, a new group of more distant islands appeared, some of them brown, some green with light sandy patches. Not a tree anywhere. There were only two things that rose from these low rounded islands : a high top-heavy castle in Shapinsay, standing by itself with the insane look of tall narrow houses in flat wide landscapes, and in Egilsay a black chapel with a round pointed tower, where St Magnus had been murdered in the twelfth century. It was the most beautiful thing within sight, and it rose every day against the sky until it seemed to become a sign in the fable of our lives.

We had two fiddles in the house and a melodeon. My two eldest brothers played the fiddle, and we were all expert on the melodeon. John Ritch, our neighbour at the Haa, was a great fiddler in the traditional country style, and he had a trick of making the bow dirl on the strings which delighted us, especially in slow, ceremonious airs such as the *Hen's March to the Midden*. Then one year we were all caught with a passion for draughts, and played one another endlessly through the long winter evenings, always wary when we met Sutherland, for he had a trick of unobtrusively replacing his men on the board in impregnable positions after they had been captured. If we pointed this out to him he would either deny it loudly or else show amazement at seeing them there. When I think of our winters at the Bu they turn into one long winter evening round the stove—it was a black iron stove with scrollwork on the sides, standing well out into the kitchen—playing draughts, or listening to the fiddle or the melodeon, or sitting still while my father told of his witches and fairicks. The winter gathered us into one room as it gathered the cattle into the stable and the byre ; the sky came closer ; the lamps were lit at three or four in the afternoon, and then the great evening lay before us like a world : an evening filled with talk, stories, games, music and lamplight.

The passing from this solid winter world into spring was wild, and it took place on the day when the cattle were unchained from their stalls in the six months' darkness of the byre, and my father or Sutherland flung open the byre door and leaped aside. The cattle shot through the opening, blind after half a year's night, maddened by the spring air and the sunshine, and did not stop until they were brought up by the stone dyke at the other end of the field. If anyone had come in their way they would have trampled over him without seeing him. Our dog Prince, who kept a strict watch over them during the summer, shrank before the sight. That was how spring began.

There were other things connected with it, such as the lambing ; I think our lambs must have been born late in the season. I have a dim picture of my mother taking me by the hand one green spring day and leading me to the yard at the back of the house to see two new-born lambs. Some bloody, wet, rag-like stuff was lying on the grass, and a little distance away the two lambs were sprawling, with their spindly legs doubled up. Everything looked soft and new—the sky, the sea, the grass, the two lambs, which seemed to have been cast up without warning on the turf ; their eyes still had a bruised look, and their hoofs were freshly lacquered. They paid no attention to me when I went up to pat them, but kept turning their heads with sudden gentle movements which belonged to some other place.

Another stage in the spring was the sowing. About that time of the year the world opened, the sky grew higher, the sea deeper as the summer colours, blue and green and purple, woke in it. The black fields glistened, and a row of meal-coloured sacks, bursting full like the haunches of plough-horses, ran down each one ; two neat little lugs, like pricked ears, stuck up from each sack. They were opened ; my father filled from the first of them a canvas tray strapped round his middle, and strode along the field casting the dusty grain on either side with regular sweeps, his hands opening and shutting. When the grain was finished he stopped at another sack and went on again. I would sit watching him, my eyes caught now and then by some ship passing so slowly against the black hills that it seemed to be stationary, though when my eyes returned to it again I saw with wonder that it had moved. The sun shone, the black field glittered, my father strode on, his arms slowly swinging, the fan-shaped cast of grain gleamed as it fell and fell again ; the row of meal-coloured sacks stood like squat monuments on the field. My father took a special delight in the sowing, and we all felt the first day was a special day. But spring was only a few vivid happenings, not a state, and before I knew it the motionless blue summer was there, in which nothing happened.

The Story and the Fable

In Glasgow

OUT of my salary I had to buy for a few pence a lunch at a neighbouring dairy ; when that was done there was not much left ; so that both for economy and health (exercise being necessary in a town, my brothers assured me) I walked to and from my work each day through a slum, for there was no way of getting from the south side of Glasgow to the city except through slums. These journeys filled me with a deep sense of degradation : the crumbling houses, the twisted faces, the obscene words casually heard in passing, the ancient haunting stench of pollution and decay, the arrogant women, the mean men, the terrible children, frightened me, and at last filled me with an immense, blind dejection. I had seen only ordinary people before ; but on some of the faces that I passed every day now there seemed to be written things which only a fantastic imagination could have created, and I shrank from reading them and quickly learned not to see. After a while, like everyone who lives in an industrial town, I got used to these things ; I walked through the slums as if they were an ordinary road leading from my home to my work. I learned to do this consciously, but if I was tired or ill I often had the feeling, passing through Eglinton Street or Crown Street, that I was dangerously close to the ground, deep down in a place from which I might never be able to climb up again, while far above my head, inaccessible, ran a fine, clean highroad ; and a soundless tremor shook me, the premonition of an anxiety neurosis. These fears might come on me at any time, and then, though I lived in a decent house, the slums seemed to be everywhere around me, a great, spreading swamp into which I might sink for ever.

I soon made a habit of escaping into the surrounding country in my free time, but even the fields seemed blasted by disease, as if the swamp were invisibly spreading there too. My nearest access to the country lay through a little mining village, where grey men were always squatting on their hunkers at the ends of the houses, and the ground was covered with coal-grit. Beyond this, if you turned to the left, there was a cinder path leading past a pit, beside which was a filthy pool where yellow-faced children splashed about. Tattered, worm-ringed trees stood round it in squalid sylvan peace ; the grass was rough with smoke and grit ; the sluggish streams

were bluish black. To the right a road climbed up the
the Hundred Acre Dyke, along which mangy hawthorns
grew. The herbage was purer here, but all that could be
seen were blackened fields, smoke-stocks, and the sooty
ramparts of coal-pits, except to the south, where lay the
pretty little town of Cathcart. These roads became so
associated in my mind with misery that after leaving the
south side of Glasgow I could never bear to revisit them.

My first years in Glasgow were wretched. The feeling
of degradation continued, but it became more and more
blind ; I did not know what made me unhappy, nor that
I had come into chaos. We had lived comfortably enough
in Orkney, mainly on what we grew ; but here everything had to be bought and paid for ; there was so much
money and so much food and clothes and warmth and
accommodation to be had for it, that was all. This new
state of things worried and perplexed my mother, and
it gave each one of us a feeling of stringency which we
had never known before. My elder brothers had already
grasped the principle of this new society, which was
competition, not co-operation, as it had been in Orkney.
The rest of us too presently came to understand this, but
my father and mother never did. Though we imagined
that we had risen in some way, without knowing it we
had sunk into another class ; for if Jimmie and Johnnie
had lost their jobs we should have had nothing left but a
small balance in a bank, which was not a responsive
adaptable thing like a farm, but would soon have run out.
We were members of the proletariat, though at that time
we had never heard the name. Happily my brothers kept
their jobs, and we did not have to become acquainted with
the abyss over which we lived. Yet somewhere in our
minds we were conscious of it. The old sense of security
was gone.

The Story and the Fable

In Prague

WE saw a great deal of Karel Čapek, who lived a few minutes' walk away from us in a rambling old house with a large garden hidden away behind it. Though he was about the same age as myself, he was already round-backed ; the brightness of his eyes and the flush on his cheeks showed that he was ill, He knew only a little English, and we only a little German, so that we had to converse in an absurd mixture of the two. He was always busy, always merry, and always supplying us with tickets to the Vinohrady Theatre. He often talked of the hardships the people of Prague had suffered during the War, and though he never said so, I imagine that his own health was undermined during that dreadful time. The attitude of the Czechs to the War was expressed in the common saying, ' The worse things become, the better ' ; they knew that they could not win their independence except by the defeat of Germany and Austria. Čapek seemed to be known and loved by everyone, and when we walked along the street with him every second or third passer-by would shout in a delighted voice, ' Oh, Karlíčku ! ' the equivalent of ' Hullo, Charley ! ' as if the mere sight of him filled them with pleasure. This warm, easy-going contact could only have been possible in a comparatively small town, and it was the first thing that made me wish that Edinburgh might become a similar place, and that Scotland might become a nation again.

Karel Čapek died shortly after the seizure of his country by Germany, whether of his illness or of a broken heart I do not know. After the Prague in which he was ' Karlíčku ' to everyone, and where he could walk about as he liked, the new Prague must have seemed a prison-yard. We met many other Czech writers. I dread to think what may have happened to them now ; even if no physical harm has come to them their life has been snatched away, and their Prague no longer exists. We spent many evenings in their houses ; we were taken into their lives. We had no premonition then that history, in Oswald Spengler's words, ' would take them by the throat and do with them what must be done.' The idea of history taking people by the throat pleased Spengler.

Our first few months in that Prague which no longer exists were happy and carefree. We had a great deal of leisure, for living was cheap and I could make enough to keep us comfortably by writing two articles a month for *The Freeman* and a weekly article for *The New Age*. It was the first time since 'fourteen that I had known what it was to have time for thinking and day-dreaming ; I was in a foreign town where everything—the people, the houses, the very shop signs—was different ; I began to learn the visible world all over again. In Glasgow the ugliness of everything—the walks through the slums, the uncongenial work—had turned me in upon myself, so that I no longer saw things, but was merely aware of them in an indirect way. In Prague everything seemed to be asking me to notice it ; I spent weeks in an orgy of looking ; I saw everywhere the visible world straight before my eyes. At this time too I realised that my fears were gone ; there was nothing to spoil my enjoyment of this new world which had been created simply by travelling a few hundred miles and crossing two frontiers. Willa and I explored the surroundings of Prague and made excursions up the Vltava, where the leaves of the cherry-trees were red against the silver stubble of the fields. We went on the river-boat to Velká Chuchle and Malá Chuchle, walked in the woods and stopped at little country inns, where we had tea with rum. Everywhere we were struck by the independence of the people.

For the first few months we did not try to meet any English people, though we knew there was a fairly large colony in the town ; we liked our solitude of two, and we wanted to see all these new things with our own eyes. As winter came on it grew very cold ; by the middle of December the river was frozen. On the theory that walking in cold, bracing weather was good for the health we set out one afternoon for a walk in the country. Paní Malá looked surprised when she heard of our intention, but, assuming that British habits were different from hers, she said nothing. All I remember of that walk is a snow-covered field on the outskirts of Prague dotted with big crows, and a black-bearded Jew in a long black fur-trimmed overcoat and a fur cap walking rapidly across it to a little cottage ; he walked as if he were walking on a city pavement, not through snow two feet deep, and this gave his progress a curious nightmare effect. The sky was shrouded, the snow dead white, the crows and the Jew glittering black. It was so cold that the longer we walked the more chilled we grew. At last we turned back, went into a *café* at the end of our street, and drank great quantities of hot tea with rum until we felt warm again. When we came out the wind had risen, and it was so cold now that we had to go into doorways to breathe. That was a particularly cold winter, we were told. The river remained frozen until the beginning of March.

During the winter we came to know the English colony. Some of them were giving English lessons, some studying Czech ; the others were mainly connected with business concerns or the Embassy. A dancing class was started where the Czechs and the English met twice a week. We joined it, and after that we heard all the gossip which flies through a foreign colony, the members of which are slightly suspicious of one another for living out of

England : there is never any convincing argument for
living out of England. We became members of the
English community, attended dances, and took part in
Carnival when it came round. But we still had three-
quarters of every day to do what we pleased with.

After the New Year the cold grew less intense, and
every morning after breakfast we went to the Kinský
Park, which was still deep in snow, to feed the birds.
This was a favourite occupation of the Prague people,
and the gardens were consequently swarming with
finches, sparrows, blackcaps, blue tits, and woodpeckers,
which were so tame that they would sit on your finger
and peck crumbs or fragments of nut from your hand.
At the end of February Holms appeared for a few days,
enveloped in an enormous long brown overcoat, in
which, with his red hair and red beard, he looked Russian.
He made a great impression on the English colony, who
kept trooping to our lodgings to have a look at him. A
young Englishman from the Midlands who had written
part of a novel which, so far as I know, has not been
finished yet, dropped in while Holms was there, carrying
a copy of *Ulysses*, which had just come out. Like many
æsthetes from the North and Midlands of England, he
was both very sensitive and very shrewd, a cross between
Aubrey Beardsley and Samuel Smiles. He was small,
dark, thin, malicious and very plucky. He had once had
a Platonic affair with Gaby Deslys while he was working
in a store in London, and amused us with stories of how
she concealed him when her lovers came to visit her ;
she would send him to the pantry to have a good meal
while she entertained the suitor of the evening—a really
humane act, for he always looked underfed. We both
came to like him, but after a while we lost sight of him ;
the English colony did not know what to make of him.

As the winter was ending Willa caught bronchitis, and

we called in a doctor who lived above us, a handsome Austrian. He had attended the same university as Otto Weininger, the author of *Sex and Character*, who, he said, had been cruelly tormented by his fellow-students, and actually involved in a sham duel staged to make him look ridiculous. The doctor related all this objectively, without showing pleasure or disapproval. He had an extraordinarily calm, disillusioned, and yet pleasant manner. The War had killed his ambition ; he did not think that the battle of life was worth waging ; all that remained to him was a sense of honour. He had left Vienna because it was no longer the Vienna he had loved before the War. He had no political convictions, and if any reference was made to politics, he looked disgusted ; he gave me more strongly than anyone else I have ever met the feeling that he had come to a place from which there was no turning back, the place which Franz Kafka says must be reached ; but in the doctor's case it did not seem to be the right place, even though he would never turn back. He did not like Prague, which as an Austrian he found provincial ; but he had no intention of leaving it. He had come to terms with a completely unsatisfactory state of things, being convinced that life itself was completely unsatisfactory. Yet he was a kind and honourable man. We saw him at intervals ; he was always pleasant and distant, like an amiable damned soul speaking to tyros who were not yet either saved or damned.

The Story and the Fable

The Good Town

LOOK at it well.   This was the good town once,
Known everywhere, with streets of friendly neighbours,
Street friend to street and house to house.   In summer
All day the doors stood open ;   lock and key
Were quaint antiquities fit for museums
With gyves and rusty chains.   The ivy grew
From post to post across the prison door.
The yard behind was sweet with grass and flowers,
A place where grave philosophers loved to walk.
Old Time that promises and keeps his promise
Was our sole lord indulgent and severe,
Who gave and took away with gradual hand
That never hurried, never tarried, still
Adding, subtracting.   These our houses had
Long fallen into decay but that we knew
Kindness and courage can repair Time's faults,
And serving him breeds patience and courtesy
In us, light sojourners and passing subjects.
There is a virtue in tranquillity
That makes all fitting, childhood and youth and age,
Each in its place.

Look well.   These mounds of rubble,
And shattered piers, half-windows, broken arches
And groping arms were once inwoven in walls
Covered with saints and angels, bore the roof,
Shot up the towering spire.   These gaping bridges
Once spanned the quiet river which you see
Beyond that patch of raw and angry earth
Where the new concrete houses sit and stare.
Walk with me by the river.   See, the poplars
Still gather quiet gazing on the stream.

The white road winds across the small green hill
And then is lost.   These few things still remain.
Some of our houses too, though not what once
Lived there and drew a strength from memory.
Our people have been scattered, or have come
As strangers back to mingle with the strangers
Who occupy our rooms where none can find
The place he knew but settles where he can.
No family now sits at the evening table ;
Father and son, mother and child are out,
A quaint and obsolete fashion.   In our houses
Invaders speak their foreign tongues, informers
Appear and disappear, chance whores, officials
Humble or high, frightened, obsequious,
Sit carefully in corners.   My old friends
(Friends ere these great disasters) are dispersed
In parties, armies, camps, conspiracies.
We avoid each other.   If you see a man
Who smiles good-day or waves a lordly greeting
Be sure he's a policeman or a spy.
We know them by their free and candid air.

It was not time that brought these things upon us,
But these two wars that trampled on us twice,
Advancing and withdrawing, like a herd
Of clumsy-footed beasts on a stupid errand
Unknown to them or us.   Pure chance, pure malice,
Or so it seemed.   And when, the first war over,
The armies left and our own men came back
From every point by many a turning road,
Maimed, crippled, changed in body or in mind,
It was a sight to see the cripples come
Out on the fields.   The land looked all awry,
The roads ran crooked and the light fell wrong.
Our fields were like a pack of cheating cards

Dealt out at random—all we had to play
In the bad game for the good stake, our life.
We played ; a little shrewdness scraped us through.
Then came the second war, passed and repassed,
And now you see our town, the fine new prison,
The house doors shut and barred, the frightened faces
Peeping round corners, secret police, informers,
And all afraid of all.

     How did it come ?
From outside, so it seemed, an endless source,
Disorder inexhaustible, strange to us,
Incomprehensible.   Yet sometimes now
We ask ourselves, we the old citizens :
' Could it have come from us ?   Was our peace peace ?
Our goodness goodness ?   That old life was easy
And kind and comfortable ; but evil is restless
And gives no rest to the cruel or the kind.
How could our town grow wicked in a moment ?
What is the answer ?   Perhaps no more than this,
That once the good men swayed our lives, and those
Who copied them took a while the hue of goodness,
A passing loan ; while now the bad are up,
And we, poor ordinary neutral stuff,
Not good nor bad, must ape them as we can,
In sullen rage or vile obsequiousness.
Say there's a balance between good and evil
In things, and it's so mathematical,
So finely reckoned that a jot of either,
A bare proponderance will do all you need,
Make a town good, or make it what you see.
But then, you'll say, only that jot is wanting,
That grain of virtue.   No : when evil comes
All things turn adverse, and we must begin
At the beginning, heave the groaning world

Back in its place again, and clamp it there.
Then all is hard and hazardous.   We have seen
Good men made evil wrangling with the evil,
Straight minds grown crooked fighting crooked minds.
Our peace betrayed us ; we betrayed our peace.
Look at it well.   This was the good town once.'

These thoughts we have, walking among our ruins.

The Labyrinth

Stone Walls . . .

WHILE the others settled down to play bridge or poker I normally read for an hour or so and then went to bed. I slept well at Gavi. It was a non-intellectual life there of discipline and exercise. I was hardening my body every day for the ordeal that surely lay ahead, for I had few illusions that the Germans would easily let us go when Italy gave up the struggle. There were too many strange and important officers in the camp, *pericolosi*, as the Italians called them—officers such as young Colonel David Stirling of the Scots Guards, the most dashing raider perhaps of all our remarkable officers in the war in the desert.

Also the fact that we were so far north excited me strongly after all those months down near the instep of Italy. Binns and Johnstone felt the same. After all, we were only a few hours in a fast train from Chiasso, a part of the Swiss frontier which was not too hard to cross. At Gavi we could talk to scores of officers who had actually been at large, who had travelled on the Italian railways, who could tell us how to buy a ticket at Milan station without arousing suspicion, who could draw plans of Como, showing where to go past the bus terminus to find the road for Chiasso and the frontier.

Not long after our arrival came the first break by officers from Gavi. It was a lower compound escape, so that even if I had been an old Gavi hand I should have had no part in it. It was one of the most remarkable achievements in all the history of escape from prison.

The central figure was a South African Hercules called Buck Palm. Buck was a loose, slouching man, with a lined, rugged heavy-jawed face and a mane of black hair as long as Samson's. He had been an all-in wrestler, a prospector and many other things besides. He rolled with long slanting hen-toed strides about the prison, talking sensibly and well to his countrymen in Afrikaans and to us in English with a strong Afrikaans accent. He was the teacher at a class which met every day after tea to go through a tremendous series of muscle-building contortions and exercises.

From a cell in the lower courtyard Buck first tunnelled a hole in the wall which led to the cellars and the large reservoir hidden below the courtyard. This hole in itself was a major triumph. Italian supervision was so un-remitting and so thorough that it seemed incredible that any hole, no matter how well concealed, could escape their daily—sometimes twice daily—searches.

Down below, day after day, and in the icy winter, Buck swam across the reservoir and tunnelled through sixteen feet of solid rock. A man less strong would never have got through. A man who had not the mining in his blood and the sting of the fall of Tobruk to avenge would never have got through. To me it is one of the fine pictures of the war ; the grim, wintry fortress up above, with lesser mortals shivering in their beds, and down in the bowels Buck, a great, muscled devil, dripping with icy water, *burning* and boring his way through solid rock. Burning in fact, for in order to split the rock he smuggled down quantities of wood and built large fires against the face. Then, when the stone was hot, he flung bucketfuls of cold water against it to crack it. Then he smashed into it with his great crowbar. What a man ! What a noble monster of a man !

It was right and just that such efforts should be success-ful. One night Buck and some of his South African friends went through the hole, swam the reservoir, and crawled through the last tunnel on to the roofs of the

Italian troops' triangular compound jutting immediately below our mess windows. They dropped into the compound and let themselves over the edge of it on a rope.

The small South African party got away. They were followed by Jack Pringle and (Baron) Cram. Pringle got down all right. The rope broke with Cram, and he injured his leg in the fall. However, he hobbled off into the darkness.

But at Gavi the sentries were always watchful. The others following on, including the tall David Stirling, found the way barred, and several of them were caught by the Italians when they were actually through the tunnel. This escape, brilliant though it was, taught me another lesson—that spectacular mass escapes are the worst kind, for they draw immediate counter-measures from the enemy. Following this break from Gavi (supposed, the Italians frequently said, to be the most secure jail in the world), two divisions of troops were immediately turned out to scour the country. Cram and the South Africans, including Buck, were still on foot and were quickly rounded up. Jack Pringle, a personable and quick-witted young man who spoke good Italian with an American accent, made a speedy get-away on the train to Milan, and thence to the banks of Lake Maggiore. He found the lake a tough proposition. Escape by water was difficult, since there were no private boats available and the Italian patrol boats were sinister things with silent electric motors and powerful searchlights which snapped suddenly on and off. All the frontier guards were on the look-out, and poor Jack, an escaping genius if ever there was one, was caught within sight of Switzerland.

The next attempt was made by our bold Brigadier Clifton. One night, when I was already in bed and the Room 14 poker game was at its noisy height, there was a sudden burst of firing from three or four different points on the battlements. This was followed by Italian screams at the brigadier, who was perched on top of the roof on the other side of our courtyard.

He had climbed out of his window (disregarding a 100-foot sheer drop), swinging on the shutter until he could scramble on to the steep old roof above. The brigadier had home-made rope wound round him, and he planned to go right along that roof and then somehow descend a couple of large precipices well sprinkled with sentry posts. The noise of his passage on the roof alarmed the sentries, and he found himself up in the sky dazzled by searchlights, and with bullets whistling past him and chipping the slates. His comment as they led him off to the punishment cell was : ' I knew I was all right so long as they were aiming at me, But I was afraid they might be aiming to miss.'

Clifton, a bald, lobsterish little man with freckles all over his muscle-rounded back, and a devilish twinkle in his forget-me-not-blue eyes, always preferred dash to caution.

Soon after this Johnny, Wally and I got to work on our own escape route. August was beginning, and the heat on the rock was stifling. The summer was slipping away. Six of us formed a team with an ambitious plan to cut through some cellars under our courtyard to underground passages which we knew existed. We believed that these passages led out of the rock on the far side from Gavi—a side which none of us had ever seen, even on our monthly escorted walks outside the fortress.

Binns, Johnson and I made up one team for the tunnelling. The other team consisted of the two New Zealanders, Jim Craig and John Redpath, and George Duncan, a long-necked Scottish Commando officer, who had been a farmer near Dumfries.

We worked steadily on alternate days. On working days the three of us would slip as soon as possible after morning roll-call into the quartermaster's stores, one of the ground-floor rooms in our courtyard. Once inside we locked the door. Often it was difficult to get in, for there was always at least one *carabiniere* wandering about the courtyard on guard. We had a team of people trained to distract the Italians' attention, talking to them until they turned away from the door so that we could walk in unobserved. There were also two high sentry posts looking down into our courtyard which had to be watched, for the sentries could see the doorway. But the sheer obviousness of the entrance was a good thing. The Italians could never have believed that we were using that room without their knowledge.

Once inside we took our apparatus out of the hole—a square hole cut by Jim and John in the wall between the room and the courtyard. The hole led into a ventilation shaft some fifteen feet deep. We hung a rope made from plaited sheets down the shaft, and it was fairly easy for a supple man to get down and up it. The remainder of the apparatus consisted of a series of iron tools forged in the cook-house fires from old bedsteads, and lamps made from margarine tins, with pyjama-flannel wicks rising out of boiled olive-oil given to us by the mess.

Two of us went down the hole at a time to work a four-hour shift on the face while the third stayed at the top to communicate with the outside world. A line of officers sat reading and sunbathing with their chairs tilted against the wall. The officer sitting against the door was always one of our other team. He passed warnings if the Italians arrived to make a search or if the *carabinieri* in the courtyard wandered so near that they might hear our hammering.

As the tempo of our work increased we were able to ask

the British authorities to organise hand-ball, improvised squash-rackets, and other games in the courtyard so that their noise would help to drown our efforts below.

The air was foul down there. There was a long series of nine large cells, all with low barrel vaults, and communicating with each other by arched openings in the thick dividing walls. The previous entrance to the cells led from number six, counting from the end one in which we worked, and it had been solidly walled-up by the Italians before the first British prisoners of war arrived at Gavi. Austrian prisoners had been incarcerated there during the First World War, and there was still pathetic evidence of their living death—evidence in the shape of old india-rubber children's balls, dates, names and inscriptions in German cut on the massive stonework, and odd rusty mugs and chamber-pots. But all the ventilation holes had been walled in, and most of the shafts had been filled with rubble, which overflowed into the dark cells. It was a sinister place, full of evil memories.

The work was a question of chipping away with chisels and a muffled hammer at the cement, levering with flimsy crowbars, and gradually, painfully, stone after massive stone, working a small shaft into the end wall. Our eyes became sore, partly from the chips, partly from the lamps ; and the foul air pinched at our chests. The hole grew very slowly, every inch representing cramp and sweat blisters.

We came out of the tunnel at tea-time, carefully cleaned ourselves in the quartermaster's stores, hid the hole in the wall with a packing-case full of spare battle-dress, and slipped out into the dazzling sunshine of the courtyard when the sentry on watch outside gave us the all clear. Then we went down to the cook-house where the cooks had saved a meal for us.

On off days we were employed on watch outside the door, in making and sharpening tools for the work, and in perfecting our clothing for the escape.

This time Wally and I were going together and Johnny was teaming up with the brigadier who, since he was too conspicuous a figure, was not working on our tunnel, but was watching it with closest interest. After talking with almost everyone in the camp who had been out, Wally and I made a good plan, and a simple one. We were going to catch a train direct from the next station to Gavi, change trains at Milan for Como, walk from Como to Chiasso, where we knew the very spot in the frontier wire that we would cross. We believed that ten hours after escaping we should be on Swiss territory. Everything was worked out, the price of the tickets, the lay-out of the stations, the Italian phrases I should have to use, our behaviour on the crowded trains.

By lashing out liberally with my hoarded tins I had bought article after article of clothing, so that now I could leave the camp quite respectably dressed in a blue, double-breasted suit (mainly adapted from naval uniform). Wally was almost as well equipped. We had forged German papers (made by an expert in the camp). I had prepared a greasy dye for my fair hair by powdering brown chalk into brilliantine (a mixture I had already tried with success at Padula).

Soon after all this work began we were alarmed to see many German troops filtering into our valley. The Sicily campaign had ended with Allied success, the Allies had gained a foothold in southern Italy. It seemed only natural that the Germans should be injecting troops into northern Italy. But what troops they looked to us, who were used all of us to the mechanised warfare of the desert ! They had old equipment, and their transport was horse-drawn. There were a great many of them, and they were settling down along the valley as though they intended to stay. Gradually we became accustomed to their presence, and, such is the optimism of man, we decided that Germans of that type would take no action against us.

Then one night as we sat at dinner a great singing shout rose from the Italian quarters below us and from the town of Gavi. We looked out, and the dark material was being torn from the windows at Gavi. Window after window came alive, until the whole singing town was sparkling with light.

The Italian Government had declared an armistice. We thought that we were free.

. . . .

'There is some bother with the Germans,' a friendly *carabiniere* said to me as I came out into the misty courtyard early the following morning.

'What sort of bother, *amico mio* ?'

'Oh,' he answered gaily. 'We are going to put them in their place. They cannot push us around as they please.'

I had never heard an Italian talking about Germans like that before, and it worried me. I moved vaguely down the courtyard, passed, unmolested by the Italian sentries, to the top of the ramp, and stood there in the deliciously fresh morning sunshine pondering the events of the night before.

It had been the most breathless night since our attempted escape from Padula. I had gone to sleep with the greatest difficulty, for I had been obliged by the movement and optimism around me to allow myself to think of Anne as something now reasonably close and attainable, and to add to the prospect of seeing her again dreams of clean linen sheets, hot water to wash with, music from a full orchestra. . . .

Earlier that night two Italian officers, the only two in the garrison who were friendly to the British, had come into our mess to shake hands with us all. They wept with joy. Our brigadier went straight into the Italian section of the camp to demand of 'Joe Grape' that we be immediately released. 'Joe' refused, stating that it would be too dangerous for us to be released while the camp was surrounded by Germans. 'Joe' said that he would hold us in Gavi by force until he received specific contrary orders from the Badoglio Government. From the windows of the mess we could see the German transport unit camped under the trees of the market-place, stolidly settling down, as though this night were exactly like any other.

Brigadier Clifton, energetic little fire-eater, had prepared an elaborate cloak-and-dagger scheme for breaking out of the camp—a scheme in which, with many officers, I had been trained to play a minor role. I believe that this scheme would have succeeded, though at the cost of some casualties. But for one reason or another it was not put into operation.

So that Armistice night we had climbed the ramp once more after dinner to be locked into our courtyard as usual by the Italians. There was much excitement and a lot of singing. They sang the *Maori Farewell*, and the *Zulu Warrior*, which began (phonetically) :

I ziga zoomba . . .
(phonetically from memory).

And a rather charming little song, the chorus of which goes :

Git away, you bumble-bee,
Git off my nose.
I ain't no prairie flower,
Ain't no bleeding rose. . . .

While the singing was at its height I had walked up and down the courtyard with Colonel Fraser. We agreed that we should have felt more comfortable outside prison and foot-slogging it for the Allied armies in the south. I had a great opinion of his judgment, and felt as he did, that since we had been made prisoners by the Germans, and not by the Italians, it would be extraordinary if the Germans allowed us to walk out. Fraser said that he was sure the Germans would seize us ; and that whenever they arrived he intended to have himself walled in at the top of the ramp at a place where John Redpath had pierced a small hole into an ancient passage-way leading through the rock. Redpath and Slater, a third New Zealander, were also going in there. The three of them had prepared a large store of food and water. . . .

.   .   .   .

Still meditating, I drifted down the ramp. Now I was on the level of the mess ; I could see the zigzag path descending towards Gavi, and I stopped thinking back.

Fifteen Italians, led by the familiarly ridiculous figure of a popinjay officer, were cautiously descending the path. As I watched I saw the patrol set out round the last corner before the highest houses of Gavi. They vanished for a moment, but later we were able to reconstruct the events that took place in the minute they were out of sight.

Two Germans in steel helmets were leaning against the wall of the first house, actually the quarters of the *carabinieri*. One of the Italian soldiers playfully levelled his rifle and said : ' *Eh eh*,' mocking at the Germans in a childish way. In reply one of the Germans shot him with his machine pistol. The Italians picked up the wounded man and, keening like witches, straggled up the hill.

Eastern cries of grief greeted the bloody body of the dying soldier as he was carried into the fortress. The sentries on the ramp levelled their rifles at me, and ordered me back to my quarters.

All the Italians now took up action stations around the ramparts, with officers crawling from position to position. What had happened was that the Germans had dispatched a company of front-line infantry to take over our fortress and assure our capture. While it was on its way they ordered the local troops, sixty men of the Veterinary Corps under a farrier-sergeant, to attack and take the fortress.

Soon after the patrol incident the farrier-sergeant fired a mortar smoke-bomb at the mighty walls. Our brigadier, watching from his room high up under the roof, saw the Italian answer. The Italian vice-commandant, a miserable and decrepit old colonel, stumbled down the slope towards Gavi with ten men and a very large white flag.

An hour later the first German troops, roughly dressed soldiers, with horse dung caked on their dusty boots, shambled stolidly on to the battlements. They greeted us with immense curiosity and even a kind of awe as they moved clumsily to take over from the Italians. Gavi fortress had not sullied its centuries-old record of instant surrender. Very soon more lively Germans under a thin and efficient young cavalry captain, troops bristling with automatic weapons, arrived to increase our guard.

The spiritual let-down at seeing these hated and efficient uniforms again at such close quarters, at finding ourselves their prisoners when we had hoped that we were free, was very terrible. Their arrival threw the whole camp into a turmoil.

Everybody rushed round the place looking for a way out on his own. That evening for the first time (since the German sentries did not know where we were not supposed to go) we were able to walk out on to the battlements above our courtyard, on the topmost pinnacle of the fortress. Several of us saw at once that it would be possible with a good rope to get down from one corner, where there was an ancient look-out turret unobserved by any German sentry. With Binns, Johnson and five others I ran down to our rooms below, and by tearing out the cord reinforcements from the canvas covers on the beds we managed in a few hours to make a hundred feet of strong pleated rope. Filling our pockets with chocolate and emergency rations, we climbed again to the ramparts. But the game was spoiled at the last moment by a bird-like Italian business man, quite a like-able and decent person, who was interpreter at the camp. He ran out of the Italian officers' mess, far below us, and waved his arms in windmill gesticulations at us, screaming to the Germans : 'Don't allow them up there. You don't know them. They are all most dangerous. . . .'

We were never allowed up there again.

When he was later asked why he did this, the interpreter was reported to have replied : 'For my wife and children.'

Brigadier Clifton now issued clear orders. A swarthy British officer from Alexandria, George Sukas, who spoke among other languages fluent Italian, had wheedled from a *carabiniere* the exact whereabouts of the secret passage for which our party had so long been tunnelling.

We soon noticed that the Germans, compared to the Italians, were sluggish guards. This was not indeed to be wondered at, for they were still befuddled in the maze of the fortress. We began to cut a new way out, work which would have been quite impossible under former conditions, with daily searches and all the complications of Italian precautions.

An entrance was to be cut from the end room in our corridor into a disused lavatory, and from the lavatory a way was to be broken to the mouth of the secret passage.

The working of this exit was entrusted to three senior

officers, Major ' Waddy ' Wadeson, of the Royal Engineers, a small, virile yellow-eyed man who had worked all over the world as a mining engineer ; Major Brian Upton, of the Essex Yeomanry, always known as ' Hack-in-the-Bush,' readily distinguishable by his bowed back and enormous red moustache ; and Commander John de Jago.

It was agonising to wait, day after day, while the three men laboriously worked their way through the bowels of the camp. The strain on them was heavy. The strain on us, who waited with freedom in Italy or what looked like permanent incarceration in Germany hanging on their efforts, was even worse. There was discontent among the younger tunnellers that the work had been given to these men. But the brigadier could not have chosen more wisely. All three were experienced jail-breakers, and ' Hack-in-the-Bush ' was the camp's genius at making anything from a skeleton key to an explosive charge.

At the end of the first day they had cut their way into the lavatory, and had chiselled in the thick lavatory wall a hole large enough to see into the passage itself.

Already Colonel Fraser, with his two accomplices, had been walled in at the top of the ramp. A friend among the Italian officers had destroyed the records, so that the Germans were unable to hold accurate roll-calls.

The brigadier launched his alternative scheme, to be put into operation if the secret passage exit failed. All officers who wished to hide were ordered to give particulars of their hiding-places, and to work with the authorities to provide and stow food and water. It was felt by some that the Germans either would not have the time or would not bother to search for officers missing when the order to move to Germany was given.

That day another company of German infantry arrived

in the camp, and we had the doubtful satisfaction of seeing the entire Italian garrison paraded below us by the Germans. The Italians handed over their arms as though they were glad to be rid of them.

'Waddy,' Jago and 'Hack-in-the-Bush' broke into the passage, only to find that two strong steel grilles barred the way. Also the mouth of the passage opened on to the ramparts near a German sentry post, so that they were obliged to work silently, and therefore slowly. By nightfall they had filed through the first grille.

Binns and I, although fully prepared to leave by the passage, decided that it would be reasonable to prepare for its possible failure. So that day we went down our old hole from the quartermaster's store and, at Wally's clever suggestion, built up a framework of wood, stones and blankets into an extremely solid shelter. We covered this over with big stones and rubble until it looked quite indistinguishable from the other rubble-piles, but it contained a space six feet by four feet in which we could lie side by side. It was a double-bluff hiding-place.

On Monday, 13th September, everything looked good. 'Waddy' and party, now working with several strong helpers, had opened both grilles. The passage had degenerated into a sewer which apparently had been blocked by a land-slide. They were tunnelling now through loose earth; and by breakfast-time they had reached the roots of the grass, and calculated that within a few hours the way would be free.

A movement order for escape by this route had been completed by the British orderly room. We were all to leave that night in batches of twenty, with half-hourly intervals between batches. There was a little hard feeling about the order of departure, which did not go by seniority. But Wally, Johnny and I, thanks to our escaping proclivities, were well up on the list.

I was sitting with Colin Armstrong and Tom Murdoch in Room 14 at ten o'clock that morning when Richard Carr arrived, breathless from running up the ramp, to tell us that the Germans had given everybody in the camp half an hour's notice to be ready to move to Germany.

After half an hour of pandemonium, with everybody charging in every direction, and the people who were going into hiding getting mixed up with people who were going away intending to make a break for it en route for Germany, Wally and I stood at the bottom of our little shaft, helping down ten other officers. The ten were all strangers to these cells—Wally and I were the only two of our original tunnelling party who had decided to hide there—and they were understandably surprised by the damp, the darkness and the stale clammy smell.

Binns had thoughtfully brought down the last of our oil-lamps, and with this we continued to perfect our camouflaged hut. Other people scrabbled out beds or hiding-places in the rubble, and all were busily at work when the senior officer there, pale-eyed Squadron-Leader Bax, ordered us sternly to stop making a noise and to put out the light.

Our hut was in the cell from which the former entrance to the line of cells had led. The other officers, obeying the nervous herd instinct, eventually all gathered in the end cell of the series at the other end from our entrance shaft and the tunnel face upon which we had worked for nearly two months. We knew that some fifty or sixty officers at least were in hiding now, and I cannot say that either of us had much confidence in the trick. We were only separated from Colonel Fraser's party by some fifty feet of rock. Tony Hay and some others were flimsily and dangerously hidden under the roof over the corridor outside Room 14. Many others, including the brigadier

184

and Tag Pritchard, were hiding in the mouth of the new escape route, hoping that the Germans would not find them in time to prevent them from digging their way out. David Stirling and Buck Palm were well hidden down a lavatory shaft in the lower courtyard. Tom Murdoch and Richard Carr had been cemented in under the stone staircase leading up from the lower courtyard to the infirmary ; and were to be fed through india-rubber tubes with hot Ovaltine and Horlick's poured in by the medical orderlies. They had a similar reverse process for ridding their almost airless hiding-place of waste liquids. Many others were hidden in the camp wood-pile. Altogether there were far too many in hiding. The only hope seemed to be that the brigadier's lot would dig themselves free. The Germans might suppose if they found an empty tunnel that all of us were already outside the fortress walls.

After an hour or two below we heard the Germans begin to loot our quarters. There was the crash of furniture being thrown from the windows of our rooms to the cobbles below, then much singing and shouting as the looters got in amongst our tins of butter and jam. After that we heard retching in the courtyard. They had been eating tinned butter by the handful.

Then the Germans came to hunt us out with picks and hand-grenades. Their search was evidently methodical. Bax's party reported that they had heard the brigadier's voice on the ramp. Almost immediately after this the enemy found Colonel Fraser's party, whom we had considered almost unfindable. The answer to this efficiency (although we did not know it at the time) was that 'Joe Grape,' who knew the fortress as well as his wife, was telling the methodical Germans which walls to break down. They could not get at Fraser and the two New Zealanders with him, but they fired rifles through a hole which they had hacked into the narrow cleft in the rock. The bullets buzzed around in the confined space until the three came out.

It was clearly only a matter of time until a search-party entered our own cells. Binns and I withdrew into our shelter and closed ourselves in with a large stone blocking the two-foot-by-one-foot-six-inch entrance. At 7 p.m., nine hours after going into hiding, we heard the first pick strike on the walled-up doorway. Binns and I lay touching in the darkness. We counted twenty-three savage strokes, then the brickwork collapsed with a rumble into our cell. Five or six Germans came in at the double. They carried some kind of lantern. Its yellow light flickered through the small interstices of our shelter. They all turned left, and searched through the empty series of cells there. We heard shouts, probably caused by the sight of the mouth of our old tunnel. Then they came clattering back past us. An instant later they challenged our friends in the end cell. They shouted at them to put their hands up and walk out singly. As they went we heard one German ask Squadron-Leader Bax, ' Are there any more British here ? '

' You can see for yourselves that there are not,' he answered curtly in German.

For two hours we lay there, cold, cramped, but in peace. The Germans seemed to have stopped searching the upper part of the fortress. But soon after nine we heard another party clattering up the ramp. We were not yet accustomed to the thunderous noise of German jack-boots in that rocky place. The search-party came straight into our cell. They searched among some of the rubble-piles in the other cells, then they collected the food store of our fellow-officers and proceeded to divide it out.

This was done in our cell, and two of them actually sat on the upper stones of our hiding-place. The ' roof ' above me was made of the frames of deck-chairs, and I could see these bend slightly under the Germans' weight. We survived two more desultory searches that night, and I blessed Binns with his heaven-sent idea of the double bluff. It looked as though we were going to get away with it, and that was worth any amount of discomfort. I never remember being more cold and cramped. The cellars ran with dampness.

By eight o'clock the following morning all noise of German presence had died down. Wally and I crawled out to stretch ourselves, breakfasted off chocolate and water, and decided that we would remain hidden until nightfall, when we would try to climb down the battle-ments. We knew where to find our rope. However, at ten o'clock we heard a large German search-party march up the ramp and halt at the hole into our cells. This time it was a real search. They tore everything to pieces in the other cells ; but because our pile of stones was small, and because it was in the half-light of the entrance cell instead of in the darkness farther inside, they did not suspect it. They were urged on with screaming, angry shouts.

When we thought once more that they had missed us a German bayonet crashed right through the stones and our wooden structure, ending within two inches of Binns's ear.

A torch beam shone through the hole and a German shouted, ' *Mensch !* '

They tore down the structure, half crushing us under-neath it, and dragged us out.

Horned Pigeon

LILIAN BOWES LYON

An Old Farm Labourer

You carved your story upon the country-side.
Your wrongs, your rights are told where needy brooks
Run gold awhile, or fouled ; here ; there.
In you sardonically a scarecrow talks,
A god evokes the venerable stillnesses
Of water and earth and air.
What stoved-in patience, what extortionate rocks
The weald you've ploughed and all the amber tide
Of autumn, punctually rolled back, lays bare !
Towns are for younger bones ; in yours abide
The old, rich dung, each crust you learnt to share,
Long years of wedlock, tedium of illnesses,
Field-mice, hunger of hawks.

Collected Poems

Death in Summer

The soldier lay on the ground, he felt the Earth
  Swell eagerly through his adolescent limbs ;
He was free of a sudden to ponder the slow birth
  Of mountains, share the articulate hush of streams.

The upstart oak, the bracken's bending crozier
  Brindled the partial light ; how long a sigh
Had stilled these rocks, what early and potent glacier
  Plotted this valley, green to man's young eye.

Lovely with sleep he turned the lock of Nature ;
  Strange was the land—oh too profound that sea !
When morning broke he seemed to have gained in stature ;
  Like other turbulent boys, fulfilled as he.

Collected Poems

COLIN MACDONALD

Lord Leverhulme and the Men of Lewis

AT the farm steading we found over a thousand people
gathered for the meeting ; mostly men, but there was
a fair smattering of women. It was a sullen crowd,
resentful of the situation which had developed. One
wrong note might have precipitated serious trouble. But
no wrong note was struck ; and if Lord Leverhulme
sensed any danger he certainly showed no sign. He
walked right into the middle of the crowd, made a little
` ring ' for himself and his interpreter, mounted an up-
turned tub (in which the farmer was wont to brew a real
knock-me-down brand of beer), raised high his hat,
smiled genially all round and said :

' Good morning, everybody ! Have you noticed that
the sun is shining this morning ?—and that this is the first
time it has shone in Lewis for ten days ? [*This was a
fact !*]

' I regard that as a good omen. This is going to be a
great meeting. This is going to be a friendly meeting.
This meeting will mark the beginning of a new era in the
history of this loyal island of Lewis that you love above all
places on earth, and that I too have learned to love. So
great is my regard for Lewis and its people that I am
prepared to adventure a big sum of money for the development of the resources of the island and of the fisheries.
Do you realise that Stornoway is right in the centre of
the richest fishing grounds in the whole world ? The
fishing which has hitherto been carried on in an old-
fashioned happy-go-lucky way is now to be prosecuted
on scientific lines. Recently at Stornoway I saw half of
the fishing boats return to port without a single herring
and the remainder with only a score of crans between

them. That is a poor return for men who spend their time and risk their lives in a precarious calling [*ejaculations of assent*]. I have a plan for putting an end to that sort of thing [*the crowd is eagerly interested*].

'The fact is, your fishing as presently carried on is a hit or a miss. I want you to make it a hit every time. How can I do that? Well, every time you put out to sea you blindly hope to strike a shoal of herrings. Sometimes you do. Oftener you do not. But the shoals are there if you only knew the spot—and *that* is where I can help you.

'I am prepared to supply a fleet of airplanes and trained observers who will daily scan the sea in circles round the island. An observer from one of these planes cannot fail to notice any shoal of herrings over which he passes. Immediately he does so he sends a wireless message to the Harbour Master at Stornoway. Every time a message of that kind comes in there is a loud-speaker announcement by the Harbour Master so that all the skippers at the pier get the exact location of the shoal. The boats are headed for that spot—and next morning they steam back to port loaded with herrings to the gunwales. Hitherto, more often than not, the return to port has been with light boats and heavy hearts. In future it will be with light hearts and heavy boats! [*Loud cheers.*]

'I have already thought out plans which will involve me in an expenditure of five million pounds! But there has been some discord between us; we have not seen eye to eye. When two sensible people have a difference of opinion they do not quarrel: they meet and discuss their differences reasonably and calmly. This is what we have met for here today—and the sun is shining! But what do I propose to do with this five million pounds? Let me tell you. . . .'

And then there appeared in the next few minutes the

most graphic word-picture it is possible to imagine—a great fleet of fishing boats—another great fleet of cargo boats—a large fish-canning factory (already started)—railways—and electric-power station ; then one could see the garden city grow—steady work, steady pay, beautiful houses for all—every modern convenience and comfort. The insecurity of their present income was referred to ; the squalor of their present houses deftly compared with the conditions in the new earthly paradise. Altogether it was a masterpiece ; and it produced its effect ; little cheers came involuntarily from a few here and there—more cheers !—general cheers ! . . .

And just then, while the artist was still adding skilful detail, there was a dramatic interruption.

One of the ringleaders managed to rouse himself from the spell, and in an impassioned voice addressed the crowd in Gaelic, and this is what he said :

' *So so, fhiribh ! Cha dean so gnothach ! Bheireadh am bodach milbheulach sin chreidsinn oirnn gu'm bheil dubh geal's geal dubh ! Ciod e dhuinn na bruadairean briagha aige, a thig no nach tig ? 'Se am fearann tha sinn ag iarraidh. Agus 'se tha mise a faighneachd* [turning to face Lord Leverhulme and pointing dramatically towards him] : *an toir thu dhuinn am fearann ?* ' The effect was electrical. The crowd roared their approbation.

Lord Leverhulme looked bewildered at this, to him, torrent of unintelligible sounds, but when the frenzied cheering with which it was greeted died down he spoke :

' I am sorry ! It is my great misfortune that I do not understand the Gaelic language. But perhaps my interpreter will translate for me what has been said ? '

Said the interpreter : ' I am afraid, Lord Leverhulme, that it will be impossible for me to convey to you in English what has been so forcefully said in the older tongue ; but I will do my best '—and his best was a masterpiece, not only in words but in tone and gesture and general effect :

' Come, come, men ! This will not do ! This honey-mouthed man would have us believe that black is white and white is black. *We* are not concerned with his fancy dreams that may or may not come true ! What we want is the *land*—and the question I put to him now is : *will you give us the land ?* '

The translation evoked a further round of cheering. A voice was heard to say :

' Not so bad for a poor language like the English ! '

Lord Leverhulme's picture, so skilfully painted, was spattered in the artist's hand !

But was it ? When the cheering died down the brave little artist looked round the crowd with eyes that seemed to pierce every separate individual. Finally he fixed a cold-steel look on the interrupter and in a clean-cut staccato accent said :

' You have asked a straight question. I like a straight question ; and I like a straight answer. And my answer to your question is ' NO.' I am *not* prepared to give you the land ' (here a compelling hand-wave that instantly silenced some protests), ' not because I am vindictively opposed to your views and aspirations, but because I conscientiously believe that if my views are listened to—if my schemes are given a chance—the result will be enhanced prosperity and greater happiness for Lewis and its people. Listen. . . .' And the indomitable little artist took up his work again in such skilful fashion that in a matter of seconds he had the ear and the eye of the crowd again—and in five minutes they were cheering him again. . . . Theatre ! Play !

But the play was not yet over. A clean-shaven æsthete—a crofter-fisherman—cut in politely at a momentary pause in the artist's work. He spoke slowly, in English, with a strong Lewis accent ; each word set square like a stone block in a building, and he made a great speech.

'Lord Leverhulme,' said he, ' will you allow me to intervene in this debate for a few moments ? (Assent signified.) Thank you. Well, I will begin by saying that we give credit to your lordship for good *intentions* in this matter. We believe you *think* you are *right*, but we *know* that you are *wrong*. The fact is, there is an element of sentiment in the situation which is impossible for your lordship to understand. But for that we do not blame you ; it is not your *fault* but your *misfortune* that your upbringing, your experience and your outlook are such that a proper understanding of the position and of our point of view is quite outwith your comprehension. You have spoken of steady work and steady pay in tones of veneration—and I have no doubt that in your view, and in the view of those unfortunate people who are compelled to live their lives in smoky towns, steady work and steady pay are very desirable things. But in Lewis we have never been accustomed to either—and, strange though it must seem to your lordship, *we do not greatly desire them*. We attend to our crofts in seed-time and harvest, and we follow the fishing in its season—and when neither requires our attention we are free to *rest and contemplate*. You have referred to our houses as hovels —but they are our *homes*, and I will venture to say, my lord, that, poor though these homes may be, you will find more *real human happiness* in them than you will find in your *castles* throughout the land. I would impress on you that we are not in opposition to your schemes of work ; we only oppose you when you say you *cannot give us the land*, and on that point we will oppose you with all our strength. It may be that some of the younger and

less-thoughtful men will side with you, but believe me,
the great majority of us are against you.

'Lord Leverhulme ! You have bought this island.
But you have not bought *us*, and we refuse to be the bond-
slaves of any man. We want to live our own lives in our
own way, poor in material things it may be, but at least
it will be clear of the fear of the factory bell ; it will be
free and independent ! '

After a short silence of astonishment there came the
loudest and longest cheers of that day. 'That's the way
to talk, lad ! ' 'That's yourself, boy,' and such like
encomiums were shouted from all quarters. One voice
demanded to know what 'Bodach an t-siapuinn ' [1] could
say to that ? Nobody thought he could say anything to
that : the enemy was annihilated !

But we had yet to grasp the full fighting qualities of
this wonderful little man, and we were soon to see him in
action, at his very best. With a sort of magical com-
bination of hand and eye he again commanded a perfect
silence ; he then spoke in modulated, cajoling tones that
showed the superb actor.

Said he : ' Will you allow me to congratulate you ?—
to thank you for putting the views of my opponents so
clearly before me ? I did know that sentiment lay at the
back of the opposition to my schemes, but I confess I had
not adequately estimated the strength of that element till
now. My friends ! sentiment is the finest thing in this
hard world. It is the golden band of brotherhood. It is
the beautiful mystic thing that makes life worth living
. . . and would you accuse me of deliberately planning
to injure that beautiful thing ? No ! No ! A thousand
times No ! Then is there, after all, so very much between
your point of view and mine ? Are we not striving after
the same thing ?—by different roads it may be, but still,

[1] The wee soap-mannie

for the same goal ? We are both out for the greatest good of the greatest number of people on this island. You have admitted, that the *young men* may believe in my schemes. May I again congratulate you ? The young people will—and do—believe in my schemes. I have in my pocket now (fetching out a handful of letters) quite a number of letters from young men in different parts of the island, and I have received a great many more of the same kind—all asking the same questions—" When can you give me a job in Stornoway ? " " When can I get one of your new houses ? " These young men and their wives and sweethearts want to give up the croft life ; they want a brighter, happier life. . . . My friends ! the young people of today will be *the* people of tomorrow. Are the older ones who have had their day going to stand in the way of the young folk ? Are we older fellows going to be dogs-in-mangers ? No ! The people of this island are much too intelligent to take up so un-Christian an attitude. Give me a chance—give my schemes a chance—give the young folks and give Lewis a chance ! Give me a period of ten years to develop my schemes, and I venture to prophesy that long before then —in fact in the near future—so many people, young and old, will believe in them, that crofts will be going a-begging—and then if there are still some who prefer life on the land they can have two, three, four crofts apiece ! '

And the crowd cheered again : they simply could not resist it, and they cheered loud and long.

The artist knew when to stop. As the cheers died he raised his hat and said : ' Ladies and Gentlemen—*Friends* —I knew the sun did not shine for nothing ! This has been a great meeting. This will be a memorable day in the history of Lewis. You are giving me a chance. I will not fail you. I thank you. Good day.' And off he walked to another round of cheering.

I tried to walk off too—unsuccessfully. An eager crowd surged round ' the man from the Board ' : ' When will the Board be dividing off the land ? '

' You do not want the land now,' said I, well knowing they did, notwithstanding the cheers.

' Want the land ! Of course we want the land, and we want it at once.'

' But you gave Lord Leverhulme the impression that you agreed with him,' said I, affecting astonishment.

' Not at all,' was the reply, ' and if he is under that impression you may tell him from us that he is greatly mistaken.'

' But why did you cheer him ? ' I inquired.

' Och ! well : he made a very good speech and he is a very clever man, and we wanted to show our appreciation—but the land is another matter.'

Highland Journey

O Wha's been Here

O WHA's the bride that cairries the bunch
O' thistles blinterin' white ?
Her cuckold bridegroom little dreids
What he sall ken this nicht.

For closer than gudeman can come
And closer to'r than hersel',
Wha didna need her maidenheid
Has wrocht his purpose fell.

O wha's been here afore me, lass,
And hoo did he get in ?
A man that deed or I was born
This evil thing has din.

And left, as it were on a corpse,
Your maidenheid to me ?
Nae lass, gudeman, sin' Time began
'S hed ony mair to gi'e.

But I can gi'e ye kindness, lad,
And a pair o' willin' hands,
And you sall ha'e my briests like stars,
My limbs like willow wands.

And on my lips ye'll heed nae mair,
And in my hair forget
The seed o' a' the men that in
My virgin womb ha'e met. . . .

A Drunk Man Looks at the Thistle

blinterin', gleaming

197

Bonnie Broukit Bairn

MARS is braw in crammasy,
Venus in a green silk goun,
The auld mune shak's her gowden feathers,
Their starry talk's a wheen o' blethers,
Nane for thee a thochtie sparin',
Earth, thou bonnie broukit bairn !
—But greet, an' in your tears ye'll droun
The haill clanjamfrie !

Sangschaw

braw, fine, gaily dressed   *crammasy*, crimson   *wheen*, a number, quantity
blethers, nonsense, foolish talk   *broukit*, dirty, neglected   *greet*, cry
haill, whole   *clanjamfrie*, collection of people

COMPTON MACKENZIE

The North Wind

[Author's Note : The date of this scene is January 1931]

IT was a small faded room, seeming all the smaller because of the large sprawling patterns of the bluish-green wallpaper ; and the gilt mirror over the fireplace had grown so tarnished with age and tobacco smoke and sea-damp that the interior dimly reflected therein added nothing to the apparent space. On the wall opposite the door hung a large steel engraving spotted with brown mould, which represented a mythical Fitzgerald saving an almost equally mythical King Alexander from the antlers of an infuriated stag, and thereby gaining the favour on which the fortunes of Clann Choinnich were supposed to have been built up. Above this engraving hung a pair of antlers mounted on a wooden shield, the *Cabar Fèidh* of the Mackenzies gained by the feat represented below. Under the engraving was a diminutive and ill-executed water-colour of Dunvegan Castle. The domination of the Mackenzies over the Macleods thus symbolised was an expression of Mistress Macleod's domination over her husband the innkeeper, she having been a Mackenzie before she married him. On either side of the engraving hung a sea-trout in a glass case, to both of which time had given a somewhat kippered appearance. The rest of the pictures showed the stock sentimentalised scenes of Highland life—sheep, shepherds, plaided lassies, shaggy cattle, hills, lochs, birds and sunsets.

There was still one of the broken-springed armchairs vacant, in which John sat down. From the sofa the face of a minister, who was lying with feet up, feet from which he had removed his boots and to which in default of slippers he had added a pair of thick grey woollen socks, bobbed up above the *Glasgow Herald* to reveal a ragged moustache, a complexion stained by excess of tea as fingers are stained by nicotine, and a pair of dark eyes inquisitive about the newcomer.

' Very cold,' he observed.

' Very cold indeed,' John agreed.

Then the moustache and yellow face and dark eyes were hidden again by the *Glasgow Herald*, and John looked round the room at the other guests.

Four commercial travellers had just finished their last rubber of solo whist. Two of them who were rising early to make the crossing to the islands went off to bed ; but one of the two that remained, a fat rubicund man in voluminous plus-fours of brown Harris tweed, came across and offered his hand to John.

' I met you once, Mr Ogilvie, in the Station Hotel at Inverness,' he reminded him.

' I remember very well,' said John, ' it's Mr MacDougal, isn't it ? '

The fat man beamed.

' Look at that now ! Well, well, you have a very good memory, Mr Ogilvie. You'll be meeting many different people of all sorts and yet you remembered my name. Well, well ! '

Mr MacDougal's companion, a slim, small dark young man with slanting eyes alight with mockery, dug him in the ribs.

' Och, go on, Seumas, who'd ever the hell be likely to forget you ? Man, you're a feature of the landscape.'

' Isht ! Less of your swearing, Alasdair MacPhee. There's a minister in the room. And you don't know who this gentleman is ? '

' I do not.'

' This is Mr John Ogilvie, Alec. You're quick enough

to blether about Home Rule for Scotland, but you don't know Mr Ogilvie. Very good, very good ! ' He laughed a high wheezy laugh of triumph over his companion.

' You're Mr Ogilvie the play-writer ? ' the dark young man asked, and the mockery vanished for a moment from his slanting eyes, leaving behind a burning, hungry look. ' Well, this is a bit of an unexpected pleasure for me,' he murmured, it seemed more to himself, as he offered his hand.

' There you are now, there you are,' Mr MacDougal wheezed complacently. ' What would you do without big James MacDougal ? You'd be nowhere at all at all. Not that I'm very much for Home Rule myself, Mr Ogilvie. What would we do without England ? '

' What would you do without your belly, James ? ' Alec MacPhee jeered. ' I'll tell you. You'd be driving that Morris Junior of yours much more comfortably than you can now.'

' I don't know so much about that, Alec. I might drive her off the road altogether if I lost so much good ballast.'

There was a general laugh at the fat traveller's retort, for by now the rest of the company were paying attention to the topic which had been raised.

' I've gathered from reports I've read of your speeches, Mr Ogilvie, that you advocate something a great deal more drastic than Home Rule in the usual sense of the words ? '

This remark came from a lanky young man with a long upper lip and light reddish hair, in plus-fours of a modest Glen Urquhart tweed, seated in the corner by the fire.

' I don't think the Northern Ireland experiment has much to recommend it,' John replied, ' if that's what you mean by Home Rule in the usual sense of the words.'

Before the new speaker could elaborate his point a
bald burly man in a faded red kilt of the MacKinnon
tartan barked with the muffled woof of a retriever with
a ball in its mouth :

' Can't stand the idea of Home Rule. Sooner be ruled
by Whitehall than Edinburgh lawyers. You fellows in
the Department of Agriculture are bad enough already.
Don't know what life would be if you got the bit between
your teeth, what ! How are you, Ogilvie ? I think we
were up at Oxford about the same time. You were at
Exeter, weren't you ? I was at Trinity. Read a lot about
you, of course. Building yourself a house, they tell me, on
the Shiel Islands. You'll find it a bit lonely, won't you ?
Can't think what you'll do with yourself all the time.'

John shook hands with Major Lachlan MacKinnon of
Drumdhu, a Skye laird of authentic lineage, whose land
had managed to stick to him in spite of the fears he had
so often and so openly expressed ever since the end of the
war that it would be raided. There was a limit, however,
even to the appetite of land-starved men, and the barren
moors and bogs of Drumdhu were beyond its capacity.
Nor had Major MacKinnon been able to persuade the
officials of the Department of Agriculture to acquire his
inheritance. Even they whose optimism about land
suitable for crofts was almost infinite shied at Drumdhu.

While the laird was exchanging courtesies with John,
the long upper lip of Mr Andrew Pirie, the representative
of the Department, lengthened in preparation for a
defence of Edinburgh.

' I'm not altogether prepared to accept your con-
demnation of Edinburgh lawyers, Drumdhu,' he said
when the opportunity came. ' I think it is generally
admitted that nowhere in Great Britain is the law more
expeditiously and more capably and more cheaply
administered than in Edinburgh. I do not agree with

Mr Ogilvie's very extreme conception of Scottish Home Rule, but I am bound to protest that one of the most potent arguments in favour of a measure—a strictly modified measure—of self-government, is the great, the very great superiority of Edinburgh lawyers over any other legal body in the world. Mind you, I'm not saying that I accept such an argument. I'm a Government servant and therefore I do not consider myself at liberty to hold any positive political opinions.'

'A lot of dummies,' Alec MacPhee scoffed.

'That may be your opinion, Mr MacPhee,' the official replied tartly. 'But I don't fancy it's the opinion of the majority.'

'The majority is made up of sheep,' snapped MacPhee.

A white-bearded man who had been dozing in the corner woke up at the magic word.

'The prices were terrible at Dingwall last autumn. Terrible, terrible,' he groaned. 'Something will have to be done by the Government or we will all be ruined. And that reminds me, Mr Pirie, I don't agree at all with the idea the Department had about cross-bred Leicesters. They're too heavy—too heavy altogether. . . .'

'We are not discussing sheep, Mr Gillies,' said Pirie. 'We're discussing Home Rule.'

The white-bearded man shook his head.

'Och, I think Mr Gladstone made a big mistake . . . a big big mistake. I was a very young man at the time, but I always used to say then that he had made a big big mistake. Mind you, I've never voted for the Tories. No, no, I wouldn't go so far as that. But I think Mr Gladstone. . . .'

'You've lost fifty years since you fell asleep, Mr Gillies,' Alec MacPhee broke in. He did not travel for an agricultural firm and did not have to handle tactfully a prospective customer. 'We're talking about today.'

' The Government will have to do something about it, or we'll all be ruined,' the white-bearded man sighed lugubriously. ' Och, well, I think I'll go up to my bed now that I've woken up. Goodnight, gentlemen, goodnight.'

' There's one of your majority, Mr Pirie,' observed MacPhee.

' Poor old Donald,' MacDougal chuckled. ' He's getting very old. But mind you, he's all there still. Och, my word, he's all there right enough. He gave me a very good order last time I was over in Loch Maddy. Now then, what about a dram, Mr Ogilvie ? Ring the bell, Alec.'

The host presented himself in the doorway.

' Three double whiskies, Mr Macleod.'

' I'm sorry, Mr MacDougal, but the bar is closed.'

' The bar is closed ? ' the fat man gasped. ' It's only just twelve o'clock. Och, man, bring us four double whiskies.'

' I couldn't serve you now, Mr MacDougal, the bar is closed.'

The host withdrew.

' There you are now,' the fat man exclaimed, ' that's what it is for a Macleod to marry a Mackenzie. She's locked the bar on him right enough. Well, well, well, isn't that terrible, right enough ? '

The host's announcement that the life of the hotel was in abeyance broke up the gathering, most of the members of which would have to be up again before five to go on board the *Puffin*. The smoking-room emptied. On his way out the minister, who had been lying on the sofa reading the *Glasgow Herald*, stuck the paper under his arm that was carrying his boots and offered his hand to John.

' I'm glad to have met you, Mr Ogilvie,' he said in the wind-blown accents of Lewis. ' I'm not a Nationalist myself. No, I feel we cannot afford to break with our southern neighbours. But there's room for improvement in many directions, especially in the island of Lewis. Yes, indeed. There's no doubt of that. We in Lewis feel we've been very badly neglected by the Government. I'm no longer living in the island myself. I accepted a call to the United Free Church at Avonside. If you're ever along my way I'll be glad to give you a cup of tea. I've just lost my sister and I am crossing to Stornoway tomorrow. I did not manage to catch the boat today. There ought to be two boats a day to Stornoway.'

This was too much for a Harrisman, who turned back indignantly in the doorway.

'Two boats a day for Stornoway!' he gasped. 'And three boats a week is enough for Tarbert.'

'But, my friend, Lewis is not Harris.'

'Och, *dhuine, dhuine*, indeed, and I hope it never will be,' the Harrisman ejaculated devoutly, and, with a courteous goodnight in Gaelic that was given rather to the collar than to the wearer of it, he passed from the conversation.

'They're very much behind the times in Harris,' the Reverend Duncan Morrison commented. 'Good people, good people, but behind the times. Well, goodnight, Mr Ogilvie. *Oidhche mhath.* Have you the Gaelic? I hope we will meet again. I gave you my card. I am between Greenock and Glasgow. Och, you're performing a great work in calling attention to the neglect of Scotland, Mr Ogilvie. I thought Mr Ramsay MacDonald would have tried to do a little more for his own country, but the world has corrupted him, they tell me. Anyway, he should bestir himself. Well, I hope we will meet again, Mr Ogilvie. Goodnight.'

Presently the only guests left in the smoking-room were Andrew Pirie, Alec MacPhee and John.

' You're not going to bed just yet, Mr Ogilvie ? ' the slant-eyed young traveller asked with a touch of eagerness.

' I haven't a bed to go to,' John replied. ' So I shall stay here.'

' You haven't a bed ? Och, that's not good enough. You'll take mine, Mr Ogilvie.'

' I wouldn't dream of it.'

' I have no room either,' the Department of Agriculture official put in. ' I don't remember when the hotel was so full.'

' You can have my room, Mr Pirie,' MacPhee suggested quickly. ' Go on, man, take it,' he urged when the official hesitated. ' I want to talk politics with Mr Ogilvie. I'll stay on in here anyway for a while if Mr Ogilvie has no objection. You'd better take my room.'

The notion of tolerable comfort for a few hours was more than Pirie could resist. Moreover, he had the dread every good civil servant has of finding himself involved in extremist politics of any kind.

' I hope you don't mind me pushing myself upon your company like this ? ' MacPhee asked when the representative of the Department of Agriculture had departed to the bed he had surrendered to him. ' But I couldn't let go of a chance like this, and I knew fine you might not like to take part in a general argument. Look now, let me pull up yon sofa in front of the fire and you can lie back and make yourself fairly snug. I'll put a couple of armchairs together for myself.'

The younger man heaped more coal on the fire, moved the furniture around, and presently came back from an expedition into the domestic fastnesses of the hotel with pillows, a couple of plaids and two brimming glasses of hot grog.

' Yon woman's a terror,' he affirmed. ' But my

mother was a Mackenzie from the Black Isle like herself, and I know the way with that same clan.'

' My great-grandmother was a Macleod from Assynt,' John told him.

' You're like me then, east and west. My father was a MacPhee of Coll, but I was born in Inverness myself. But that's not what I wanted to tell you, Mr Ogilvie. What I wanted to say was " Go ahead, man." I'm a member of the Party. I've been a member for three years, but we're too slow. " Ca' canny " may be a good slogan for business, but it's no slogan at all for a country that's dying from the top down. And you know that. Weren't they all dead men blethering away in here tonight ? I never heard you speak in public, but I've read all you've written about Nationalism and I know you're right when you say that it's too late to talk about Home Rule in terms of a plank on the Liberal platform, and that Scotland must assert her sovereign independence or perish as a nation. O God, man, isn't it you that's right ? '

' I think I am,' John agreed. ' But the problem is whether there's vitality enough left to feed the nation with the courage and endurance to assert those sovereign rights. So much of our Nationalist propaganda has been concentrated on telling people that if we managed our own affairs we should manage them more profitably ; but there's no vision of true independence inspiring such an argument. When you press that kind of Nationalist you find he's using a municipal drain-pipe as a telescope for the future. His Scottish Parliament is hardly more than a glorified County Council. He's not prepared to sacrifice half a crown, much less imperil his own liveli-hood. And if he's not willing to face material loss he's right to be canny. I believe that the kind of independence a few of us dream of would involve ten and perhaps twenty years of hardship and bitter self-denial. I believe that any such complete separation from England as those few of us dream of would for a long while be fatal to all prosperity except the prosperity of the nation's soul. Those who contend that the maintenance of the Union is more than ever necessary at a time when the economic trend is toward amalgamation, and when industry believes that the secret of success is rationalisation—foul word for a foul process—are justified from their point of view. It maddens me to hear those sentimental Nationalists moaning about the flight of industry to the south, and hoping to check it by artificial legislation from Edinburgh instead of Westminster. Nothing can stem that flight of industry except so radical a readjustment of the economic life of this country as would involve not merely separation from England but probably even withdrawal from the Empire and any further subjection to Anglo-American finance.'

'Not even you would advocate that on a public platform,' said MacPhee.

'I've always asserted that it was a mistake to fetter the Party's declaration of its aims with the proviso that the country's sovereign independence was to be sought only within the British Commonwealth of Nations.'

'Scotland never would go out of the Empire.'

'Probably not,' John agreed. 'But it would be more logical to leave that decision to a free Scotland. I object for the same reason to this demand for a programme. It turns us into one more political party. If we have no confidence that sovereign independence will improve the re-creation of our national life, sovereign independence is not worth winning. But as I said just now, the doubt always at the back of my mind is whether the vitality is really there, whether it is not too late. Tell me, MacPhee, why do you think independence worth winning ?'

'Didn't you say just now that it would be soon enough to say why when we were after winning it?'

'Ah, that didn't mean I haven't my own vision of a free Scotland,' John replied. 'The point I was making was that we could not afford to present the country with a compromise programme designed to please the greatest number of people and so win their votes. Let me put it this way—if tomorrow you were offered a job in London with a salary of a thousand a year and the prospect of a certain steadily rising income, would you take it?'

The younger man pitched the stub of his cigarette into the fire as if with it went a part of himself.

'I suppose I would.'

'You wouldn't feel that such a surrender of your own independence made it rather ridiculous to worry any more about the independence of your country?'

'I wouldn't want to go to London, but what kind of a chance like that would I ever find in Scotland today?'

'In a Scotland that cut itself off completely from England you mightn't be able to earn even half of what you're earning in it today.'

'May I ask you a question, Mr Ogilvie?'

'Ask away,' John told him.

'If the independence of Scotland meant that never another play of yours was put on the stage in England, would you still work for that independence?'

'I've asked myself that question and I think I can say " yes " with complete conviction. But our two cases are not really similar. I have the advantage, because in the first place an artist always has at any rate a little more personal independence than a man on a salary, and in the second place—how old are you?'

'I'm twenty-two.'

'I shall be fifty in October next year. I have enjoyed my economic opportunity. But thirty years ago on the last day of the nineteenth century old Torquil Macleod of Ardvore told me that I ought to settle in Assynt and devote myself to working to preserve the old Highland habit of life and way of thought. Perhaps if he had encouraged my political views, which were then very much what they are today, I might have thought his suggestion less impractical. But old Ardvore abhorred the notion of Home Rule, and as for separation he thought it merely fantastic. For him Home Rule was synonymous with radicalism, and to a Highland laird of thirty years ago radicalism sounded as unpleasant as socialism sounds today. I don't have to tell you that the profound opposition to the national movement among the lairds and business men of Scotland is entirely inspired by a fear of socialist experiments at the expense of their pockets. Our friend Drumdhu declared just now that Home Rule would mean the Highlands being ruled by Edinburgh lawyers, and he prefers Whitehall. Mind you, I think there's a good deal to be said for that point of view. Well, to come back to what I was telling you, the notion of settling down in Assynt at the age of eighteen to learn Gaelic, encourage homespun and preserve the old Gaelic culture seemed to me an idle dream.'

' So it would have been if there was nothing left to preserve it for,' MacPhee agreed.

' That's what I told Ardvore. He wanted me to take a wife from our own people and bring up a large family in the traditions of our race. I remember I told him I would only do that if the traditions of our race could be practically demonstrated to the rest of the world. And Ardvore said they had been practically demonstrated in the building up of the Empire.'

MacPhee muttered an ejaculation of disgust.

' Oh yes,' John continued with a smile. ' I felt exactly as you feel about it, because at that date I was just suffering

from the first violent reaction to the Boer War. You
can't feel a bit more strongly the reaction against the
mood of the Great War.'

'Do you know Glen Strathfarrar?' the young man
asked.

'That lovely wilderness!' John sighed.

'Two hundred men from Glen Strathfarrar fought in
the wars against Napoleon, fifty men fought in the
Crimea, two men fought in the last war, and if there's
ever another war there'll be none to fight in it from Glen
Strathfarrar. *A dhia*, the making of the Empire left
Scotland like a shot salmon. Small wonder you turned
your back on Ardvore's proposal.'

'And then I met Norman MacIver,' John went on.
'Did you ever come across him?'

'The tailor in Melvaig?'

'Yes.'

'It's he that has the eyes to see,' MacPhee averred.

'He has indeed. It was from him I heard first of
Michael Davitt's idea that the Highlands and Islands
should throw in their lot with Ireland. But he argues it
is too late now to save the *Gaidhealtachd*.'

'It's not too late, it's not too late,' MacPhee cried.

'Yet you would take a thousand-a-year job in London,
Alasdair.'

The young man's eyes lighted up at hearing himself
called by his Christian name.

'Not if I thought there was a chance to give Scotland
back its life,' he declared.

'What with?'

'With my own blood if that would serve.'

A silence fell. The coal in the grate subsided, and
flames licked the sooty mouth of the chimney. John
looked back to the door of the inn in Lochinver and to
the thin January sunlight in which the old laird of Ardvore

was waving him farewell just thirty years ago. And anon from the jolting omnibus he was watching the isolated blue-grey shape of Suilven, snow-sprinkled on the summit, recede and sink out of sight below the bleak rolling moorland like a ship below the horizon.

It seemed to him that now for the first time he was beholding it again.

'Tell me about yourself, Alasdair,' he said, breaking the silence.

'There's little enough to tell. My father is a grocer in Inverness. The idea was that I would become a minister. My mother came from the only village in the Black Isle where they keep the Gaelic. Her father is Alasdair Mackenzie. He has written plenty Gaelic poetry. I don't suppose you've heard of him?'

'Wasn't he crowned bard at one of the Mods?'

'He was.'

'I've read some of his work. A genuine poet.'

'A better poet than most of them, perhaps,' the grandson allowed. 'But his poetry ran to religion, which is why my mother was so set on my becoming a minister. My own idea was different, and my career at Inverness Academy was not very brilliant. I made it clear that it would be a big waste of money to send me to Aberdeen University. Luckily my elder brother Donald was already in the shop, and I got a job as traveller for Loudoun and Gray, the big Glasgow biscuit makers. Och, it's not a bad job. It takes you into the heart of the country. I cover the west from Lochinver to Mallaig with Skye and the Long Island and the Small Isles. I've just driven through Glenmoriston and Glenshiel. It's great in the winter-time. There's not much snow here in Portrose; but, man, it lay deep in the glens. My Austin seemed just a wee toy and myself a bairn's doll.'

'Are you a poet yourself?' John asked.

' I have written some Gaelic verse, right enough. But it frightens the An Comunn people. The Highland Society is a very respectable body of men, Mr Ogilvie. They don't admit any violent political emotion later than the 'forty-five.'

' I don't think we must laugh at An Comunn too much. The language would have been in a much worse way without the work they've been doing for the last forty years.'

' Och, what's the annual Mod now? Just a society function the success of which is judged by the amount of money it makes. And anyway, what is the use of keeping a language alive for a dying people? Look round this room, Mr Ogilvie. Doesn't it sum up the Highlands of today? That steel engraving of a legend which was never worth believing anyhow—a nineteenth-century piece of snobbery spotted by damp and flies. That washy water-colour of Dunvegan hardly fit for a schoolgirl's auto-graph album. Those two sea-trout to catch the eye of the rich sportsman and persuade him the hotel's bad food is compensated for by the fishing obtainable in the land of bens and glens and heroes. Those rosy maidens from the lone shieling who are smiling so sweetly because next week they'll be meeting their friends again on the Jamaica Bridge in Glasgow. And that meditative shepherd! Ay, ay, meditating on the prices his hoggets fetched at Dingwall last week. That's the reason for so noble an expression of Celtic gloom and dignity. Land of bens and glens and heroes! What is it now? Rabbits and bracken; Indian pedlars on bicycles hawking cheap silks and French letters; inshore fishing destroyed by English trawlers; unemployment; education planned to make good North Britons but bad Scotsmen, and to fill the minds of children with the belief that a city man is a bigger fellow than a countryman; ministers without

scholarship and scholars without religion ; tinned salmon
and tinned lobster ; Midlothian porridge like clay and
Glasgow bread like chalk ; plus-fours, Government
officials, pink asbestos tiles, and the *People's Journal*.'

' Yes, but can't the same kind of thing be said about
England ? ' John suggested. ' I'm not convinced—I wish
I were !—that the independence of Scotland would
change these signs of what is called progress. I've been
rather disappointed by the way Ireland has developed
since the Treaty. It's rather too much of a not very good
imitation of England at present. The pillar-boxes have
been painted green, but their shape remains. And as much
may be said of their legal and financial and economic
system. They've all been painted green, but in truth the
shape was better suited to England's cruel red. True,
there's a censorship of books, contraception is officially
discouraged, and it is recognised that the Irish language
must prevail ; but the country has not shaken off that
air of faded provincialism which hangs over our own
country. Contemporary Dublin is more a metropolis
than Edinburgh, largely I think, because it was farther
away from Belfast than Edinburgh from Glasgow,
and therefore avoided the complacency about its own
superiority with which the nearness of Glasgow has
infected Edinburgh. Princes Street has always seemed so
obviously an authentic metropolitan thoroughfare compared with Sauchiehall Street that Edinburgh people have
not noticed the rapid decline of Princes Street during
the last twenty-five years. I think Perth should be the
capital of a sovereign Scotland, Alasdair, and the King
crowned again at Scone.'

' Will a sovereign Scotland want a coronation ? ' the
young man asked. ' I think a sovereign Scotland must be
a republic.'

' I should prefer an autocratic monarch until the

country has emerged from provincialism,' said John. ' I wish the Prince of Wales would give up trying to persuade the people of these islands of their imperial destiny and take the throne of Scotland, leaving his brother to rule constitutionally over all the rest.'

'The Prince of Wales! You're not serious, Mr Ogilvie?'

' Perfectly serious. Scotland needs an autocrat, but you can't expect so proud a country to accept a Mussolini. And the kind of revolution that's necessary in our national life could not be carried out by following traditions of the English Civil Service. That's the mistake they've made in the Irish Free State. When the Treaty was signed the civil servants threw down their pens and sat back to watch the new State collapse under the administration of young men in Fedora hats and Burberrys with an automatic in one pocket and a packet of gaspers in the other. Unfortunately the young men picked up the pens with their nicotine-stained fingers and proceeded to get on with the job, and almost before they knew it, had turned into good little bureaucrats. They had dyed the red tape green, and though green tape may be better it remains tape and has the same capacity for strangulation. Let me give you a few of my ideas about the revolution I fancy for this country, and if you agree with them you'll have to agree that they couldn't be put into effect by a nation which relied on Parliamentary institutions. The whole world is passing through a period of upheaval. It will be time to return to Parliamentary institutions when the fires below the surface are again quiescent.'

' Isn't that what's been happening in Italy ? '

' Yes, and so far the experiment has been in many ways a success. The trouble there, however, is that Mussolini, like all self-made dictators, must continually go forward or run the risk of a reaction. If he comes to an end of his capacity for useful internal reform he will have to maintain his position by external aggression. Hence this wearisome braggadocio in all his speeches about Italy's mission in the world. If he were a truly wise and great man he would retire from the helm now and restore to Italy a free Parliament which would know how to profit by the example he has set of constructive energy. That's why I made the point about an autocratic monarch. He'd run less risk of having his head turned by his own position. In any case he could not hope to compensate for any failure of internal reform by a policy of external aggression. Even if the spirit of the people of Scotland was inclined in that direction their geographical situation would make such ambitions absurd. Obviously Scotland would be no more likely to contemplate aggression than Norway, and it would have to make every effort to achieve self-sufficiency.'

' To feed ourselves in fact,' Alasdair observed.

' That first of all, of course,' John agreed. ' And it would involve nationalisation of all the land as an immediate first step, or as I should prefer to say the restoration of the trusteeship for all the land into the hands of the King, by whom the tenure of it would be granted on a system of mutual obligation. Private ownership would never be freehold, but so long as it was used for the common good no man could be dispossessed of his tenure.'

' What about the deer forests ? How could they be used for the common good ? '

' Well, first of all we must admit that there *are* great tracts unfit for cultivation ; but, as once upon a time, all sporting rights would again be vested in the King, and it would lie with him and his advisers to decide what was the best use to make of such land for the common good. At any rate, the private sporting estate would have to go, and the rights of all salmon rivers would have to revert to the trusteeship of the King. That salmon would require protection is obvious, but not less obvious is the protection required by our other fish. With the support of Norway we should be able to secure the thirteen-mile limit for territorial fishing waters that was to be asked from the North Sea Convention by the Scottish Fisheries Act of 1896.'

' Eighteen ninety-six ? '

' Yes, and never put into full operation all these twenty-five years through the opposition of the big English fishing interests. We cannot afford to ruin the spawning grounds to keep the cities of the south supplied with cheap fish. We have seen our best herring market destroyed because the British Government has had a quarrel with the Soviets. We want Russian wheat in return for our fish. The grass growing on the quays of Leith will not make bread. But mind you, Alasdair, we'll have to eat more oatmeal, and not this fine-ground Midlothian stuff. Do you realise that you have never tasted proper porridge? Twenty-five years ago the wash that's served as porridge now in Scotland would have been considered uneatable even at a railway meal. Scots used to moan because they couldn't get real porridge over the Border, and now they all eat Anglicised porridge from the Cheviots to the Pentland Firth. And we must grow more rye. The black bread of Germany at which we scoff is worth ten times that foul chalk-like Glasgow bread you mentioned. That's fit for nothing except to make plaster tombstones for its victims.'

' And all the people like it better than home-made bread, *amadain truaigh* ! '

' Poor fools indeed,' John echoed.

' That's going to be a big problem. Whatever we make of the land it will be hard nowadays to persuade people not to leave it for the towns.'

' That desertion of the country for the cities seems a world-wide tendency, and when country people cannot escape from what they believe to be a prison they import into the country as much as they can of city life. Hence your tinned lobster and your cheap silks. I believe that if transport were made free, or at any rate if the rates were equalised on the same principle as the post, the population would adjust itself much more equally. It's not the time that tells against travel but the money it costs. I would have sixpenny and threepenny electric trains worked by our own water-power running almost continuously night and day, and sixpenny boats from the islands. And I would charge freightage by weight and space only, regardless of distance. Of course, that would mean nationalisation of the railways and all ferry services.'

' Wouldn't that mean burdening the State with a huge capital investment ? '

' No, because with the death of every holder of railway shares his shares would revert to the country. The original capital invested in railways has long been paid back in interest. Furthermore, arterial roads would have to be constructed along which people would be prohibited from building.'

' And what about the finance ? '

' The King's money should be the King's money again, and of course all banks would have to be nationalised and amalgamated in a Royal Bank of Scotland. I've a notion we might require a double rate of currency—one for internal and the other for external requirements. The value of the latter would depend on our export. For what the country consumed itself of its own produce prices and wages could be regulated to encourage at once producer and consumer. More or less what I'm advocating is what is called Social Credit—the creation of purchasing power for the community. Did you ever read any of Major Douglas's books ?'

' I never have.'

' You'd find it worth while.'

' But what would we do about our share of the present National Debt ?'

' I am afraid we should have to repudiate our share of that, though I think it might be possible to make a fair bargain by leasing our harbours to England, the harbours I mean suitable as naval bases.'

' That would mean the Firth of Forth,' said Alasdair. ' A little ignominious for the capital of an independent Scotland.'

' But Perth is to be the capital of my Utopian Scotland. No, obviously one would prefer not to lease the naval bases, but I don't see how England would get on without them, and if war ever broke out again between England and Germany it would certainly mean their occupation by English naval forces, with all the tiresome complications of violated neutrality. I saw enough of that at Salonica in 1915.'

' But wouldn't that drag us into one of England's wars ?' Alasdair still objected.

' No small nation can ever be safe from violation in a general war. . . .'

The North Wind of Love

KENNETH BUTHLAY

The Salmon

I'll love you, dear, I'll love you
Till China and Africa meet,
And the river jumps over the mountain
And the salmon sing in the street.

W. H. Auden

I GOT up on a Sunday morning
    And I didn't need a beer,
For I could hear the music
    And all the people cheer.

I knew there would be bus-loads
    Of combined brass bands
And policemen cavorting on dolphins
    And bunting festooning the stands.

I knew there must be magnolias
    In all the charwomen's hair,
And the Provost of Auchinshuggle
    Waltzing with a bear.

And gondolas meeting the buses
    With cargoes of macaroons,
And beaver-crested guardsmen
    Peddling in platoons.

And all the lovers diving
    For jewelry and bouquets,
And oysters drinking Guinness
    In flooded cabarets.

And a long-haired walrus conducting
    With a most meticulous beat
For the rows and rows of salmon
    Singing in the street.

' O pink and spotted salmon,'
  The people they would moan,
' O philharmonic salmon,
  What purity of tone ! '

And after the salmon folksongs
  In four-part harmony,
They would sing the great finale
  Of the Choral Symphony.

Though the whole world were water
  And the deity celluloid,
The salmon would sing triumphant
  And *Freude* would conquer Freud.

But when I leaned out of the window
  I heard no noble song,
But only the plaintive church bells
  Admonishing the throng.

And when I walked into the sunlight
  The sun was an evil star,
For I saw the Salvation Army
  Marching forth to war.

The poke-bonneted Sunbeams
  Were mobilising souls
With Torch-Bearer escorts
  And illuminated scrolls.

With banners and with cornets,
  With blasts in brassy tones,
The Army went marching over
  My heart on the cobble-stones.

I prayed for a singing salmon
    Or at least a poetical cod,
But all I could see was a poster :
    THY GOD IS A JEALOUS GOD.

And then I knew that the salmon
    Had been and gone in the night,
And the Corporation Transport
    Had removed the river from sight.

And China and Africa also
    Had been warned by a mutual friend
That the salmon had gone from the city
    For love was at an end.

Scottish Student Verse 1937–47

GEORGE BLAKE

The Football Match

THE surge of the stream was already apparent in the
Dumbarton Road. Even though only a few wore favours
of the Rangers blue, there was that of purpose in the air
of hurrying groups of men which infallibly indicated
their intention. It was almost as if they had put on
uniform for the occasion, for most were attired as Danny
was in decent dark suits under rainproofs or overcoats,
with great flat caps of light tweed on their heads. Most
of them smoked cigarettes that shivered in the corners of
their mouths as they fiercely debated the prospects of the
day. Hardly one of them but had his hands deep in his
pockets.

The scattered procession, as it were of an order almost
religious, poured itself through the mean entrance to the
subway station at Partick Cross. The decrepit turnstiles
clattered endlessly, and there was much rough good-
humoured jostling as the devotees bounded down the
wooden stairs to struggle for advantageous positions on
the crowded platform. Glasgow's subway system is of
high antiquarian interest and smells very strangely of age.
Its endless cables, whirling innocently over the pulleys,
are at once absurd and fascinating, its signalling system a
matter for the laughter of a later generation. But to
Danny and the hundreds milling about him there was no
strange spectacle here : only a means of approach to a
shrine ; and strongly they pushed and wrestled when at
length a short train of toy-like dimensions rattled out of
the tunnel into the station.

It seemed full to suffocation already, but Danny, being
alone and ruthless in his use of elbow and shoulder,
contrived somehow to squeeze through a narrow door-

way on to a crowded platform. Others pressed in behind him while official whistles skirled hopelessly without, and before the urgent crowd was forced back at last and the doors laboriously closed, he was packed right among taller men of his kind, his arms pinned to his sides, his lungs so compressed that he gasped.

'For the love o' Mike . . .' he pleaded.

'Have ye no' heard there's a fitba' match the day, wee man ?' asked a tall humorist beside him.

Everybody laughed at that. For them there was nothing odd or notably objectionable in their dangerous discomfort. It was, at the worst, a purgatorial episode on the passage to Elysium.

So they passed under the river, to be emptied in their hundreds among the red sandstone tenements of the South Side. Under the high banks of the Park a score of streams met and mingled, the streams that had come by train or tram or motor car or on foot to see the game of games.

Danny ran for it as soon as his feet were on earth's surface again, selecting in an experienced glance the turn-stile with the shortest queue before it, ignoring quite the mournful column that waited without hope at the Unemployed Gate. His belly pushed the bar precisely as his shilling smacked on the iron counter. A moment later he was tearing as if for dear life up the long flight of cindered steps leading to the top of the embank-ment.

He achieved his favourite position without difficulty : high on one of the topmost terraces and behind the eastern goal. Already the huge amphitheatre seemed well filled. Except where the monstrous stands broke the skyline there were cliffs of human faces, for all the world like banks of gravel, with thin clouds of tobacco smoke drift-ing across them. But Danny knew that thousands were still to come to pack the terraces to the point of suffocation, and, with no eyes for the sombre strangeness of the spectacle, he proceeded to establish himself by setting his arms firmly along the iron bar before him and making friendly, or at least argumentative, contact with his neighbours.

He was among enthusiasts of his own persuasion. In consonance with ancient custom the police had shepherded supporters of the Rangers to one end of the ground and supporters of the Celtic to the other—so far as segregation was possible with such a great mob of human beings. For the game between Glasgow's two leading teams had more in it than the simple test of relative skill. Their colours, blue and green, were symbolic. Behind the rivalry of players, behind even the commercial rivalry of limited companies, was the dark significance of sectarian and racial passions. Blue for the Protestants of Scotland and Ulster, green for the Roman Catholics of the Free State ; and it was a bitter war that was to be waged on that strip of white-barred turf. All the social problems of a hybrid city were to be sublimated in the imminent clash of mercenaries.

The Celtic came first, strangely attractive in their white and green, and there was a roar from the western end of the ground. ('Hefty-looking lot o' bastards,' admitted the small, old man at Danny's side.) They were followed by a party of young men in light-blue jerseys ; and then it seemed that the low-hanging clouds must split at the impact of the yell that rose to greet them from forty thousand throats. The referee appeared, jaunty in his shorts and khaki jacket ; the linesmen, similarly attired, ran to their positions. In a strange hush, broken only by the thud of footballs kicked by the teams uneasily practising, the captains tossed for ends. Ah ! Rangers had won and would play with the sou'-westerly wind, straight towards the goal behind which Danny stood in his eagerness.

This was enough to send a man off his head. Good old Rangers—and to hell with the Pope ! Danny gripped the iron bar before him. The players trotted limberly to their positions. For a moment there was dead silence over Ibrox Park. Then the whistle blew, a thin, curt, almost feeble announcement of glory.

For nearly two hours thereafter Danny Shields lived far beyond himself in a whirling world of passion. All sorts of racial emotions were released by this clash of athletic young men ; the old clans of Scotland lived again their ancient hatreds in this struggle for goals. Not a man on the terraces paused to reflect that it was a spectacle cunningly arranged to draw their shillings, or to remember that the twenty-two players were so many slaves of a commercial system, liable to be bought and sold like fallen women, without any regard for their feelings as men. Rangers had drawn their warriors from all corners of Scotland—lads from mining villages, boys from Ayrshire farms and even an undergraduate from the University of Glasgow. Celtic likewise had ranged the industrial belt and even crossed to Ulster and the Free State for men fit to win matches so that dividends might accrue. But for such as Danny they remained peerless and fearless warriors, saints of the Blue or the Green as it might be ; and in delight in the cunning moves of them, in their tricks and asperities, the men on the terraces found release from the drabness of their own industrial degradation.

That release they expressed in ways extremely violent. They exhorted their favourites to dreadful enterprises of assault and battery. They loudly questioned every decision of the referee. In moments of high tension they

raved obscenely, using a language ugly and violent in its
wealth of explosive consonants.

Yet that passionate horde had its wild and liberating
humours. Now and again a flash of rough jocularity
would release a gust of laughter, so hearty that it was as
if they rejoiced to escape from the bondage of their
own intensity of partisanship. Once in a while a clever
movement by one of the opposition team would evoke
a mutter of unwilling but sincere admiration. They were
abundantly capable of calling upon their favourites to use
their brawn, but they were punctilious in the observation
of the unwritten laws that are called those of sportsman-
ship. They constituted, in fact, a stern but ultimately
reliable jury, demanding of their entertainers the very
best they could give, insisting that the spectacle be staged
with all the vigour that could be brought to it.

The Old Firm—thus the evening papers conventionally
described the meeting of Rangers and Celtic. It was a
game fought hard and fearless and merciless, and it was
the rub of the business that the wearers of the Blue scored
seven minutes from half-time.

The goal was the outcome of a movement so swift
that even a critic of Danny's perspicacity could hardly
tell just how it happened. What is it to say that a back
cleared from near the Rangers' goal ; that the ball went
on the wind to the nimble feet of Alan Morton on the
left wing ; that that small but intense performer carried
it at lightning speed down the line past this man in green
and white and then that ; that he crossed before the
menace of a charging back, the ball soaring in a lovely
curve to the waiting centre ; and that it went then like
a rocket into a corner of the Celtic net, the goalkeeper
sprawling in a futile endeavour to stop it ?

It was a movement completed almost as soon as it was

begun, and Danny did not really understand it until he read his evening paper on the way home. But it was a goal, a goal for Rangers, and he went mad for a space.

With those about him he screamed his triumph, waving his cap wildly about his head, taunting most foully those who might be in favour of a team so thoroughly humiliated as the Celtic.

From this orgasm he recovered at length.

' Christ ! ' he panted. ' That was a bobbydazzler.'

' Good old Alan ! ' screeched the young man behind. ' Ye've got the suckers bitched ! '

' A piece of perfect bloody positioning,' gravely observed the scientist on Danny's left.

' Positioning, ma foot ! ' snorted Danny. ' It was just bloomin' good fitba ! Will ye have a snifter, old fella ? '

So they shared the half-mutchkin of raw whisky, the small man politely wiping the neck of the bottle with his sleeve before handing it back to Danny.

' That's a good dram, son,' he observed judicially.

Half-time permitted of discussion that was now, however, without its heat, the young man behind exploiting a critical theory of half-back play that kept some thirty men about him in violent controversy until the whistle blew again. Then the fever came back on them with redoubled fury. One-nothing for Rangers at half-time made an almost agonising situation ; and as the Celtic battled to equalise, breaking themselves again and again on a defence grimly determined to hold its advantage, the waves of green hurling themselves on rocks of blue, there was frenzy on the terraces.

When, five minutes before time, the men from the East were awarded a penalty kick, Dannys' heart stopped beating for a space, and when the fouled forward sent the ball flying foolishly over the net, it nearly burst. The Rangers would win. ' Stick it, lads ! ' he yelled

again and again. ' Kick the tripes out the dirty Papists ! '
The Rangers would win. They must win. . . . A spirt of
whistle ; and, by God, they had won !

In immediate swift reaction, Danny turned then and,
without a word to his neighbours, started to fight his
way to the top of the terracing and along the fence that
crowned it to the stairs and the open gate. To the feelings
of those he jostled and pushed he gave not the slightest
thought. Now the battle was for a place in the Subway,
and he ran as soon as he could, hurtling down the road,
into the odorous maw of Copland Road station and
through the closing door of a train that had already
started on its journey northwards.

The Shipbuilders

The Clyde

THE *Estramadura* went down the river on the Wednesday
afternoon, and Leslie Pagan travelled with her.

He was busy and preoccupied while the tugs moved
her from the basin in their fussily efficient way. She was
still his own, and the more precious for being the last he
had in that kind. His heart was in his mouth when her
cruiser-stern cleared the pierhead with only a foot to
spare. He was haunted by daft fears that this winch
would not function and that hollard fail to hold the pull
of the tow-ropes. The extinction of a series of lights on
the promenade deck at one moment gave him the panic
notion that the dynamos had broken down. Knowing
well that the apprehension was excessive, he was haunted
by a sense of the fallibility of the intricate and inter-
dependent mechanisms of the ship ; her security, the
thousands of pounds of value she represented, resting
perhaps on an abraded inch of insulation on a mile or so
of electric cable.

As soon, however, as she was fair in mid-channel, her head down-stream and her beautiful light hull towering over the riverside buildings, he suddenly resigned his creation to chance and the skill of the pilot. At another time he would have been fretfully active until her anchor-chain rattled over the Tail of the Bank, dodging now into the engine-room, now up steel ladders to where the steering-gear churned forward and back again with its own queer air of independence, and then hurrying to the bridge and the battery of tell-tale lights up there. But now he did nothing, keeping in a mood of uneasy detachment out of the way of busy men in overalls. He found a corner for himself on A deck, well forward below the navigating bridge, and in that retired position stood for a long time—watching, as it were, the last creation of his own hands pass forever beyond him.

It was in a sense a procession that he witnessed, the high tragic pageant of the Clyde. Yard after yard passed by, the berths empty, the grass growing about the sinking keel-blocks. He remembered how, in the brave days, there would be scores of ships ready for the launching along this reach, their sterns hanging over the tide, and how the men at work on them on high stagings would turn from the job and tug off their caps and cheer the new ship setting out to sea. And now only the gaunt dumb poles and groups of men workless, watching in silence the mocking passage of the vessel. It was bitter to know that they knew—that almost every man among them was an artist in one of the arts that go to the building of a ship ; that every feature of the *Estramadura* would come under an expert and loving scrutiny, that her passing would remind them of the joy of work, and tell them how many among them would never work again. It appalled Leslie Pagan that not a cheer came from those watching groups.

It was a tragedy beyond economics. It was not that

so many thousands of homes lacked bread and butter.
It was that a tradition, a skill, a glory, a passion, was
visibly in decay, and all the acquired and inherited loveli-
ness of artistry rotting along the banks of the stream.

Into himself he counted and named the yards they
passed. The number and variety stirred him to wonder,
now that he had ceased to take them for granted. His
mental eye moving backwards up the river, he saw the
historic place at Govan, Henderson's of Meadowside at
the mouth of the Kelvin, and the long stretch of Fairfield
on the southern bank opposite. There came Stephen's
of Linthouse next, and Clydeholm facing it across the
narrow yellow ditch of the ship-channel. From thence
down river the range along the northern bank was almost
continuous for miles—Connell, Inglis, Blythswood and
the rest : so many that he could hardly remember their
order. He was distracted for a moment to professionalism
by the lean grey forms of destroyers building for a foreign
power in the sheds of a yard that had dramatically
deserted Thames for Clyde. Then he lost himself again
in the grim majesty of the parade. There came John
Brown's, stretching along half a mile of waterfront at
Clydebank, the monstrous red hull of Number 534
looming in its abandonment like a monument to the
glory departed ; as if shipbuilding man had tried to do
too much and had been defeated by the mightiness of his
own conception. Then came, seeming to point the
moral, the vast desolation of Beardmore's at Dalmuir,
cradle of the mightiest battleships and now a scrap-heap,
empty and silent forever, the great gantry over the basin
proclaiming stagnation and an end.

Even where the Clyde opened out above Erskine, with
the Kilpatricks green and sweet above the river on the
one hand and the wooded fat lands of Renfrewshire
stretching to the escarpment of Misty Law on the other,

the sight of a legend—FOR SALE—painted large on the walls of an empty shed reminded him with the effect of a blow that Napier and Miller's were gone, shut down, finished, the name never to appear again on a brass plate below the bridge of a good ship. And he suddenly remembered that there lay on his desk at the office a notice of sale of the plant at Bow, Maclachlan's on the Cart by Paisley. His world seemed visibly to be crumbling. Already he had been appalled by the emptiness of Lobnitz's and Simons's at Renfrew, and the sense of desolation, of present catastrophe, closed the more oppressively upon him.

As they rounded the bend by Bowling, passing close under the wooded crags of Auchentorlie on the one hand and, as on a Dutch canal, past the flats of Erskine on the other, his eye was taken by the scene ahead. The jagged noble range of the Cowal hills made a purple barrier against the glow of the westering winter sun. Now he was lost for a space in wonder that this cradle and home of ships enjoyed a setting so lovely. Through the gap of the Vale of Leven he could see the high peak of Ben Lomond, and his fancy ranged up those desolate, distant slopes. But then the dome of Dumbarton Rock, the westernmost of the chain strung across the neck of Scotland, brought him to think of the mean town at its base, and of Denny's yard in the crook of the Leven behind it, and of the lovely, fast, small ships they could build, and of the coming of the turbine. And another yard there, Macmillan's, derelict.

Past Dumbarton, the river opening to the Firth, the scene took on an even more immediate grandeur. The sands of the Pillar Bank were showing in golden streaks through the falling tide. The peninsula of Ardmore was a pretty tuft of greenery thrust out towards the channel. Dead ahead lay the mouth of the Gareloch, backed by the jagged peaks on the western side of Loch Long. A man could almost feel the freshness of the open sea coming to meet him over the miles of island, hill and loch ; and Leslie Pagan marked how the fresher and larger waves slapped against the sides of the *Estramadura*, and could almost imagine that the ship responded with quiver and curtsey to their invitation.

That openness of the river below the derelict timber ponds of Langbank, however, is deceptive ; for still the channel must run round the end of the bank and close into the Renfrewshire shore. There are miles of waste space there over the shallows, and Glasgow is more than twenty miles away before a ship of size has more than a few feet of water between her keel and the bottom. Port Glasgow and Greenock look across miles of sand and sea to the Highland hills, but the yards there must launch their ships into narrow waters ; so that the man who had built the *Estramadura*, scanning the shores, saw thereabouts an even thicker crowding of berths than he had marked on the upper reaches.

It was another roster of great names, older, more redolent even than those that had become namely about Glasgow with the deepening of the Clyde. Ferguson's, Duncan's, Murdoch's, Russell's, Hamilton's. . . . Even he could not be sure that he had them right ; there had been so many changes. Out on Garvel Point, under the old marooned Scots mansion-house, stood Brown's—the ' Siberia ' of the artisan's lingo. There came Scott's East Yard—was it not once Steele's, where the clippers were built ? There came the Greenock and Grangemouth, once the artisan's ' Klondike.' Then Scott's Mid Yard ; then Caird's, the last of the lot—closed down. It was queer to see how Newark Castle survived in its pink grace and antiquity among the stocks and gantries.

Here history went mad—the history of the countryside

and the history of shipbuilding in fantastic confusion. Here they had moved a sixteenth-century church stone by stone that a yard might be extended, and with it carted away the poor bones of a poet's love. This town of Greenock, sprawling over the foothills of Renfrewshire, had had its heart torn out to make room for ships. It was as if a race had worshipped grim gods of the sea. And now the tide had turned back. Greenock's heart lay bare and bleeding—for the sake of a yard that had never cradled a ship since strangers, afire with the fever of war-time, took it and played with it and dropped it. Never again, in any calculation of which the human mind was capable, would the Clyde be what it had been.

That was incredible, surely. The fall of Rome was a trifle in comparison. It was a catastrophe unthinkable, beside which the collapse of a dynasty or the defeat of a great nation in battle was a transient disturbance. How in God's name could such a great thing, such a splendid thing, be destroyed?

As they swung the *Estramadura* to anchor at the Tail of the Bank, Leslie Pagan wrestled with this enormity. He saw the million ships of the Clyde as a navy immortal and invincible. Launches, yachts, tugs, hoppers, dredgers, tramps in every conceivable shape and size, tankers, destroyers, cruisers, battleships, liners, and now the largest and last of them all, the Cunarder on the stocks at Clydebank—there was nothing the Clyde could not do in this business of ships. Out of this narrow river they had poured, an endless pageant, to fill the ports of the world.

Why had he forgotten, passing Port Glasgow, that John Wood had built there the *Comet*, the first effective thing, using steam, of all? Or, sailing by Denny's, that there were shaped the perfect historic lines of the *Cutty Sark*? The last, mightiest Cunarder of all up at Clydebank ; and here in Greenock Robert Duncan had built the first—the *Britannia*, all of wood, a mere two hundred odd feet long, only fit to cross the Atlantic in fourteen days under the drive of her two primitive engines. (She could have been housed handily on the boat-deck of the *Estramadura*.) He remembered—for the great stories came crowding—how the name and tradition were immortalised by that *River Clyde*, built in Port Glasgow, which carried the soldiers to the bloody and splendid assault on the heights above V Beach.

But the story was to end, or so he thought in his misery.

The Shipbuilders

DOUGLAS YOUNG

Fermer's Deein

HE turns awa frae life,
    frae the sun and the sterns,
wi hardly a word for his wife,
    or a curse for his bairns,
forfochten wi rowth o strife
    and man's puir concerns.

He's tyauvt wi kye and corn
    and scarce thocht why,
aamaist sin he was born.
    Nou Daith stilps by,
ohn hope, faith, fear, or scorn,
    fegs, he's blye.

A Braird o Thristles

sterns, stars   *forfochten*, worn out by fighting   *rowth*, abundant
tyauvt, worked hard. been embarrassed   *stilps*, stalks with long strides
ohn, without   *blye*, cheerful, blithe

Last Lauch

THE Minister said it wald dee,
    the cypress buss I plantit.
But the buss grew til a tree,
    naething dauntit.

It's growan stark and heich,
    derk and straucht and sinister,
kirkyairdie-like and dreich.
    But whaur's the Minister?

A Braird o Thristles

236

BERNARD FERGUSSON

Across the Chindwin

I COULD not have had a more congenial set of officers.
Only three had seen service before : Duncan Menzies of
my own regiment, whom with much intrigue I had
secured as Adjutant ; John Fraser, who commanded my
Burma Rifles and was also second-in-command ; and
Denny Sharp, my Air Force officer from New Zealand.
Duncan had been the only platoon commander in my
battalion who was not wounded or killed in Tobruk ;
John had been taken prisoner by the Japanese in Myitkyina
in the previous campaign, and escaped, reaching India by
the Chaukkan Pass in the height of the monsoon ; and
Denny had fought in Malaya, escaping via Sumatra.
We were pretty mixed in origin. Two were ex-
regular N.C.O.s, three were undergraduates, two were
business men from Burma, a professional footballer, a
lad straight from school, a medical student from Liver-
pool, a land agent from South Wales, a civil engineer
from Yorkshire, a builder from Hertfordshire, a doctor
from Glasgow, a gentleman of leisure from Cornwall.
Duncan was the only one whom I knew previously ; our
acquaintance had begun one dark night in Tobruk when
he opened fire on me with a tommy-gun and a Bren-gun
as I came in off patrol. This was, of course, a great link
between us. He and John were my intimates and my
stalwarts ; I had no secrets from them, and they made a
team which can never have been bettered. We had the
same tastes, the same views, the same sense of humour,
and were all Scots (though Duncan was a Rhodes Scholar
from South Australia) ; and, if I may mix metaphors,
although we lived cheek by jowl we always saw eye
to eye.

Among the new arrivals was a youthful Punjabi Mussulman armourer called Abdul. He answered variously to Abdul the Armourer, Abdul the Bulbul or Abdul the Damned. He turned out to be a stout fellow, and as armouring was hardly a whole-time job Duncan made him his *syce*. From then on it was a question which he adored most—Duncan or the horse.

Our march began at railhead, and to avoid congestion on the lines of communication we marched mostly by night. Generals cheered us on our way, and the Commander-in-Chief addressed us in a speech which we shall not forget. As he walked round my column his eye fell on his old acquaintance Peter standing solid in the ranks, and he said, 'Hullo, what are you doing here?' Peter rolled a resigned eye on him and replied, 'Just the same as usual, sir—followin' the Major.'

On the evening of 15th February we left the roadhead, and a nightmare march over a shocking track brought us into the Chindwin valley. I got my first view of the 'Jordan,' as it had come to be known, from a clearing on the way down, where three of us column commanders sat and stared through glasses across the broad river and the miles and miles of rolling jungle away to the eastward. It was a solemn moment; for one knew only too well that many of the laughing high-spirited troops following us down the hill would cross that river only once. Often in Burma I thought of that view and looked forward to the day when I should see it again; but although I eventually came out by that identical track I never turned my head.

There was something of congestion where the other columns were crossing, and as I was the last in the order of march I asked and was given permission to try my luck at a deserted village three miles farther up-stream. With John and a small party of Burma Riflemen, and with Peter, I pushed on down to the river ahead of the column by an even viler track than that by which we had come, and an hour before dusk reached the bank. A native boat happened to be passing, and we all hid while Jameson hailed it. While John and his men made preparations to receive the column, Jameson and I crossed to the east side to find a spot suitable for landing the animals and scrambling up the bank. As darkness fell the column arrived, and I ordered a meal to be prepared and eaten, determining to start the crossing at 9 P.M.

Nothing went right that night. The stream was very swift, and the river five or six hundred yards wide ; and every rope we tried to get across fouled a snag and stuck fast. Using the native boat, I got Tommy Roberts's machine-guns and mortars across as a bridgehead, but the rafts which we had knocked up from the ruined houses were too cumbersome for easy handling, and could not be got across without a rope. By four-thirty in the morning we were tired and discouraged, and I knocked off for two hours. When we started again at half-past six our luck turned, and from then on everything went well. My two spot swimmers stripped and dived for the ropes, and by seven the rafts were buzzing to and fro across the river like shuttles. The work went on all day without interruption, and soon after dark, with the exception of two mules which had managed to get a rope round their necks and drowned themselves, the whole column— stores, men and animals—were in bivouac on the far side.

Astonishing as it may sound, there is practically nothing to record for the next fortnight. We played hide-and-seek with strong enemy patrols, which always missed us. Two passed within three miles of my columns within twenty-four hours. We had two supply droppings for all the columns in our group, each lasting three days, and were not interrupted. At the second we got mail ; we should have got it at the first as well, had not the pilot concerned dropped it accurately on to some Japanese instead of on us. Once I marched across a track between a Jap patrol and the coolie party carrying its baggage. We tipped the coolies not to tell the Japs they had seen us, because, having got so far without being tumbled to, it seemed a pity to give the show away. They accepted the tip all right, but I doubt if they held their tongues.

At the beginning of March, when we had done about a hundred miles from the Chindwin, I was detached from the main body and sent off on my own to do a job for which my column had been earmarked before leaving India—the blocking of the Bonchaung Gorge, through which runs the main line from Shwebo to Myitkyina. One evening of pouring rain I received my *congé* from the Brigadier, with orders to push ahead. I did so most gladly ; for it was an irksome business being tied to the others, and it is always pleasant to be on one's own. We marched thirty-two miles with one brief halt, and then turned eastward up a long valley which, owing to its freedom from Japs and its general peaceful atmosphere, we dubbed 'Happy Valley'. We went to sleep at four in the morning on a wooded hill two miles from its mouth, and did not wake until noon.

I had resolved, if I could, to blow the Bonchaung and slip across the Irrawaddy without a further supply drop, since I reckoned the country would get a bit hot for us after the big bang. We had drawn seven days' rations at the last supply drop on the 24th February, and I was prepared to spin it out for ten if need be ; but everything hinged on how much rice we could get for ourselves and how much forage for the animals. We found that mules would cheerfully eat paddy and bamboo, and the horses bamboo ; and although the horses went a bit off colour the mules throve. In the Happy Valley we got as much rice as we could carry, thanks to the efforts of Duncan and the Karen Subedar, who went on ahead warning the villagers to prepare stuff for us. All was ready for a dash across country to the railway.

A short easy day to recover from the long march was followed by two marches of twenty-two and twenty-five miles. The high pass at the head of the Happy Valley was luckily not held, and on the night of the 5th March we bivouacked only three miles from the railway. We had collected the first of many woeful tales of forced labour and of requisitioned foodstuffs, and gathered the welcome news that we were well inside the main Japanese garrisons. Small posts existed in most railway stations, and the line was regularly patrolled, but our information was that the enemy was not really thick on the ground in this particular area. The only definite news we could get of his dispositions was of a post some eight miles south of where I was camped, and another about twelve miles north. The incredible truth was that we had arrived within three miles of the railway, after marching for three weeks through enemy-occupied country, without firing a shot.

I had supposed that we would have to do our fell work (I always thought of it as ' fell work ' or ' nefarious activities ') by night, and David Whitehead, my technical blowing-up expert, had warned me that with the best will in the world it would take half as long again. As the opposition was apparently going to be so slight, I resolved to do it by daylight. I went into a trance for half an hour, and then emerged and gave my orders to those concerned sitting round the fire. John Fraser with half his Karens was to leave at dawn, cross the railway, and reconnoitre the crossing of the Irrawaddy, some three days' march away. Half my demolition experts, with a platoon as escort, were to go and blow the Bonchaung

Gorge on to the railway line. I myself would take the main body and the rest of the demolition experts to Bonchaung railway station and blow up the great bridge there, of which we had plans, sending on the unwanted mouths and animals to a bivouac in the jungle beyond, where we would join them. Finally, as it seemed a pity not to let the Japs share in the day's high jinks, I thought I would send Tommy Roberts, John Kerr and about forty men to beat up the Jap post to the south.

That night, as Duncan and I lay by the fire, we discussed the incredible luck which had brought us within striking distance of our main objective without interruption and with only one casualty—a man who had fallen asleep at a halt and been lost. We agreed that whatever the outcome of the expedition we wouldn't willingly be elsewhere, and Duncan quoted, ' And gentlemen in in England now a-bed. . . .' Hoping that our luck would hold on the morrow, we went to sleep at last.

At six in the morning John set off with his wireless set and his Karens. The demolition experts spent the morning tinkering with their mysterious toys, and I ran through the plan again. All the parties except John's were to meet me in two days' time on a small stream some thirty miles away ; and any who failed to make it by a certain hour were to carry on ten miles farther and meet me at my rendezvous with John on the evening of the 8th or early morning of the 9th. All officers knew that I intended to cross the Irrawaddy at Tigyaing on the 9th, if John's information was encouraging. At eleven-thirty Tommy and the demolition party set off together, since their way coincided for the first mile to a certain village ; and I was to follow an hour later to the same village, from which a track was alleged to run to Bonchaung station.

I marched off with the main body soon after noon, and at once met Fitzpatrick, a mounted orderly, galloping back up the track towards me. He brought a message from Jim Harman, commanding the gorge demolition party, to say that Tommy had bumped the enemy in the village and was fighting them ; and that Jim, quite rightly, had avoided trouble and was making straight for his objective with his escort. Not knowing the strength of the opposition, but thinking that it wasn't likely to be much, I still thought it better not to involve the main body, so sent it across country to the station to start its fell work, while I pushed on with a rifle platoon to see how the scrap was going.

, The fight was practically over by the time I arrived, only one Jap light machine-gun still holding out, which was soon silenced. Tommy had already gone on, leaving only a small party behind. Fifteen Jap dead were lying about, and four British, with another poor chap dying. He recognised me when I gave him morphia.

Leaving the platoons to find a way for their animals, Peter and I pushed on to the station. The alleged track didn't exist, and the going was atrocious ; even without animals to cumber us it took two hours to do the three miles. At last we slid through thick undergrowth into the dry river-bed which we knew the bridge spanned farther down. Soon we heard the chink of metal ; and there, sitting on the bridge seventy or eighty feet above our heads, were David Whitehead, Corporal Pike and their assistants, with their legs dangling in space. I stood in the river-bed and shouted my news up to them, and then went on to find Duncan and see his dispositions.

Four hours later, at a warning from David, we held our breaths for the big bang. I had decided against waiting for a train, dearly though I would have liked to catch one just crossing the bridge ; for I knew that one Jap had escaped from Tommy's battle, and also that Mike Calvert and his column were raising Cain not far to the south. It seemed on the whole unlikely that trains in that neighbourhood would be running strictly according to Bradshaw just then. So I told David to complete the nefarious act : muleteers stood to their animals, I took a new purchase on my eyeglass, and we waited. David had warned us that there would be two bangs, the first a baby one and the second ' quite a big one.' The baby was startling enough ; the big one five minutes later must have been heard thirty miles off. John Fraser heard it away in his bivouac by the Meza River, across twelve miles of jungle and hill ; Mike Calvert heard it far to the south ; and Tommy Roberts and Jim Harman's detachments nearly jumped out of their skins. The flash alone was stupendous. In its light we saw the mules standing among the bushes, loaded and ready to move, and the tense faces of officers and men with their packs already on their backs and their rifles in their hands, bracing themselves for the bang that was to follow. We had blown the Bonchaung Bridge.

We waited twenty minutes while David crawled out along the remains of the bridge to assess the damage. One hundred-foot span rested with one end in the river-bed ; the middle span of forty feet had been blown clean from its piers and lay slewed across the sand below. The piers themselves were torn and jagged ; altogether it was a very gratifying affair, and even David expressed himself as satisfied. We marched on down the track until we met Alec's guides ; and just as we entered his bivouac area, a minute or two before midnight, we heard another terrific explosion followed by a sliding, slithering sound, and knew that hundreds of tons of rock and soil had fallen on to the line in the gorge. We flung ourselves on the ground, and slept the grateful sleep of the successfully nefarious until first light.

Next day we marched some twenty miles and forded

the Meza River about three in the afternoon. There was
no news of Japs, although Aung Pe, the Karen Jemadar,
asked in every village. At about 4 P.M. I had got the
column wedged in a patch of jungle which, cut and slash
as we would, was utterly impassable for animals ; so I
made one of what Duncan used to call my ' weak
decisions,' and said, ' To hell with this ; we'll bivouac
here.' Next morning I sent Duncan and a small party
across to the rendezvous while I took the column and
animals round by a track. Tommy arrived soon after me,
and for the first time we heard his version of the fight
two days before. I waited beyond the allotted time for
the Gorge party, and then heard on the wireless from
John Fraser that they had already joined him at the
second rendezvous. This delay put back the programme
by twenty-four hours, and it wasn't till the evening of the
9th that I finally met John's guides and reached his
bivouac.

John's preliminary reports had been encouraging.
Tigyaing, where I had directed him to investigate the
possibilities of crossing, was a fairly large town on the
Irrawaddy shown on the map as a steamer station ; for
it seemed to me that the Japs wouldn't expect us to cross
at a town marked in nice big capital letters, but were
more likely to seek us skulking up secluded creeks. John
had told me on the wireless that the gamble looked like
coming off, and that he could hear of no garrison in the
town at all. Since then he had moved to within three
miles of it and sent in his spies, who confirmed his early
information and declared that there were ample boats on
the water-front. My only worry was that the enemy
should have devined our intention. John had by now
been in the area some time, and the presence and movement of my party, Tommy's party and Jim Harman's
party could hardly have been unnoticed. Indeed, we had

all of us had to buy food ; for it was now five days since we left the Happy Valley and fifteen since we drew our seven days' rations at the last supply drop. However, we had some reason to hope that at any rate our present exact whereabouts were unknown, because we had moved in after dark ; and all parties had been inducing the locals to believe that we were bound elsewhere, by asking searching questions about routes which we had no intention of taking. I pondered the prospects, decided they were good, gave out preliminary orders for the crossing, ate some rice and went to sleep.

Alas for our belief that our whereabouts were unknown. The first thing next morning some local inhabitants arrived with presents of milk, bananas and other good things, walking straight into our sentries with unerring direction. I received them graciously and gratefully, although disconcerted, with Duncan murmuring in my ear, ' *Timeo Danaos et dona ferentes.*' John suggested that the sooner he was off the better. I agreed, and, taking two platoons for bridgehead and cordon, he marched into the town. An hour later a Jap aircraft circled overhead and dropped a shower of leaflets, printed in English, Urdu, Karenni and Burmese, addressed to ' The Pitiable Anglo-Indian Soldiery,' telling us that all our forces had been defeated in the great battle on 3rd March, and that not a man had been able to recross the Chindwin. We were to desert our cruel and selfish British officers and hand ourselves over (carrying the leaflet) to the nearest Nippon soldiers, who would treat us etc., etc. At the same time they dropped another leaflet printed in Burmese on the inhabitants of Tigyaing, telling them that we were stragglers, and bidding them apprehend us and take us to Shwebo.

I could not believe that the Japs would go to all this fuss and bother if they were confident of reaching us in time to prevent our crossing, although the report which John now wirelessed to me from the town that there were fifty to five hundred Japs in Tawma (eight miles south of me) was a little disturbing. But John added that the boats were collecting quickly, and a glance at the map showed me that there were extensive marshes between Tigyaing and Tawma which would take some little time to negotiate, so the show went on. All the same, the tension, not to say the drama, was certainly mounting, and it continued to do so all day until the excitement in the evening.

At what I judged to be the right moment we left the bivouac and marched to the town. I found my cordon position to my taste, and marched through it into the main street. All the inhabitants were out to see the fun, and it looked as if we ought to give them value for their money. So, having sited machine-guns and mortars on a commanding hill that covered all approaches, I ordered that all movements within the town should be carried out in the best Buckingham Palace guard style, that marching should be in threes and rifles at the slope. The only thing I could do nothing about was our beards, but perhaps they would think we were some sort of Beefeater. I also read out to the troops the leaflet which had been dropped on them, because I thought it would do the inhabitants good to see them laughing at it. I wasn't disappointed. Finally, I made a stirring speech, explaining that we were not the glorious reconquering British Army *this* time, but that we had come in to kill Japs, to find out what conditions were like (and we were appalled at them), and generally to say, ' Cheer up ! the time will come.'

On the water-front John's second-in-command, Pam Heald, looked something like a harvest thanksgiving. He had announced that we wanted food, and that, unlike the Japs, we were in the habit of paying for it. There he stood, surrounded by rice, melons, potatoes, a hundred and thirty-seven eggs, chickens, and two packets of cheroots per man. He also bought as a private transaction with (so he assured me) his own money two tins of butter, two of Porage Oats, and one of tinned oysters. I think they cost him twenty rupees each (about 27s). The town appeared to have plenty of rice and cheroots, but, like everywhere else we went in Burma, no luxuries were obtainable (not even at these fancy prices), and all shops other than rice-shops were pathetically empty. Everyone was dressed in rags. Only in one village outside Tigyaing was sugar to be found, and many had no salt.

The crossing-place was from a sand-bank in the middle of the river to which we had to wade. Here the boats which we had commandeered (so that the owners could not be accused by the Japs of helping us) were already engaged in ferrying across the bridgehead platoon. The rest of the troops and animals were disposed here and there about the town and beaches with a view partly to defence and partly to the order in which they were to cross. It was really a very pretty sight : the shining varnished boats with high Venetian prows skimming across the blue river laden with troops, with the powerful torsos of the boatmen heaving to get the best out of the current ; the gold-tipped pagoda dominating the town and sparkling in the sun ; the long line of men and animals wading the shallows and stringing across the sand. The water was as warm as tea, and refreshing to the twenty or so naked men who were urging the mules into the river, to follow the boats which were towing them across to the other side. The crossing-place was over a thousand yards wide, and too far to swim them free, although one or two of the wise ones followed their friends across. Every animal was got safely across in the end, with the exception of John's charger, which ran away and was never caught.

It was a feather in the cap of Bill Smyly, the animal transport officer, and others concerned that every mule which crossed the Chindwin also crossed the Irrawaddy, except for two killed in Tommy's battle and two more which, wounded there, did not show signs of recovery and were eaten. (In passing, let me say that mule meat is good ; better than horse, and in my view better than water-buffalo. There is no need to be fastidious about it, and if anybody ever tries to enlist your sympathy by saying that he had to eat mule, you will be quite justified in withholding it. He won't have done so badly.)

Things had gone famously, and by dusk only about forty men and the last half-dozen recalcitrant animals were left after three hours' work, the most ambitious crossing we had ever done proving the most expeditious as well. But just at sunset the watching crowd on the river wall across the shallows suddenly dispersed, and all the boatmen ran away. Two crews we managed to retain at the point of the revolver. The symptoms were only too clear : they meant Japs. John extracted from them that two hundred Japs were marching up our bank from the southward. At this moment somebody on the far bank chose to send a message through the signal lamp which I had established on the far bank earlier in the day. Then the infinitesimal spark had done valuable work without being visible, except to the watchful terminal on my side ; now in the dusk the flashing light broadcast to the whole world the news that we were crossing. In vain my terminal signalled, ' Stop ! Shut up ! You are ordered to close ! ' For twenty minutes the unlucky lamp went on flashing until to my tormented eyes it looked like the red glare on Skiddaw rousing the burghers of Carlisle ; it might almost have been visible from there.

At last the next boat-load across stopped it, but not before the damage had been done.

With only the last two crews to work the boats—the current was too tricky for amateurs, though a crew of Karens managed to fetch up somewhere on the far side, half a mile down-stream—the little knot of men and the last few animals still waiting on the beach gradually dwindled. Each boat held about six besides the crew, but if animals were to be towed the freeboard was not great enough to make the boat's trim secure against their struggles. Not expecting this sudden reduction in the rate of crossing, I had withdrawn the last of my cordon and machine-guns. All I had to protect me was a couple of Brens sited on the sand-bank and pointing towards the shore. Before the last of the light had gone, a Jap reconnaissance plane, an Army 97, flew over us at five or six hundred feet. It seems incredible that it did not see us, even though we all froze and tried to look like jetsam ; but there was practically no light left, and at all events it didn't open up.

At last all the animals were across except John's charger, which had taken fright at the aircraft and run away into the dusk towards the town. Nelson, his Karen groom, had gone after it ; the Sergeant-Major, Peter, and a handful of others had got into the last boat but one ; the last of all was just approaching the beach under an armed guard of one Karen. Duncan, John, the Karen Colour-Sergeant, Nelson, and I were positively the only people still on the beach, and I had just said, ' This is where General Alexander makes his final tour of the beaches to make sure that not a single British soldier is left ! ' when from the southern outskirts of the town light machine-guns, and if my memory is correct a mortar, opened fire on us. Nelson came haring back through the darkness. The approaching boat hesitated, but the Karen guard pointed his rifle at the oarsmen, and it grounded a few yards out. The Sergeant-Major shouted for permission to push off, which I naturally granted, though he still insisted on being assured that we were all right before he would go ; and ' General Alexander's ' party waded out and embarked. I was the least lucky ; I was afraid that the boat, laden to the gunwales as it was, might stick, and pushed it out till I was waist deep, forgetting that Peter had been filling my pack with good things all afternoon, and that it now weighed fully a ton. I got my elbows on to the gunwale, but couldn't heave myself aboard until Nelson and Po Po Tou, the Colour-Sergeant, hauled me in by the scruff of my neck and the underside of my pack, and deposited me in a kneeling position on a thwart, with my head under the matting canopy, and the boat half-full of water.

There followed a most uncomfortable crossing. Whenever I tried to shift to a more comfortable position, the boat rolled again, and more water came over the side. I couldn't see a thing—not the other boat, nor the flashes from the Jap light machine-guns, nor how we were getting on ; I had cramp in my arms and legs, and my head kept bumping that infernal canopy. That fifteen hundred yards of water was the most unpleasant bit of boating I have ever done. Yet the thought kept running through my head that I was probably the first British officer ever to have crossed the Irrawaddy on all-fours.

On the far side I found that Tommy Roberts—ex-regular N.C.O. and splendid soldier—had organised a first-rate defence in case of a follow-up : he was quite prepared to fire on us in case we were Japs. There was a slight hold-up while the last stores and mule-loads were being sorted. In due course we found Alec's guides, a little apprehensive about the sound of firing, not knowing that it had begun too late to do any harm ; and so to bed, after a busy day.

The next few days were dull ones of hard unprofitable marching. I wanted to reach a secluded village in a remote valley to have our long-overdue supply drop. I was fairly confident that the Japs wouldn't be able to trace us, having taken certain steps, of which the nature is a trade secret. But the going was exceedingly bad.

For two or three days we had been unable to wireless H.Q., failing to find them on the air at the prescribed times. Before crossing the Irrawaddy, I had told them that I hoped to have supplies dropped, in the secluded village I have mentioned, on 12th March ; but what with one thing and another I was behind schedule. On the 12th we were floundering our way up a dry river-bed when we heard aircraft overhead ; and a few minutes later, for the first time since our crossing, we got H.Q. on the air. They told us that what we had just heard had been aircraft destined for us with supplies, and that having missed the bus we must wait till the 14th. Irritating though this was, all of us were immensely cheered to know that both H.Q. and the R.A.F. had our interest sufficiently at heart to send us supplies ' on spec. ' on such a vague message, in case our wireless had broken down, or some trouble had befallen us.

On the 14th we were duly at the prescribed place ; and at 11 A.M. we were cheered by the sound of engines heading towards us. Within a few minutes the first welcome canopies had opened and were drifting down on us. Accurately and regularly they floated down, all in the right area ; and by noon mules and men had done their work : five days' supplies had been issued to all ranks, animals were eating proper fodder, and all of us reading our mail. I had a letter from my regiment, requiring an answer by return of post, asking whether I would come back immediately to take over second-in-command ; Private Lumsden had a letter from a firm of solicitors in Calcutta to say that his aunt had left him eleven thousand rupees, and would he fill in and return the enclosed form. My father enclosed a cutting from the local newspaper at home containing an account of the unveiling of a memorial to the former minister of our parish : this survived many changes and chances, only to be made into cigarettes on our way out to India five weeks later.

I had asked for a good many articles of clothing to be dropped on us, and waited until the next afternoon for them to arrive in a supplementary drop, but they didn't. Again I had trouble in getting through on the wireless, or I could have found out the position without this delay. I eventually moved off at 3 P.M. on the 15th, and by bad luck was spotted an hour later crossing a patch of open paddy-field by an enemy reconnaissance plane which continued to plague us during the next week or so but never again spotted us. This and the two aircraft (unless it was the same one) which had flown over us at Tigyaing, dropping pamphlets and scaring John Fraser's horse, were the only enemy planes we saw during the whole time ; every other was British, a marked contrast to one's experience in other campaigns.

There followed a week so unpleasant that I take leave not to recall it in detail. Water was scarce, and had to be dug for, which involved long periods of waiting until the hole filled up with a muddy liquid which we had perforce to drink. The heat was intense, and the shelter scanty, for the trees were young and afforded little shade. The only life which flourished was red ants, and they in abundance. And lastly, for reasons which I cannot go into, I could neither forage nor have a supply drop, so that the five days' rations we got on the 14th had to last us till the 23rd. We had been hungry before the drop on the 14th, but we were worse now. Perhaps it was as well we didn't realise that we would be very much worse yet.

There were one or two pleasant incidents all the same. After a long period of drouth we came to a stream with 18 in. of water, and we all bathed. One of my Karens saw a Jap patrol, and although by himself flung two grenades into it before beetling off; he was one and they were fifty. Two more reported a Jap garrison in a certain village; we whistled up the R.A.F. and they got their kail through the reek within a few hours. And we bumped another column who had crossed the Irrawaddy south of us, had had the super-supply drop of all time, and were eating tinned fish and bread-and-butter pudding. These were the first allies we had seen for twenty-two days.

Hearing that (for perfectly good reasons) I couldn't have another supply drop till the 23rd, I sent a wireless message to the Brigadier : ' O.K. ; but see Psalm 22, verse 17.' (' I may tell all my bones : they look and stare upon me.') I got no change out of him : only a reference to ' It is expedient that one should die for the people.' I was amused at this, but wasn't sure that my *entourage* would be, and substituted some innocuous reference for public consumption.

Unfortunately when the 23rd at last arrived, the supply drop went wrong in that one of the aircraft bringing food failed to take off (as I afterwards discovered) ; and instead of the ten days' food for which I had asked we got only three. Some of us had had nothing to eat for two days, and all had starved at least for one, so this was a grave disappointment. Even so, however, we had something to laugh at : a shower of silver coins which descended on our heads, followed more slowly by a torn bag attached to a parachute with a note tied to it, which read :

'Enclosed please find Five Thousand Rupees.' An hour's diligent search in the jungle produced most of it.

My orders were now to rendezvous with Brigade Headquarters, which, together with other columns, was some thirty miles north of me. We did a bit that night, slept and went on at moonrise. At nine next morning we heard the sound of a brisk battle, and knew that some of our chaps were having a scrap. We pushed on, but the going was worse than I had hoped when giving a forecast of what time I could arrive ; so I told the column to make for a certain stream where I hoped they would find water, and went on to the rendezvous myself, with Heald and an escort of Karens, leaving the column to follow under John. I told them that if I hadn't got back to them on their stream by four o'clock the following morning they were to push on to another river-bed ten miles farther north, where I would meet them ; and with that I went ahead.

I failed to find anyone waiting for me at the rendezvous (or what I took to be the rendezvous) ; so telling Pam Heald to go on watching for them, I went back to the stream where I had arranged to meet the column. I gave Pam similar instructions : to wait until eight the next morning, and then to push on to the next rendezvous, where we would all join up. Confident that I would find the column, I took no map with me, although I studied Pam's for ten minutes before I left ; my own I had left with Duncan. Like a fool also, I had come on 'light,' leaving my pack and all my rations on my horse. Taking Jameson, my faithful Karen interpreter, I said goodnight to Pam ; and at about 9.30 P.M. left for the column rendezvous four miles to the southward.

If the night which followed wasn't the nastiest of my life, I am at a loss to know which can have been worse.

Poring mentally over the map which I had studied,

I marched due south by compass till I hit the stream which I believed to be the one I had given as Rendezvous. Then I turned east along it to find the confluence, marked large and generous on the map, which I had given as pin-point. I found a place where the stream ran into a marsh, but that was all. No marsh had been shown on the map : I couldn't remember one within twenty miles. I at once developed that sinking feeling in the stomach which I associate with Paddington Station and going back to school. Was I on the right stream, and was I far enough along it ? I pushed down it for a mile, the most atrocious going, through prickly bamboo, the greatest scourge of Burma jungle, and then retraced my steps. The meeting-place just couldn't be so far east as that, and there was no other confluence of the requisite size. Therefore, I reasoned, I must be on the wrong stream, and the right one must be farther south.

I returned to the spot where I had hit the stream, and started off due south. I crossed various ridges, but had marched an hour and more before I reached a watershed, and although I thrust on downhill until I reached the main stream I was perfectly certain that I was much too far south. So I turned and went back to the first stream, turned east along it again to see if there was anyone at the marsh, and again drew a blank. It was now close on four o'clock, the hour at which I had told the column to move ; and I could picture them rousing up, rubbing their eyes, and loading up the animals. What other chukkers I took I cannot remember ; but I know I went back a good two miles to the westward to see if there was a suitably prominent confluence there. There wasn't.

Dawn was now breaking, and I had two hours to get back to Pam. I returned to what I thought was the spot where I had first hit the stream, but Jameson and I couldn't agree on where it was. This shook me a lot, because the

Karens are normally far better than I in jungle. I gave him his head at first, but after half a mile I was convinced he was wrong, and indeed he himself looked anything but confident. We went back to my starting-point, as opposed to his, and went off on a bearing of due north. I had no map, and my study of Pam's before leaving had not included the country round the new rendezvous : I had not the vaguest idea of how to get there. The country we were going through seemed to bear not the slightest resemblance to our route of last night ; it was thick as the devil, and we had to slash a track where I was positive we had been able to walk free the night before. Jungle seen in the evening, with the shadows all stretching eastward, looks very different to the same jungle next morning, when they stretch west. Jameson was despondent and pessimistic, and so was I ; it was seven o'clock, Pam was also due to move shortly, and we were very weary. I reckoned we had done twenty-two miles since leaving Pam, and we had marched all the previous day and much of the previous night. And we were jolly hungry.

At a quarter to eight Jameson and I struck a jungle mere ; and as we were arguing whether or not we had seen it the night before, we heard the unmistakable crashing sound of troops marching through teak jungle. Thirty seconds later we saw our column converging on us ; and at the same moment Pam popped his head through the bushes on our other flank. I have never been more aware of God's mercy.

They, too, had failed to find the alleged confluence, and had had patrols up and down the same stream all night long. Duncan himself had walked miles in the effort to find me, but our various visits to the marsh and the stream had failed to coincide. The point where we eventually met was only five hundred yards from Pam, one of whose sentries had reported the approach of unidentified troops, and about three miles from the non-existent confluence. I ordered an immediate halt for the benefit of myself and Jameson, and had a breakfast of two biscuits (all I could afford) and an hour's sleep before pushing on.

While I was sleeping Duncan got a new rendezvous out of H.Q. on the wireless ; and next morning, having picked up one day's rations which they had left for us, we walked in on H.Q. and its attendant columns an hour after dawn. It was twenty-six days since we had last seen them, and we had a great reunion. I reported to the Brigadier, and spent the rest of the day having a sleep.

The decision had now been taken to return to India. Our principal objects had been achieved : we had blown the railway (Mike Calvert had done so in something like seventy places), gained a great mass of valuable intelligence, and got the Japs marching and counter-marching furiously in all directions. But the blow about returning to India was the necessity of abandoning the bulk of our mules and equipment. They had served their purpose, and would now be a hindrance rather than a help ; but it was a wrench all the same, and poor Bill Smyly went about with a long face at the thought of leaving the faithful animals whom he had nursed all the way from India. Yet it had its advantages in that our rate of movement was much greater than it could possibly have been had they all been coming with us. Our hand would have been forced anyhow, because they had started anthrax, and were going down like flies. I intended, in accordance with orders from above, to retain only an essential half-dozen to carry wireless, some medical stores, and, at least as far as the Irrawaddy, some of my hard-hitting weapons.

Next morning at moonrise we started for the Irrawaddy.

The Blades of Harden

Ho ! for the blades of Harden !
  Ho ! for the driven kye !
The broken gate and the lances' hate,
  And a banner red on the sky !
The rough road runs by the Carter ;
  The white foam creams on the rein ;
Ho ! for the blades of Harden !
  ' There will be moonlight again.'

The dark has heard them gather,
  The dawn has bowed them by,
To the guard on the roof comes the drum of a hoof
  And the drone of a hoof's reply.
There are more than birds on the hill tonight,
  And more than winds on the plain !
The threat of the Scotts has filled the moss,
  ' There will be moonlight again.'

Ho ! for the blades of Harden !
  Ho ! for the ring of steel !
The stolen steers of a hundred years
  Come home for a Kirkhope meal !
The ride must risk its fortune,
  The raid must count its slain,
The March must feed her ravens,
  ' There will be moonlight again ! '

Ho ! for the blades of Harden !
　Ho ! for the pikes that cross !
Ho ! for the king of lance and ling
　—A Scott on the Ettrick moss !
The rough road runs by the Carter,
　The white foam creams on the rein ;
And aye for the blades of Harden
　' There will be moonlight again ! '

Whaup o' the Rede

ERIC LINKLATER

Sealskin Trousers

I AM not mad. It is necessary to realise that, to accept it as a fact about which there can be no dispute. I have been seriously ill for some weeks, but that was the result of a shock. A double or conjoint shock : for as well as the obvious concussion of a brutal event, there was the more dreadful necessity of recognising the material evidence of a happening so monstrously implausible that even my friends here, who in general are quite extraordinarily kind and understanding, will not believe in the occurrence, though they cannot deny it or otherwise explain—I mean explain away—the clear and simple testimony of what was left.

I, of course, realised very quickly what had happened, and since then I have more than once remembered that poor Coleridge teased his unquiet mind, quite unnecessarily in his case, with just such a possibility ; or impossibility, as the world would call it. ' If a man could pass through Paradise in a dream,' he wrote, ' and have a flower presented to him as a pledge that his soul had really been there, and if he found that flower in his hand when he woke—Ay, and what then ? '

But what if he had dreamt of hell and wakened with his hand burnt by the fire ? Or of chaos, and seen another face stare at him from the looking-glass ? Coleridge does not push the question far. He was too timid. But I accepted the evidence, and while I was ill I thought seriously about the whole proceeding, in detail and in sequence of detail. I thought, indeed, about little else. To begin with, I admit, I was badly shaken, but gradually my mind cleared and my vision improved, and because I was patient and persevering—that needed discipline—

I can now say that I know what happened. I have indeed, by a conscious intellectual effort, *seen and heard* what happened. This is how it began. . . .

How very unpleasant ! she thought.

She had come down the great natural steps on the sea cliff to the ledge that narrowly gave access, round the angle of it, to the western face which today was sheltered from the breeze and warmed by the afternoon sun. At the beginning of the week she and her fiancé, Charles Sellin, had found their way to an almost hidden shelf, a deep veranda sixty feet above the white-veined water. It was rather bigger than a billiard table and nearly as private as an abandoned lighthouse. Twice they had spent some blissful hours there. She had a good head for heights, and Sellin was indifferent to scenery. There had been nothing vulgar, no physical contact, in their bliss together on this oceanic gazebo, for on each occasion she had been reading Héaloin's *Studies in Biology*, and he Lenin's *What is to be Done ?*

Their relations were already marital, not because their mutual passion could brook no pause, but rather out of fear lest their friends might despise them for chastity and so conjecture some oddity or impotence in their nature. Their behaviour, however, was very decently circumspect, and they already conducted themselves, in public and out of doors, as if they had been married for several years. They did not regard the seclusion of the cliffs as an opportunity for secret embracing, but were content that the sun should warm and colour their skin ; and let their minds be soothed by the surge and cavernous colloquies of the sea. Now, while Charles was writing letters in the little fishing hotel a mile away, she had come back to their sandstone ledge, and Charles would join her in an hour or two. She was still reading *Studies in Biology*.

But their gazebo, she perceived, was already occupied, and occupied by a person of the most embarrassing appearance. He was quite unlike Charles. He was not only naked, but obviously robust, brown-hued, and extremely hairy. He sat on the very edge of the rock, dangling his legs over the sea, and down his spine ran a ridge of hair like the dark stripe on a donkey's back, and on his shoulder-blades grew patches of hair like the wings of a bird. Unable in her disappointment to be sensible and leave at once, she lingered for a moment and saw to her relief that he was not quite naked. He wore trousers of a dark-brown colour, very low at the waist, but sufficient to cover his haunches. Even so, even with that protection for her modesty, she could not stay and read biology in his company.

To show her annoyance, and let him become aware of it, she made a little impatient sound ; and turning to go, looked back to see if he had heard.

He swung himself round and glared at her, more angry on the instant than she had been. He had thick eyebrows, large dark eyes, a snub nose, a big mouth. 'You're Roger Fairfield !' she exclaimed in surprise.

He stood up and looked at her intently. 'How do you know ?' he asked.

'Because I remember you,' she answered, but then felt a little confused, for what she principally remembered was the brief notoriety he had acquired, in his final year at Edinburgh University, by swimming on a rough autumn day from North Berwick to the Bass Rock to win a bet of five pounds.

The story had gone briskly round the town for a week, and everybody knew that he and some friends had been lunching, too well for caution, before the bet was made. His friends, however, grew quickly sober when he took to the water, and in a great fright informed the police, who called out the lifeboat. But they searched in vain, for the sea was running high, until in the calm water under the shelter of the Bass they saw his head, dark on the water, and pulled him aboard. He seemed none the worse for his adventure, but the police charged him with disorderly behaviour, and he was fined two pounds for swimming without a regulation costume.

'We met twice,' she said, 'once at a dance and once in Mackie's when we had coffee together. About a year ago. There were several of us there, and we knew the man you came in with. I remember you perfectly.'

He stared the harder, his eyes narrowing, a vertical wrinkle dividing his forehead. 'I'm a little short-sighted too,' she said with a nervous laugh.

'My sight's very good,' he answered, 'but I find it difficult to recognise people. Human beings are so much alike.'

'That's one of the rudest remarks I've ever heard!'

'Surely not?'

'Well, one does like to be remembered. It isn't pleasant to be told that one's a nonentity.'

He made an impatient gesture. 'That isn't what I meant, and I do recognise you now. I remember your voice. You have a distinctive voice and a pleasant one. F sharp in the octave below middle C is your note.'

'Is that the only way in which you can distinguish people?'

'It's as good as any other.'

'But you don't remember my name?'

'No,' he said.

'I'm Elizabeth Barford.'

He bowed and said, 'Well, it was a dull party, wasn't it? The occasion, I mean, when we drank coffee together.'

'I don't agree with you. I thought it was very amusing

264

and we all enjoyed ourselves. Do you remember Charles Sellin ? '

' No.'

' Oh you're hopeless,' she exclaimed. ' What is the good of meeting people if you're going to forget all about them ? '

' I don't know,' he said. ' Let us sit down, and you can tell me.'

He sat again on the edge of the rock, his legs dangling, and looking over his shoulder at her, said, ' Tell me : what is the good of meeting people ? '

She hesitated and answered, ' I like to make friends. That's quite natural, isn't it ? But I came here to read.'

' Do you read standing ? '

' Of course not,' she said, and smoothing her skirt tidily over her knees, sat down beside him. ' What a wonderful place this is for a holiday. Have you been here before ? '

' Yes, I know it well.'

' Charles and I came a week ago. Charles Sellin, I mean, whom you don't remember. We're going to be married, you know. In about a year, we hope.'

' Why did you come here ? '

' We wanted to be quiet, and in these islands one is fairly secure against interruption. We're both working quite hard.'

' Working ! ' he mocked. ' Don't waste time, waste your life instead.'

' Most of us have to work whether we like it or not.'

He took the book from her lap, and opening it read idly a few lines, turned a dozen pages and read with a yawn another paragraph.

' Your friends in Edinburgh,' she said, ' were better off than ours. Charles and I, and all the people we know, have got to make our living.'

' Why ? ' he asked.

' Because if we don't we shall starve,' she snapped.

' And if you avoid starvation—what then ? '

' It's possible to hope,' she said stiffly, ' that we shall be of some use in the world.'

' Do you agree with this ? ' he asked, smothering a second yawn, and read from the book : ' *The psychical factor in a germ-cell is beyond our analysis or assessment, but can we deny subjectivity to the primordial initiatives ? It is easier, perhaps, to assume that mind comes late in development, but the assumption must not be established on the grounds that we can certainly deny self-expression to the cell. It is common knowledge that the mind may influence the body both greatly and in little unseen ways ; but how it is done, we do not know. Psychobiology is still in its infancy.*'

' It's fascinating, isn't it ? ' she said.

' How do you propose,' he asked, ' to be of use to the world ? '

' Well, the world needs people who have been educated —educated to think—and one does hope to have a little influence in some way.'

' Is a little influence going to make any difference ? Don't you think that what the world needs is to develop a new sort of mind ? It needs a new primordial directive, or quite a lot of them, perhaps. But psychobiology is still in its infancy, and you don't know how such changes come about, do you ? And you can't foresee when you *will* know, can you ? '

' No, of course not. But science is advancing so quickly——'

' In fifty thousand years ? ' he interrupted. ' Do you think you will know by then ? '

' It's difficult to say,' she answered seriously, and was gathering her thoughts for a careful reply when again he interrupted, rudely, she thought, and quite irrelevantly.

266

His attention had strayed from her book to the sea beneath, and he was looking down as though searching for something. ' Do you swim ? ' he asked.

' Rather well,' she said.

' I went in just before high water, when the weed down there was all brushed in the opposite direction. You never get bored by the sea, do you ? '

' I've never seen enough of it,' she said. ' I want to live on an island, a little island, and hear it all round me.'

' That's very sensible of you,' he answered with more warmth in his voice. ' That's uncommonly sensible for a girl like you.'

' What sort of a girl do you think I am ? ' she demanded, vexation in her accent, but he ignored her and pointed his brown arm to the horizon :

' The colour has thickened within the last few minutes. The sea was quite pale on the skyline, and now it's a belt of indigo. And the writing has changed. The lines of foam on the water, I mean. Look at that ! There's a submerged rock out there, and always, about half an hour after the ebb has started to run, but more clearly when there's an off-shore wind, you can see those two little whirlpools and the circle of white round them. You see the figure they make ? It's like this, isn't it ? '

With a splinter of stone he drew a diagram on the rock. ' Do you know what it is ? ' he asked. ' It's the figure the Chinese call the T'ai Chi. They say it represents the origin of all created things. And it's the sign manual of the sea.'

' But those lines of foam must run into every conceivable shape,' she protested.

' Oh, they do. They do indeed. But it isn't often you can read them. There he is ! ' he exclaimed, leaning forward and staring into the water sixty feet below. ' That's him, the old villain ! '

From his sitting position, pressing hard down with his hands and thrusting against the face of the rock with his heels, he hurled himself into space, and straightening in mid-air broke the smooth green surface of the water with no more splash than a harpoon would have made. A solitary razor-bill, sunning himself on a shelf below, fled hurriedly out to sea, and half a dozen white birds, startled by the sudden movement, rose in the air crying, ' Kitti-wake ! Kittiwake ! '

Elizabeth screamed loudly, scrambled to her feet with clumsy speed, then knelt again on the edge of the rock and peered down. In the slowly heaving clear water she could see a pale shape moving, now striped by the dark weed that grew in tangles under the flat foot of the rock, now lost in the shadowy deepness where the tangles were rooted. In a minute or two his head rose from the sea, he shook bright drops from his hair, and looked up at her laughing. Firmly grasped in his right hand, while he trod water, he held up an enormous blue-black lobster for her admiration. Then he threw it on to the flat rock beside him, and swiftly climbing out of the sea, caught it again and held it, cautious of its bite, till he found a piece of string in his trouser pocket. He shouted to her, ' I'll tie its claws, and you can take it home for your supper ! '

She had not thought it possible to climb the sheer face of the cliff, but from its forefoot he mounted by steps and handholds invisible from above, and pitching the tied lobster on to the floor of the gazebo, came nimbly over the edge.

' That's a bigger one than you've ever seen in your life before,' he boasted. ' He weighs fourteen pounds, I'm certain of it. Fourteen pounds at least. Look at the size of his right claw ! He could crack a coconut with that. He tried to crack my ankle when I was swimming

268

an hour ago, and got into his hole before I could catch him. But I've caught him now, the brute. He's had more than twenty years of crime, that black boy. He's twenty-four or twenty-five by the look of him. He's older than you, do you realise that ? Unless you're a lot older than you look. How old are you ? '

Elizabeth took no interest in the lobster. She had retreated until she stood with her back to the rock, pressed hard against it, the palms of her hands fumbling on the stone as if feeling for a secret lock or bolt that might give her entrance into it. Her face was white, her lips pale and tremulous.

He looked round at her, when she made no answer, and asked what the matter was.

Her voice was faint and frightened. ' Who are you ? ' she whispered, and the whisper broke into a stammer. ' What are you ? '

His expression changed, and his face, with the water drops on it, grew hard as a rock shining under sea. ' It's only a few minutes,' he said, ' since you appeared to know me quite well. You addressed me as Roger Fairfield, didn't you ? '

' But a name's not everything. It doesn't tell you enough.'

' What more do you want to know ? '

Her voice was so strained and thin that her words were like the shadow of words, or words shivering in the cold : ' To jump like that, into the sea—it wasn't human ! '

The coldness of his face wrinkled into a frown. ' That's a curious remark to make.'

' You would have killed yourself if—if——'

He took a seaward step again, looked down at the calm green depths below, and said, ' You're exaggerating, aren't you ? It's not much more than fifty feet, sixty

269

perhaps, and the water's deep. Here, come back ! Why are you running away ?'

'Let me go !' she cried. 'I don't want to stay here. I—I'm frightened.'

'That's unfortunate. I hadn't expected this to happen.'

'Please let me go !'

'I don't think I shall. Not until you've told me what you're frightened of.'

'Why,' she stammered, 'why do you wear fur trousers ?'

He laughed, and still laughing caught her round the waist and pulled her towards the edge of the rock. 'Don't be alarmed,' he said. 'I'm not going to throw you over. But if you insist on a conversation about trousers, I think we should sit down again. Look at the smoothness of the water, and its colour, and the light in the depths of it : have you ever seen anything lovelier ? Look at the sky : that's calm enough, isn't it ? Look at that fulmar sailing past : he's not worrying, so why should you ?'

She leaned away from him, all her weight against the hand that held her waist, but his arm was strong and he seemed unaware of any strain on it. Nor did he pay attention to the distress she was in—she was sobbing dryly, like a child who has cried too long—but continued talking in a light and pleasant conversational tone until the muscles of her body tired and relaxed, and she sat within his enclosing arm, making no more effort to escape, but timorously conscious of his hand upon her side so close beneath her breast.

'I needn't tell you,' he said, 'the conventional reasons for wearing trousers. There are people, I know, who sneer at all conventions, and some conventions deserve their sneering. But not the trouser convention. No, indeed ! So we can admit the necessity of the garment, and pass to consideration of the material. Well, I like sitting on rocks, for one thing, and for such a hobby this is the best stuff in the world. It's very durable, yet soft and comfortable. I can slip into the sea for half an hour without doing it any harm, and when I come out to sun myself on the rock again, it doesn't feel cold and clammy. Nor does it fade in the sun or shrink with the wet. Oh, there are plenty of reasons for having one's trousers made of stuff like this.'

' And there's a reason,' she said, ' that you haven't told me.'

' Are you quite sure of that ? '

She was calmer now, and her breathing was controlled. But her face was still white, and her lips were softly nervous when she asked him, ' Are you going to kill me ? '

'Kill you? Good heavens, no ! Why should I do that?'

' For fear of my telling other people.'

' And what precisely would you tell them ? '

' You know.'

' You jump to conclusions far too quickly : that's your trouble. Well, it's a pity for your sake, and a nuisance for me. I don't think I can let you take that lobster home for your supper after all. I don't, in fact, think you will go home for your supper.'

Her eyes grew dark again with fear, her mouth opened, but before she could speak he pulled her to him and closed it, not asking leave, with a roughly occludent kiss.

' That was to prevent you from screaming. I hate to hear people scream,' he told her, smiling as he spoke. ' But this '—he kissed her again, now gently and in a more protracted embrace—' that was because I wanted to.'

' You mustn't ! ' she cried.

' But I have,' he said.

' I don't understand myself ! I can't understand what has happened——'

271

' Very little yet,' he murmured.

' Something terrible has happened ! '

' A kiss ? Am I so repulsive ? '

' I don't mean that. I mean something inside me. I'm not—at least I think I'm not—I'm not frightened now ! '

' You have no reason to be.'

' I have every reason in the world. But I'm not ! I'm not frightened—but I want to cry.'

' Then cry,' he said soothingly, and made her pillow her cheek against his breast. ' But you can't cry comfortably with that ridiculous contraption on your nose.'

He took from her the horn-rimmed spectacles she wore, and threw them into the sea.

' Oh ! ' she exclaimed. ' My glasses !—Oh, why did you do that ? Now I can't see. I can't see at all without my glasses ! '

' It's all right,' he assured her. ' You won't need them. The refraction,' he added vaguely, ' will be quite different.'

As if this small but unexpected act of violence had brought to the boiling-point her desire for tears, they bubbled over, and because she threw her arms about him in a sort of fond despair, and snuggled close, sobbing vigorously still, he felt the warm drops trickle down his skin, and from his skin she drew into her eyes the saltness of the sea, which made her weep the more. He stroked her hair with a strong but soothing hand, and when she grew calm and lay still in his arms, her emotion spent, he sang quietly to a little enchanting tune a song that began :

> ' *I am a Man upon the land,*
> *I am a Selkie in the sea,*
> *And when I'm far from every stand*
> *I am at home on Sule Skerry.*'

After the first verse or two she freed herself from his embrace, and sitting up listened gravely to the song. Then she asked him ' Shall I ever understand ? '

' It's not a unique occurrence,' he told her. ' It has happened quite often before, as I suppose you know. In Cornwall and Brittany and among the Western Isles of Scotland ; that's where people have always been interested in seals, and understood them a little, and where seals from time to time have taken human shape. The one thing that's unique in our case, in my metamorphosis, is that I am the only seal-man who has ever become a Master of Arts of Edinburgh University. Or, I believe, of any university. I am the unique and solitary example of a sophisticated seal-man.'

' I must look a perfect fright,' she said. ' It was silly of me to cry. Are my eyes very red ? '

' The lids are a little pink—not unattractively so—but your eyes are as dark and lovely as a mountain pool in October, on a sunny day in October. They're much improved since I threw your spectacles away.'

' I needed them, you know. I feel quite stupid without them. But tell me why you came to the University— and how ? How could you do it ? '

' My dear girl—what is your name, by the way ? I've quite forgotten.'

' Elizabeth ! ' she said angrily.

' I'm so glad, it's my favourite human name. But you don't really want to listen to a lecture on psychobiology ? '

' I want to know *how*. You must tell me ! '

' Well, you remember, don't you, what your book says about the primordial initiatives ? But it needs a footnote there to explain that they're not exhausted till quite late in life. The germ-cells, as you know, are always renewing themselves, and they keep their initiatives though they nearly always follow the chosen pattern except in the case of certain illnesses, or under special direction. The direction of the mind, that is. And the glands have got a lot to do in a full metamorphosis, the renal first and then the pituitary, as you would expect. It isn't approved of —making the change, I mean—but every now and then one of us does it, just for a frolic in the general way, but in my case there was a special reason.'

'Tell me,' she said again.

'It's too long a story.'

'I want to know.'

'There's been a good deal of unrest, you see, among my people in the last few years : doubt, and dissatisfaction with our leaders, and scepticism about traditional beliefs —all that sort of thing. We've had a lot of discussion under the surface of the sea about the nature of man, for instance. We had always been taught to believe certain things about him, and recent events didn't seem to bear out what our teachers told us. Some of our younger people got dissatisfied, so I volunteered to go ashore and investigate. I'm still considering the report I shall have to make, and that's why I'm living, at present, a double life. I come ashore to think, and go back to the sea to rest.'

'And what do you think of us ? ' she asked.

'You're interesting. Very interesting indeed. There are going to be some curious mutations among you before long. Within three or four thousand years, perhaps.'

He stooped and rubbed a little smear of blood from his shin. ' I scratched it on a limpet,' he said. ' The limpets, you know, are the same today as they were four hundred thousand years ago. But human beings aren't nearly so stable.'

'Is that your main impression, that humanity's unstable ? '

'That's part of it. But from our point of view there's

something much more upsetting. Our people, you see, are quite simple creatures, and because we have relatively few beliefs, we're very much attached to them. Our life is a life of sensation—not entirely, but largely—and we ought to be extremely happy. We were, so long as we were satisfied with sensation and a short undisputed creed. We have some advantages over human beings, you know. Human beings have to carry their own weight about, and they don't know how blissful it is to be unconscious of weight : to be wave-borne, to float on the idle sea, to leap without effort in a curving wave, and look up at the dazzle of the sky through a smother of white water, or dive so easily to the calmness far below and take a haddock from the weed-beds in a sudden rush of appetite. Talking of haddocks,' he said, ' it's getting late. It's nearly time for fish. And I must give you some instruction before we go. The preliminary phase takes a little while, about five minutes for you, I should think, and then you'll be another creature.'

She gasped, as though already she felt the water's chill, and whispered, ' Not yet ! Not yet, please.'

He took her in his arms, and expertly, with a strong caressing hand, stroked her hair, stroked the roundness of her head and the back of her neck and her shoulders, feeling her muscles moving to his touch, and down the hollow of her back to her waist and hips. The head again, neck, shoulders and spine. Again and again. Strongly and firmly his hand gave her calmness, and presently she whispered, ' You're sending me to sleep.'

' My God ! ' he exclaimed, ' you mustn't do that ! Stand up, stand up, Elizabeth ! '

' Yes,' she said, obeying him. ' Yes, Roger. Why did you call yourself Roger ? Roger Fairfield ? '

'I found the name in a drowned sailor's pay-book. What does that matter now ? Look at me, Elizabeth ! '

275

She looked at him and smiled.

His voiced changed and he said happily, ' You'll be the prettiest seal between Shetland and the Scillies. Now listen. Listen carefully.' He held her lightly and whispered in her ear. Then kissed her on the lips and cheek, and bending her head back, on the throat. He looked and saw the colour come deeply into her face.

' Good,' he said. ' That's the first stage. The adrenalin's flowing nicely now. You know about the pituitary, don't you ? That makes it easy then. There are two parts in the pituitary gland, the anterior and posterior lobes, and both must act together. It's not difficult, and I'll tell you how.'

Then he whispered again, most urgently, and watched her closely. In a little while he said, ' And now you can take it easy. Let's sit down and wait till you're ready. The actual change won't come till we go down.'

' But it's working,' she said, quietly and happily. ' I can feel it working.'

' Of course it is.'

She laughed triumphantly, and took his hand.

' We've got nearly five minutes to wait,' he said.

' What will it be like ? What shall I feel, Roger ? '

' The water moving against your side, the sea caressing you and holding you.'

' Shall I be sorry for what I've left behind ? '

' No, I don't think so.'

' You didn't like us, then ? Tell me what you discovered in the world.'

' Quite simply,' he said, ' that we had been deceived.'

' But I don't know what your belief had been.'

' Haven't I told you ? Well, we in our innocence respected you because you could work, and were willing to work. That seemed to us truly heroic. We don't work at all, you see, and you'll be much happier when you

276

come to us. We who live in the sea don't struggle to keep our heads above water.'

'All my friends worked hard,' she said. 'I never knew anyone who was idle. We had to work, and most of us worked for a good purpose ; or so we thought. But you didn't think so ? '

'Our teachers had told us,' he said, 'that men endured the burden of human toil to create a surplus of wealth that would give them leisure from the daily task of bread-winning. And in their hard-won leisure, our teachers said, men cultivated wisdom and charity and the fine arts ; and became aware of God. But that's not a true description of the world, is it ? '

'No,' she said, 'that's not the truth.'

'No,' he repeated, 'our teachers were wrong, and we've been deceived.'

'Men are always being deceived, but they get accustomed to learning the facts too late. They grow accustomed to deceit itself.'

'You are braver than we, perhaps. My people will not like to be told the truth.'

'I shall be with you,' she said, and took his hand. But still he stared gloomily at the moving sea.

The minutes passed, and presently she stood up and with quick fingers put off her clothes. 'It's time,' she said. He looked at her, and his gloom vanished like the shadow of a cloud that the wind has hurried on, and exultation followed like sunlight spilling from the burning edge of a cloud. 'I wanted to punish them,' he cried, 'for robbing me of my faith, and now by God, I'm punishing them hard. I m robbing their treasury now, the inner vault of all their treasury ! I hadn't guessed you were so beautiful ! The waves when you swim will catch a burnish from you, the sand will shine like silver when you lie down to sleep, and if you can teach the red sea-ware to blush so well, I shan't miss the roses of your world.'

'Hurry,' she said.

He, laughing softly, loosened the leather thong that tied his trousers, stepped out of them and lifted her in his arms. 'Are you ready?' he asked.

She put her arms round his neck and softly kissed his cheek. Then with a great shout he leapt from the rock, from the little veranda, into the green silk calm of the water far below. . . .

I heard the splash of their descent—I am quite sure I heard the splash—as I came round the corner of the cliff, by the ledge that leads to the little rock veranda, our gazebo, as we called it, but the first thing I noticed, that really attracted my attention, was an enormous blue-black lobster, its huge claws tied with string, that was moving in a rather ludicrous fashion towards the edge. I think it fell over just before I left, but I wouldn't swear to that. Then I saw her book, the *Studies in Biology*, and her clothes.

Her white linen frock with the brown collar and the brown belt, some other garments, and her shoes were all there. And beside them, lying across her shoes, was a pair of sealskin trousers.

I realised immediately, or almost immediately, what had happened. Or so it seems to me now. And if, as I firmly believe, my apprehension was instantaneous, the faculty of intuition is clearly more important than I had previously supposed. I have, of course, as I said before, given the matter a great deal of thought during my recent illness, but the impression remains that I understood what had happened in a flash, to use a common but illuminating phrase. And no-one, need I say? has been able to refute my intuition. No-one, that is, has found an alternative explanation for the presence, beside Elizabeth's linen frock, of a pair of sealskin trousers.

I remember also my physical distress at the discovery. My breath, for several minutes I think, came into and went out of my lungs like the hot wind of a dust-storm in the desert. It parched my mouth and grated in my throat. It was, I recall, quite a torment to breathe. But I had to, of course.

Nor did I lose control of myself in spite of the agony, both mental and physical, that I was suffering. I didn't lose control till they began to mock me. Yes, they did, I assure you of that. I heard his voice quite clearly, and honesty compels me to admit that it was singularly sweet and the tune was the most haunting I have ever heard. They were about forty yards away, two seals swimming together, and the evening light was so clear and taut that his voice might have been the vibration of an invisible bow across its coloured bands. He was singing the song that Elizabeth and I had discovered in an album of Scottish music in the little fishing hotel where we had been living :

> ' I am a Man upon the land,
> I am a Selkie in the sea,
> And when I'm far from any strand
> I am at home on Sule Skerry ! '

But his purpose, you see, was mockery. They were happy, together in the vast simplicity of the ocean, and I, abandoned to the terror of life alone, life among human beings, was lost and full of panic. It was then I began to scream. I could hear myself screaming, it was quite horrible. But I couldn't stop. I had to go on screaming. . . .

Sealskin Trousers and Other Stories

GEORGE CAMPBELL HAY

Ardlamont

RAIN from windward, sharp and blinding ;
 sweet to hear my darling tramping
on her way, the seas unminding,
 swinging forefoot wounding, stamping.

Steep to windward ridges breaking,
 huddled down in flocks before her ;
light she throws her head up, shaking
 broken seas and spindrift o'er her.

Wind on Loch Fyne

To a Loch Fyne Fisherman

CALUM thonder, long's the night to your thinking,
night long till dawn and the sun set at the tiller,
age and the cares of four and a boat to keep you
high in the stern, alone for the winds to weary.

A pillar set in the shifting moss, a beacon
fixed on the wandering seas and changing waters,
bright on the midnight waves and the hidden terrors ;
the ancient yew of the glen, not heeding the ages.

Set among men that waver like leaves on the branches,
still among minds that flicker like light on the water.
Those are the shadows of clouds, the speckled and fleeting ;
you are the hill that stands through shadow and sunlight.

Little you heed, or care to change with changes,
to go like a broken branch in the grip of a torrent ;
you are your judge and master, your sentence unshaken,
a man with a boat of his own and a mind to guide her.

Wind on Loch Fyne

The Smoky Smirr o Rain

A misty mornin' doon the shore wi a hushed an' caller air,
an' ne'er a breath frae East or West tie sway the rashes there,
a sweet, sweet scent frae Laggan's birks gaed breathin' on its
   ane,
their branches hingin' beaded in the smoky smirr o rain.

The hills aroond war silent wi the mist alang the braes.
The woods war derk an' quiet wi dewy, glintin' sprays.
The thrushes didna raise for me, as I gaed by alane,
but a wee, wae cheep at passin' in the smoky smirr o rain.

Rock an' stane lay glisterin' on aa the heichs abune.
Cool an' kind an' whisperin' it drifted gently doon,
till hill an' howe war rowed in it, an' land an' sea war gane.
Aa was still an' saft an' silent in the smoky smirr o rain.

Wind on Loch Fyne

GEORGE SCOTT-MONCRIEFF

Lowland Portraits

[By *Lowlands* here the author intends not the Central Lowlands only but all Scottish lowland areas where burghs have
been long established—e.g. the south-west, south-east and
north-east of Scotland]

Kirkcudbright

THE most attractive of the Galloway burghs is unques-
tionably Kirkcudbright. A little larger than Gatehouse,
it is better planned, less elongated, less of the Scottish
tendency to a high-road community, being on no main
road, but an outpost at the estuary of the Dee. At high
tide the great breadth of water around it makes a brilliant
setting. There are whole blocks of fine eighteenth-
century houses in its streets : classical austerity in the
homespun of a not-too-finished stone, suited to a remote
and rural township. These houses were the town
mansions of the gentry in the days when provinces were
also units. . . .

The Isle of Whithorn

The best of the Galloway villages is the Isle of Whithorn,
although, like Kirkcudbright, its charm depends partly
upon the tide. The ' Isle ' itself is a peninsula, a green spit
of land, well shaped, without houses except for the
laroch of the Norman church that replaced the *candida
casa* built by St Ninian when he brought Christianity to
the Picts of his native place in the year 397. The houses
are built above a sea wall along a curve of land running
out to the Isle. Many of them are white, and some a dark
ox-blood red. Towards the seaward end is a white kirk,

built out over the water and facing the single line of houses, like a white-cassocked preacher addressing his congregation. It was so built because the laird would not feu ground for building a Free Kirk. . . .

The Galloway Pattern

Its most personal characteristic is the small scale of everything. The hills are small and the mountains are small. The fields are small, rarely level ; they climb the foothills and embrace small outcrops of rock that the plough skirts with liquid curves. Most of the roads are still small, not driven like thongs across the country, unregarding of its contours, but winding, rising and falling, so that driving along them one has that sense of contact with the landscape which is denied by the modern trunk road. The native cattle are small. The Galloway Beltie, black or dun with a wide neat white belly-band, is still a familiar within the knobbly dyked enclosures ; but the native pony, stocky and muscular, is almost extinct. Shakespeare makes mention of the old Galloway nag, and the author of *Lithgow's Rare Adventures*, writing in 1632, says ' this country aboundeth in Bestiall, especially in little Horses, which for mettall and Riding, may rather be termed bastard Barbs, than Gallowedian Nagges.' He himself rode south, *en route* for Russia, on one of them. Lord Stair a hundred years later, Ambassador in Paris, was making gifts of Galloway ponies to the French nobility. They were probably kin to the Norwegian pony and owed their origin to the Viking invasions. The original Galloway sheep were small, with fine wool, similar to the Shetland and the old Highland breeds. But, like the Highlands, Galloway went over to the blackfaced, whose wool is so coarse it is used chiefly for carpets.

Anwoth

Over the hill from Gatehouse lies Anwoth Auld Kirk, long since deserted in favour of an ungainly successor. Yet the first kirk was built for the ministry of Samuel Rutherford, one of the most striking figures of the Kirk, a poet-evangelist, not merely worthy but imaginative. (' These things take me so up, that a borrowed bed, another man's fireside, the wind upon my face—I being driven from my lovers and dear acquaintance, and my poor flock—find no room in my sorrow. I have no spare or odd sorrow for these ; only I think the sparrows and swallows that build their nests in the kirk of Anwoth blessed birds. Nothing has given my faith a harder back-set till it crack again than my closed mouth.') The auld kirk is now a laroch, prettily set within its graveyard. There are some good stones here, including one of those Covenanters' tombs with epitaph in vigorous rhyme, to be found in many small Galloway kirkyards and almost peculiar to the province (in which, unlike most places, the Covenanters were more persecuted than persecuting).

The Old House of Park

It is hard for us to conceive the rightness of mind that, for example, evolved the Old House of Park : made it perfect with apparently no intention other than to build a house to measure, while today thousands of architects must strive with textbook and theory and rarely achieve anything half so satisfying. Park stands grandly, an angle house of the transition period—between tower and mansion—that is perhaps the most interesting of all in Scottish architecture. The heavy chimneys, the bold gables, give sense of might and height ; the low unsymmetrical wings, flung out at a slightly later date, with their broad hipped-roofs and wide chimney-stacks, add depth and repose. At the back the elevation is relieved by the low dormers and by a single-storied projection, a neat buttock. There is as much, or more, artistry in Park than in any picture Raeburn ever painted : for the price of a cheap Raeburn it could be saved, renovated into the loveliest of homes without the slightest prejudice even to the fenestration. . . .

White Hares

I have been with the shepherds shooting white hares on the tops around Black Law. We clambered up into a clinging mist, and trudged through snow-patches ; high up the red bog grasses were encased in sheaths of ice. The earth and one's fellow-shooters loomed queerly and disappeared as strangely. The foreman shepherd's flask contained claret, the chill taken off it by his person : it seemed to me more cordial than whisky. He shared it with me as we lunched above a gully through which water spouted and mingled spray with the mist. I had long completely lost my bearings, and supposed, as we descended, that it was Manor that coiled through the valley which sprang suddenly from the mist, but it was Megget Water that flows into St Mary's Loch. Until now we had seen hardly a hare, but as we descended on Megget we could see them, mottled white against the uncovered ground, feeding on the low country. They ran up towards us and the guns blazed ; but we were widely spaced, and far more were hit than were killed, which is the sad thing to white hare shooting. . . .

Traquair

Six miles down the river from Peebles lies Innerleithen, well situated but a dull sprawling place. A road here crosses Tweed, runs through a pleasant slip of a village— with two delightful miniature houses, one empty and ivy-grown, the other spruce in yellow wash—and passes the gates of Traquair that have not been opened since Prince Charles Edward passed through them. Great toothy bears surmount the gateposts, and between them the grass-covered drive dips to a glimpse of the house. Traquair is a building that has grown over many years, the latest part dating from the end of the seventeenth century. It is one of the most impressive houses in Scotland and peculiarly Scottish in character. The grey harled walls rise straight up, breaking at three stages into single turrets, one a stair tower, one almost a bartizan ; deep-roofed wings enfold a court fronted by a further pair of gates. The north side is still more austere, but the line falls to the east, and in front are two terraces flanked with pavilions with ogival roofs. Yet there is nothing that could aptly be called grim about Traquair ; rather the spatial grace enwrapping its austerity gives it a quality of supremely unconscious romanticism.

Smailholm

Smailholm is the one tower remainng essentially untouched and complete of that simplest type that once stood freely across the Border country. At the north of the county of Roxburgh, it stands high on a grassy rock ; simple box form with small windows, one dormer and a cap-house to the parapet which runs along two sides only. The roof pitch is crow-stepped, but all the slates away and the poor back of the vaulting exposed to the rains. Around are two other rocky knolls and then a view for miles ; southwards to the three Eildon stacks. To the north lies a pool of water, with an islet, in which Smailholm reflects and seems momentarily a placid castle, Narcissus-like in self-admiration, then again asserts the tremendous austerity of its outline against the mad moon-mountains of the landscape. Its walls are speckled like the Scotch Grey hens that peck by the road-end farmstead, dark and light, a hard-looking stone, with red ashlar angles and scant dressing to the windows ; one is impressed with recollection of glints of brickwork amongst soiled city walls. And once more Smailholm is graceful by dint of its eminence, the slight softening of its pattern and form where the roof and the dormer and parapet emerge from the barrack walls. Wild thyme, tormentil, yellow bedstraw, and violas grow amongst the rocks and the gorse. Smailholm when it seems to blossom in summer becomes elemental, in winter it is barren with the dead grasses. . . .

Kelso

Kelso looks bigger than it is, for it is well planned, not untidily developed, but with streets running out of a central square. It is a charming town : in particular, Bridge Street, where there is a double row of pilastered shops—may they remain intact, and no chain store smash into them with vulgar frontage framing shoddy goods. These pilastered shops reap additional charm from curving to the ruined abbey, whose arcading is so fine that even as a ruin it has aesthetic, as distinct from romantic or associative or speculative significance. The stone is pale, there is good detail, and the round arches mount grace-fully to the tower's summit. It is seen today much as it was left by the pimping earl. For contrast it is worth looking at the Free Kirk along the pleasant strand leading to the gateway to Floors : surely there is nowhere more tortured stonework than that to be seen on this too well-preserved edifice. . . .

The Black Laird

Through much of the sixteenth century Henry VIII's troops savaged the land. By the time Queen Mary came back from France it was to a country in the extremity of tumultuous suffering ; a hopeless kingdom. Near Roxburgh stood the tower of Ormiston, whose founder in the twelfth century had been a man pious and civilised, a benefactor of Melrose. Hertford destroyed the tower, but it was rebuilt by the Black Laird in a day in which insecurity and moribund religion had bred all bloody excess. The Black Laird shared in Darnley's murder at Kirk o' Field. For a subsequent crime he was taken and hanged. He became penitent after his manner and left a telling testament : ' With God I hope this night to sup. . . . Of all men on the earth I have been one of the proudest and most high-minded, and most filthy of my body. But specially, I have shed innocent blood of one Michael Hunter with my own hands. Alas, therefore, because the said Michael, having me lying on my back, having a pitchfork in his hand, might have slain me if he pleased, but he did not, which of all things grieves me most in conscience. . . . Within these seven years I never saw two good men, not one good deed, but all kinds of wickedness.' . . .

Dumfries

Despite impoverishment, and despite the unfortunate overdressed red sandstone of the villas on its outskirts (that Dumfriesshire sandstone is villainous stuff, temptingly easily worked), Dumfries is a gay and inspiriting county town. Down to Whitesands and Devorgilla's bridge runs a small street whose shops burst with their goods on to the pavements. The tolbooth, the Midsteeple, is on an island site in the High Street, its red stone mellowed. It was finished in 1707, but the blazon is *pre-Anschluss* ; alongside it a delightful figure of the town's patron, St Michael, with a beard, a skirt and a crozier, standing indifferently on top of a small worm-like dragon. Burns's house is as nicely done as could have

288

been expected, which is to say that it is not offensive. His mausoleum in the neighbouring kirkyard is of the Greek Revival, a classical dome covering pastoral statuary. The guide will insist that you go into the corner that you may see every button on the bard's breeks, so cunningly and realistically has the artist done his work (but there are better buttons to be seen in Edinburgh, from Princes Street Gardens, on the back of the white marble upholstery on the chair of the eminent philanthropist, Dr Guthrie). . . .

The Old Road

In coaching times the stage from Berwick left the coast abruptly, hedging a little south again, past the policies of the grand Adam house of Paxton, and the church at Ladykirk built by James IV and meetly capped by Robert Adam. Making along the province of Merse for Greenlaw, then the county town of Berwickshire, the coach turned north to Lauder and into Midlothian. On the road between Greenlaw and Lauder there is still a pair of gatehouses of that peculiarly pleasant and absurd period, the early pseudo ; cottages each with one gable castellated and fitted with blind Gothic windows, and each bearing a milestone and a clock whose painted hands show the times at which the coaches passed, north and south. This road was the old route, along which marched armies north to Bannockburn and south to Flodden ; for fertile though Berwickshire is, its fertility has been won by its farmers from marsh and moor. The coast road was the wilder and, with the profound cutting of the Pease Burn, deterred the traveller. . . .

Farmers

The improving farmer may be mean, tyrannous and close-fisted, but he has a redemption that the industrialist lacks. He cannot be an absentee employer, sitting back and waiting for his profits : he cannot lose touch with his work or his men. This intimacy and concern save him from a degrading detachment, so that money is never the dominating motive of his enterprise. The very risk and uncertainty of his craft is a safeguard—the weather cannot be hoodwinked by the conscientious development of low cunning which for the business man can mitigate the trade depressions which are part and parcel of his world. The farmer, moreover, is creating a wealth more real than that of the manufacturer : a fundamental wealth. Like the gold reserve that should exist to back bankers' loans, the land should be treasured as a positive source of wealth behind all industrialist development. . . .

East Lothian

East Lothian is the heart of Lothian and one of the loveliest counties of the Lowlands. Its landscape lies in horizontal planes of colour : the ruddy twigs of stripped copses, green of grass, darker green of turnip and kale, dark-and bright-red ploughland. I suppose it is the rise and fall of the ground, neither too flat nor too broken, that makes the effect so marked. At harvest there are strokes of bronze-red wheat stubble ; and, earlier, stretches of mellowing grain. Towards Dunbar the earth is as red as the guts of man. Women work in the fields in deep poke-bonnets, telescopic-like crinolines and covered with bright-coloured stuffs. They look up at one, red faces framed and framing the flash of teeth. Old jumpers and oddments many-coloured wrap their bodies against the sea winds. They merit the brush of a Renoir, but their high-cheek-boned faces are as Scots as his girls are French. Right up the spur of East Lothian the tilled fields stretch with a final flourish of intensive cultivation to the crest of the cliffs at Tantallon. The pitted screen-wall of the castle stands tremendous, dwarfing the abrupt Bass beyond, whose white lighthouse buildings look like something erected by an old seaman inside a bottle. . . .

Progress

Not so many years ago, within the memory of the middle aged, there were weavers living in three thatched cottages where there is now a wide gap. There was a tailor and a cobbler. There was a baker, whose assistant is still here to draw his old-age pension. The neighbouring smithy is now shut up, with boards across the window, and piles of old iron, red with rust like dead leaves, about the door. The permanent officials regard the village with stern distaste : the houses have no water supply. True, hundreds of thousands of gallons of water pass close by from ample reservoirs to the big town. The reservoirs are lochs in the same parish as the village ; they bring in a large revenue to the county council : but seemingly the village has no claim upon them or even upon the expense of tapping the springs on the slope, save such as will supply two or three pumps down the street. If the villagers insist upon water, it will be charged to their individual rate—an impossible tax upon the dwindling population. As they can, the authorities condemn the houses, and shift the people into the box-like structures that they are busy building underneath the slag-heaps of the mining township four miles away. The people of the village—miners or labourers—want to keep their homes, preferring to live in the country even under present conditions, and cycle to their work ; but the grim clerks have the Law behind them, which deems free choice of domicile a luxury not for the poor. . . .

Fife

In Fife alone amongst Scottish counties is it still possible to go from one small burgh to the next over a considerable area and find in each good houses and a fine parish church, perhaps a tolbooth too. In this Fife is comparable to parts of England. But the buildings themselves, and the countryside despite its low lying, are in no way English. Fife is appropriately situated between the country of Lothian and that of Angus. It is almost insular, with the sea to three sides : the country well farmed and wooded, with little moorland ; the climate bright, dry and cold.

Ceres

The most attractive village in Scotland is Ceres, near the county town of Cupar. Ceres does not cling to the road, but drapes itself graciously about its kirk and burn. Its people still celebrate the return of the men from Bannock-burn. Nearby a free-standing tower of yellow ashlar looks afar over the countryside. Here lived that cultured gentleman, Sir John Scot of Scotstarvit. Sir John edited the works of Scottish poets, for printing in Holland. He was also responsible for saving the maps of Timothy Pont and for their eventual publication by Blaue. He vented his spleen upon Government in a volume with the title, *The Staggering State of Scottish Statesmen*. He used the garret of his tower as a study ; an excellent chamber, with its sunny parapet walk and wide view.

Nairn

The town of Nairn is not beautiful. It was largely the creation of the eminent Dr Grigor, whose statue, that of a fat man in verdigris and a big-brimmed hat with what may be a Nairn cape (a diminutive Inverness) falling back from his wide shoulders, stands in a prominent position from which it is shortly to be moved. Dr Grigor (1814–86) spent the winter in Italy, the summer in Nairn where he built himself a Florentine villa that was terribly cold and had to be reconstructed after his death. He sent his Italian patients to Nairn and his Nairn patients to Italy. Nairn became noted as a resort.

Lowlands of Scotland

ADAM DRINAN

The Men of the Rocks

CRYSTAL long-boat shadowily moving
curlew home to constant moorland
rounding point to an ancient mooring
    leeward of the skerries

a wan grief of unanimous oars
a weary heave of ghostly rowlocks ;

home to the long hill-fortressed harbour
arms hauling, voices hailing,
starved seagulls' drunken harmony
    dirge on the wind drifting :

' Swirl of a deep year over our heads
sleep of a deep year round our eyelids.

Nightly, moonily, nightly oaring
the barnacled hulk from the black sea-floor
a moon and a night and a moon borrowing
    in every year of doom

loom of land piercing our dream
release-image pleasing our gloom.

Night of the first moon.   Lay in the anchorage.
Curing-, storing-, landing-places
glowed on shore in grander days
    when the rippled world was young.

What those ribs left sprung on shingle,
if they are not our fathers' ships ?
Patterned wefts for the ghosts of fishers
these tattered nets the wind quivers.
Who but the geese and the seagulls forage
   where the old men flourished ?

No place here for dead sea-warriors,
no stay here for the brave sea-wanderers :
one look checked us, turned us, warning us
   back to the blank of the sea.

Night of the next moon.   Beached and landed.
Oats, and cattle, and a strath once shaggy ;
tales ran warm here ; women sang
   when the furrowed world was young.

What will we gather in the time of hairst
if it will not be bracken and heather ?
Who from the hill will answer, other,
lonelier, than the pipe of plover ?
What has he got that seized and feued it ?
   Dead birds and solitudes !

He that of Indian plains made serfdom
wastes our glens to take his freedom,
Such was our home-come.   Back to the doom, come
   back yet a year to the sea !

Night of the last moon.   Moored in port
summoning out our sons and daughters,
an old call of an old order
   when the wrinkled world was young.

What these passages narrow, secluded,
hard, to the sea-soft, feeling foot ?
Whose these voices drawn, dreary,
harsh to our island-subtle ears ?
Who responds ? who grasps ? who governs ?
   where are our children gone ?

Cold, cold, cold the sea
cold the sea, and glistening ! '
   (Their stiff arms fixed at the elbow)

' Cold, cold, cold the sea
the sea, the snake, and the exile ! '
   (Their shirts as seals' fur wettened)
' Bitter to the young a young world's death
Better for the old a youth of legend ! '

Ship of glass in water melting
under the bubbly lipper settling
heads bobbing on waves' swell
   men that have been are seals.

Men that have been are seals, swimming
save for my friend on a rock, sitting.
Tears his human eyes have dimmed.
   We gaze at each other on the skerries.

The Men of the Rocks

MORAY McLAREN

The Commercial Traveller

A WEST HIGHLAND commercial traveller is a man whose whole livelihood depends upon his vivacious and un-affected charm. He has to do more than persuade nice quiet shopkeepers in south-country towns to buy a particular kind of thing that they don't want. He has to deal with a romantic and remote peasantry on the shores of lochs and in Atlantic islands : a peasantry who are passionately hospitable to the stranger and the friend, but who are suspicious of the bagman and the Englishman. The West Highland commercial traveller has, therefore, to approach as a stranger, and then by the charm and the vivacity of his manner make himself so much a friend that he can for ever after appear in this light to these particular people again. He must be bilingual, for many of his clients have only the Gaelic ; he must have no easy tricks of a hearty manner ; there must be no slappings on the back and bull-like roars of : ' How are you, old chap ? ' Nor must he ever be shy and at a loss for the word. Embarrassment would make his clients uneasy, boisterous-ness repel them. Sometimes he will be so far afield that the direct method of barter will appeal most to the natives, and he will exchange his packets of tea, or what-ever it is, for yards of the odorous and rich-looking tweed which the remoter islanders weave, and which are so beloved by London business men. Dealing with remote peoples, who have not only the sensitiveness of the Celt but the wisdom of a lonely race, he must have one element of the gentleman—he must neither condescend to, nor be afraid of those who are less *au fait* with the world than he is. Let me say at once that he is himself usually no romantic or even impressive figure ; he preserves the splendid bounderdom of his kind when he is amongst his kind, or away from the Highlanders ; but he has a genius, a hidden quality, which on his travels emerges out of his pre-urban ancestry and makes admirable that trade which we are accustomed to look upon with such unmerited condescension.

I was not aware of these qualities in the West Highland commercial traveller when I sat in the little bar at Roy Bridge Inn, for at first I saw nothing worthy of remark in my companion, and I had not seen the type at work, as I did afterwards in the Outer Hebrides. My friend was a little cock sparrow of a man of about fifty, with vivacious eyes and a funny mobile mouth. . . .

. . . He reminded me of those impertinent little Glasgow Boy Scouts whom John Buchan writes about—capable of the more vigorous and amusing side of Glasgow vulgarity, but quite incapable of the Glasgow mass sentimentality, which has no good side and is merely the complement to Glasgow brutality. I forget how we got into conversation, for at the beginning I was too sleepy to remember much. I think he showed his curiosity at my bedraggled and exhausted appearance ; for the Scots, even the most respectable of them, have an affection for vagabondage, which was frequently discovering itself to me in the half-envious curiosity which my now very shabby look awoke in the people I met on the way. I must say here—so fearful am I of being thought to play without true qualification the picaresque role—that there was about me no romantic abandonment of dress or manner, induced by carefully exposed rents in my clothes, or dishevelled hair. It was merely that my tiredness, my clothes too rough to demand care, my healthy and now sunburnt skin, spoke of a freedom of purpose and direction, appealing to the savage which, have as I already said, lies so near the surface of the Scotsman's mind.

The little commercial traveller then, I think, in some such way opened the conversation with me. My vanity, which is never sleepy, aroused the rest of me ; and I soon was talking to him about travel, about France, the Germanies, and, finally, about Scotland. He showed such detailed knowledge of the parts of the country into which I was going—of the Western Highlands and Islands—of the names of all the most interesting people to see in the most remote villages, that my curiosity silenced me and allowed me to listen to story after story (not particularly amusing in themselves, but catching something from his own vivacity), of his bartering travels in Skye, Morar, Sutherland and the Outer Hebrides. Frequently he would return in his narratives, as he did in his journeys, to the respectable Glasgow suburb which was his home ; and would tell me of the local ' footba' club,' of which he was evidently the doyen and for which he used to go through the extremely risky feat of refereeing. I had often seen jokes in the comic papers about the dangers of refereeing, but had supposed them to be would-be humorous exaggerations, like the jokes about people being killed in the fight for buses and tubes. If only one learned to take one's *Punch* a little more seriously, what a lot one would learn ! Now, however, I was enchanted by and, indeed, believed the sagas of the Gorbals' football club referee, and perceived that what I had always looked upon as incredible happened every Saturday afternoon in Glasgow. My friend at the end of his stories used to twist up his lips into a squeezed and contorted smile, as if he had been sucking a lemon. This was impressive as well as being funny, and made one wonder how much that smile meant and what that was in words inexpressible was contained in that curious grimace. There was about the man a neatness, a precision of manner, which made very ridiculous the thought of him being subjected to physical indignities every Saturday afternoon. After one story of how he had been removed from the pavilion and out of the football ground, hidden in a laundry basket, so that he should escape the fury of the crowd, he drew up his lips into so strange a contortion, and for so long a time, that I laughed loudly to his face, and was relieved to see that he joined me easily and unoffendedly. After that he perceived his own genius—or that element of it that amused me—and told stories, all of which ended up with his own discomfiture and all of which were crowned with the contortion and the laugh. It was three o'clock before we went to bed.

The next morning broke for me very cheerless. The hopeless grey that is not quite white of a Highland mist pressed against my bedroom window-pane. I had been too tired to sleep well, and I awoke at an indeterminate hour that was neither early nor late. It was not so late that I could console myself with the thought that in fact, if not in sense, I had had many hours' sleep ; it was not so early that I could turn over and say to myself, ' If you cannot sleep any more you can at least rest.' I got out of bed and came downstairs, knowing that only the rich quality of a Scottish breakfast could revive me to anything like my normal energy.

I had, however, not only this consolation awaiting me, but also a very kindly offer from my little companion, the cause of my exhaustion. He, who had already breakfasted, was waiting for me, and upon my arrival offered to give me a lift on to the shores of Loch Lochy in his car. I was tired. I had childish memories (possibly quite unjust) that told me that the country between Loch Lochy and Roy Bridge was dull, the weather was horrible and above all I liked the companionship of my lift offerer : so I accepted.

. . . On some of the business calls I accompanied my friend so as to see him actually on the job. I despair of being able to describe his manner of persuasion. It was partly an application of his natural Gaelic ease and charm, and partly the use of a genius for understanding what would please those to whom he was talking. By this genius, which he loved to exercise, even when not for profit, he had found out from me that I was most amused by his vivacity and by the thought of his being placed in undignified positions. It was this discovery on his part that had enabled him to keep me up till three that morning. As with me he used the stories of his football experiences, so with a crofter or village shopkeeper he would make a quite direct appeal to the emotion of surprise, caution, friendliness or whatever else that he knew was dominant in his client's mind. I perhaps make him out too much of a play-actor, and to counteract this impression let me say at once that to whomever he was appealing he always remained in appearance, gesture and manner the perky little vivacious Glasgow tradesman that he was by nature. He was never so crude as to change his voice, save when he had occasion to use the Gaelic. It was only the things he said, the sentiments which he attacked in his audience that changed. He was too clever to rely upon the use of any personality in manner save his own natural one.

When we were approaching in the not very late and foggy afternoon the place where we proposed to spend the night, we learnt that the local Member of Parliament was expected to arrive. This man, as it turned out afterwards, was to make a speech at the village hall at the beginning of a small local concert. We heard a good deal about this concert from the clients as we got nearer our destination and passed quite a number of Highlanders walking in on their way to the festivities. About a mile from the village we stopped the car and offered a lift to two fine-looking girls accompanied by their brother. The commercial, who loved to show off his vivacity to the sex, said to the young man, ' Can you drive, mannie ? ' And on hearing ' Yes,' at once surrendered the wheel to him (for I had long ago told him that I could not drive) and got into the back seat along with me and the two girls.   I was at once very much cold-shouldered, for I was confronted with two handsome girls who to whatever I said would only reply, ' Yes-s-s-s ' with that fading sibilance which, however charming to listen to, is not the best thing for dispelling shyness.   My friend quickly took the situation in hand, and sitting down between them put an arm round each of their waists and poured forth a series of Glasgow music-hall songs about being ' happy where the girls are ' and others of that kind.   They were soon, of course, giggling happily, and what with the banging, rattling of the car, the unending songs of the commercial, the giggling of the girls and my own laughter, we approached the village in a fairly gay and somewhat ludicrous way.

As we turned the corner and swung into the little street we saw gathered together in a little knot by the school-house a collection of local worthies, headed by the minister.   They were evidently awaiting the arrival of the legislator.   I felt a little embarrassed to come before this austere gathering in such a way, but my friend at once leapt to the occasion again.

He did not stop his singing and did not remove his arms from the girls' waists, but as the car drew up by the schoolhouse, shouted out, ' Good-evening to you, gentlemen.   I'm glad to see so many of my constituents here to welcome me.'   This was said in that absurd voice which a Scotsman assumes when he imagines himself to be imitating the haw-haw type of Englishman.   He then stood up in the car, and thrusting one hand under his overcoat tails, started to make a speech. There was a pause amongst the waiting crowd. Many of them I could see either recognised the commercial from his previous visits or suspected on other grounds that this funny little creature, now more than ever looking like a cock sparrow with his tail thrust out, could not be the man they were waiting to welcome. The minister, how-ever, who was new to the district and who had evidently been deputed to be the one to do the welcoming, waited irresolutely. He did not dare to take no notice—for he clearly did not know the Member by sight—and it was just possible that this gesticulating little absurdity might be he arrived drunk ; also he could not overcome his suspicion sufficiently to make an overture of greeting, which would commit him. The minister stood at the front of the crowd, and those at the back who knew for certain that this was not the Member were, for the moment, not bold enough to come forward and say so to their deputed chief. They could not believe that he would be taken in : they waited for him to make the first move, either of anger or amusement. I do not suppose that the whole scene lasted more than two minutes, but to the giggling girls and to me, uneasy and ashamed, it seemed to go on for hours.

The speech was not a very successful, but certainly vivacious, imitation of the platitudinous nonsense that is usually produced on such occasions. After a minute the minister, so it seemed to me, made up his mind that this was a fraud and was about to move away, when his suspicions on the other side—that this might really be the Member, but in a state of drunkenness—were aroused by the conclusion of the speech, in which my friend in the name of the Liberal Party invited the entire village to come with him to the hotel bar and have a drink. He added, as he saw the eye of the hotel proprietor, whom he knew, brightening at this tremendous invitation, that he had unfortunately no money with him, but would ask Donald MacLean to put the whole account down to the Lloyd George Fund. At this Donald, the hotel proprietor, gave such a shout of laughter that without any abrupt or unpleasant exposure the whole thing was quite easily and suddenly taken by everyone as a joke, and those who had been taken in at the start, anxious that their gullibility should not be discovered, were the loudest and most genial in their expression of amusement. Those who knew my friend came forward to greet him and introduced him to the minister, who to my admiration did not show any annoyance. The whole party then, with that carelessness for time-tables and programmes, which is the mark of the Celt all over the British Isles, left the schoolhouse where they had gathered to greet the approaching Member of Parliament, and wandered towards the hotel where Donald was soon busy dealing out whiskies in the bar and in the sitting-room.

The day had been cold and misty, my blood was chilled by sitting in the car, so I settled down with great satisfaction to my warming drink—I had chosen that most delicious of all warm drinks, a rum and hot milk—and looked at my surroundings with pleasure. We were in a warm well-furnished room, with deep rugs on the floor to welcome the feet, and many 'trophies of the chase,' as they are always called, hung on the wall to interest the eye. Highland hotels may be expensive, but they never have a mean effect. The profession of inn-keeper has always been considered a gentlemanly one in the north of Scotland, either (as David Balfour said) because of the tradition of Highland hospitality, or because the profession is one which allows one to be fairly successful and at the same time drunken and lazy.

The result is that the 'great hall' or reception room of many Highland hotels looks as if it belonged to a great gentleman's house. It is large, gives off an air of comfort, and unbelievably fat salmon in glass cases ornament the walls ; while the proud heads of the red deer stare at one out of the lofty gloom. The chairs and sofas are always comfortable, the whisky admirable.

This room in which I now found myself looked very well with the tall Highland farmers and estate agents in their thick tweeds which smelt deliciously because of the mist in the air. They were standing about and talking in that soft, almost feminine, voice which the strongest of Highlanders always has. I, who was near the fire, noticed that my friend was in another corner of the room talking to a group of men, and now and again the conversation amongst them seemed to turn on me, for I noticed that they looked at me frequently ; and at last the schoolmaster announced that as the evening was coming on we had better move down to the village hall, where the concert was to be held and the speeches made. As the people began to go out of the room and I to wonder if I should follow them to the concert, he came up to me and said :

'Can you tell me now, sir : is it not true that you are a great comic ?'

'There's none alive that's greater,' I replied, not quite getting what he was driving at, 'and as I know none that's dead, that's the highest praise I have.'

'Ah, that's true, that's true,' continued the schoolmaster in that clear Inverness-shire voice which quite evades any of the usual hackneyed attempts at phonetic dialect spelling so beloved by the local colourists. 'And now so kind a gentleman as yourself even though he is on holiday will not grudge to help me in my concert. We have a fine piper, a fine Gaelic singer, a piano player and a reciter, but the people here are sad for the want of a comic.'

As soon as I understood what he wanted I began the usual process of polite refusal when, to my disgust, my commercial friend came up to the group that was beginning to gather round me and said :

'He'll sing for ye, gentlemen, only don't press the little man too far. He's the finest coamic in Gorbals and that's saying all I can. Ye'll sing them yon coamic song you gave me last night,' he said turning to me. I remembered in confusion that I had been so warmed and genial at Roy Bridge the previous night that I had sung my French song. And here I made my fatal mistake. Instead of flatly denying that I could sing a note I went on, with deprecatory gestures and noises, to imply that I may have sung or squealed a note or two, but that sort of thing was merely a bar-parlour trick and was no use for singing before an audience. I soon understood my error when they all closed in on me and said that that was all nonsense. This was not the Albert Hall and any old comic song was good enough to go down. In vain, I protested that I could not sing before an audience at all ; that the song was not a comic one.

'Coamic !' said the commercial with a wicked wink at me. 'Coamic ! I laughed till I was nearly deid. Ye're jist bashful, my friend. Get him on the platform, gentlemen, and he'll bring the house down.'

Now there was so much talking and general noise that I almost hoped that in the confusion the whole project might drop, and remained silent neither consenting nor denying. And then without given reason or apparent impetus, the crowd began to move off to the hall where I gathered the meeting and concert were to take place. It is one of the most amusing and, to the Saxon, most irritating qualities of the Celt, that he can, contemptuous

306

of time, leave an arrangement unfinished, a discussion, an essential argument unclinched, hanging in the air and move off, implying that in some unspoken way everything has been made clear. The initiated (so will his maddening behaviour suggest) are now, by some secret understanding, all at one, and there is no further need with clumsy words and reiteration to make redundant what has already been so easily comprehended by the subtle. It was in this way that the crowd around me in the height of the talk and babble melted away : and I was left wondering whether I had offended by my downrightness of refusal or weakly given in through my timidity.

When the hotel was quite empty, save for servants, I had a whisky to fortify me further and settled down in front of the fire. I decided that clearly I was not expected to do anything. Even Celtic casualness could not suppose that I had really consented to make a fool of myself in public to amuse these dignified villagers. I should, after the speech was over, go down myself and sit at the back of the hall. I knew how easily Highland enthusiasm was aroused and how easily it could be deflected. I should be allowed to sit quietly and listen to what promised to be an amusing exhibition of local manners and customs. So, quite full of courage, I came out of the hotel at about six o'clock and walked down the collection of few houses which served as a street, and, deciding to while away a few minutes so that the concert might be in full swing before I entered, I went into the little post office-cum-general stores to buy a few stamps, postcards and bars of chocolate for my next day's journey.

The post office was just about to close, for the proprietor of the little cottage, a charming old Highlander with a voice as soft as a child's, was evidently anxious to seize the very first moment to be off to the concert.

There were two little girls standing in the shop as I entered, who, with the slow, unspeaking, ungiggling curiosity which Northern children seem always to have, looked at me long and embarrassingly. At last one of them broke silence, and I heard her say to her companion in that slow whispering voice, for the sounds and meanings of which I was already becoming so sharp, ' Jeannie, yon's the hoamic.' The last word, which was intended to be ' comic,' was drawn out incredibly long on the first syllable, and through the whole sentence there ran the sighing sound of the Gaelic speech.

' My children,' I said as I struck a foolishly affected attitude, ' daughters of my friends, let me assure you that however comic I may look, however well may your fathers have entertained me to their admirable whisky, however melodiously may your handsome brother have besought me, nothing is going to persuade me to expose myself to the laughter of this happy valley.' The only reply to this remark was a repetition—this time as if in explanation of my folly, ' Jeannie, yon's the hoamic.'

Return to Scotland

DONALD G MACRAE

The Pterodactyl and Powhatan's Daughter

AMERICAN poets have seen their country
as a brown girl lying serene in the sun,
as Powhatan's daughter with open thighs,
her belly a golden plain of wheat,
her breasts the firm and fecund hills,
each sinuous vein a river, and in each wrist
    the pulse of cataracts.

She has rejected no lover, not the
fanatic English nor the hungry Scot,
the trading Dutchman nor the industrious
continental peasant, used to oppression,
the patient stolen negro nor the
laborious Asiatic, schooled to diligent,
    ingenious labour.

By all her lovers she has been fruitful,
has multiplied all numbers, lying
indolent, calm and almost asleep,
only her lake-eyes watchful, expectant
of new wanderers from further shores
seeking her young immortal body,
    waiting unsated.

She is patient this girl with her black hair tumbled,
with her earth-bedded, receptive body outstretched,
relaxed and leisured, at ease in the sun.
In her veins the sun-warm blood is coursing,
swift running through the golden body,
obedient to the steadfast heart's command,
    the unending beat.

Not such is our land.   It is a skeleton
crushed by the long weight of years, the bone
hard stone, the skin tight on the sinew,
the flesh wasted by long years of hunger.
It is a stone land, a hard land of bone,
of lean muscle and atrophied membrane
     ridged over ribs.

This is a pterodactyl land,
lean survivor of ice and the frost,
sea and the parching sun, which,
the last of its kind, is now dying
by inches, blinking and bleeding through the
death shroud of mist, the dissolving film
     of steady rain.

We dwell on the stiffening corpse of Scotland,
starved lice on a pauper's body
chill on a marble slab.   Should we leave ?
Should we follow our fathers' pattern,
make love to Powhatan's daughter,
westward refurrow the weary sea ?
     We had better not.

She too is a myth : we'd be wise to forget
our symbols, turn from the romantic vision,
the loose-thought personified images of countries,
to study and learn to read, painfully,
the facts of these matters aright, then nourish—
if we have heart—some slight sober hope
     of tomorrow.

Poetry Scotland No. 3

JAMES FERGUSSON

Portrait of a Gentleman

I HAVE known him, in a sense, ever since my childhood. Whenever any of my brothers or I came home after long absence at school or elsewhere, it used to be a regular ritual for someone to say, 'Have you said "How do you do?" to Sir Adam yet?' Being thus reminded of a neglected duty, one would go into the dining-room, place oneself opposite to the big portrait over the black marble Victorian mantelpiece, and make the established inquiry, accompanied by a respectful bow. Sometimes this salutation was extended to his father and grandfather or a few other favourites among The Ancestors; but it was to Sir Adam that one felt chiefly bound to report oneself, as it were, on revisiting the family roof-tree.

Sir Adam never unbent so far as to return my bow, though I always glanced up at him to see if he would. Sometimes—if, for instance, I had been near the bottom of my class last term—his eye was a trifle cold, sometimes it rested on me with grave approval, occasionally it looked almost benevolent. But anything approaching to geniality would have been foreign to the dignified pose in which Raeburn's brush had set him there, calm and upright in his big armchair. There he sat—and there, for that matter, he still sits—in his sober brown coat, with his hair neatly powdered, his legs, in their black silk breeches, composedly crossed, his hands, their fingers interlocked, resting on his knee, and his chair turned a little aside from the table on which lies the letter he has just been reading. He looks exactly the figure described in his obituary notice of September 1813—'this venerable and respectable Baronet.'

It was many years before I came—I might almost say

'presumed'—to make Sir Adam's closer acquaintance. The outlines of his life, the fact that he died a bachelor at the age of eighty, and a few family traditions illustrating the extreme propriety of his conduct—these at least were familiar to me ; and I was dimly aware that he had been a great planter of trees and had laid out most of our favourite paths through the surrounding woods. The phrase 'in Sir Adam's time,' applied to plantations, paths or farm-houses, denoted to me a vague epoch a little subsequent to the Creation ; and it was beyond my youthful imagination to conceive what appearance the hills and woods of my home might have borne before his constructive hand had been laid upon them. He remained a kind of peak in history, an eminent and dominating figure of the past. No doubt Raeburn's art, and the position of his portrait in the place of honour, had much to do with forming this impression.

I knew that in certain long drawers in another room there lay a vast collection of Sir Adam's correspondence ; but it was not until a few years ago that I began to explore them. What I found there introduced me for the first time to the vivid realities of life in eighteenth-century Scotland. It taught me that history was not after all a dead thing belonging only to the past. And also it led me at last to appreciate the significance of that letter on the table in Sir Adam's portrait.

Sir Adam had been what is known as a voluminous correspondent. From about 1756 till a few months before his death he seemed to have preserved almost every letter of importance he received, and, in many cases, copies of his answers. From this mass of documents and some research in books, it was possible to piece together in fascinating detail large periods of his industrious life in the Scotland of Boswell and Burns : his 'grand tour' as a young man, his interests and friendships, his career at the Scottish Bar and in Parliament, and his loving and methodical care for the family estate to which he succeeded in 1759.

For several years now the exploration and reconstruction of Sir Adam's life has been one of my major interests. I have not yet got to the end of his correspondence. Sometimes I doubt if I ever shall. He was a man who never left a letter unanswered, and seldom wrote in one sentence what could be more politely expressed in three. Many people would call him a dull correspondent. To me he is a perpetual delight. As he winds his way through clause within clause of each elaborate paragraph, with that neat and flourishing handwriting, as careful in his old age as in his youth, and with grammar so faultless and punctuation so meticulous that any one of his letters might be printed without editing as it stands, I follow him with the appreciation of a musical critic listening to the unravelling of a well-scored fugue. Today I know him as intimately as a favourite uncle ; and neither long-windedness, formality nor an almost total absence of humour obscures my admiration of him.

His letters contain no original thoughts, and his frequent good advice to his nephew and heir consists chiefly of gracefully expressed platitude. But his sincerity is never in doubt ; his advice, if trite, is invariably sound, for he was a very wise and sensible man ; and no-one practised more thoroughly the virtues of honesty, industry and public service which he preached. He deserved Burns's eulogy of him—' aith-detesting, chaste Kilkerran ' —and he was too sympathetic to be a prig.

I will not write of his long political career—he was a good politician, but not made for a statesman—nor of the entertaining but complicated electioneering intrigues which form the subject of many of his letters. Nor, for the sake of space, will I touch on his clashes with Boswell, his friendship with that versatile and charming man George Dempster of Dunnichen (whose letters to him I have published elsewhere) or their tireless efforts, including an arduous journey through the greater part of the Hebrides, to work out a scheme for checking High- land emigration by establishing fishing stations on the West Coast. Sir Adam's long life and wide acquaintance with politicians and men of letters would fill a book. It is only one side of his busy career that concerns me now : the activities that transformed the fields, woods and roads of his corner of Ayrshire, and thereby provided his most enduring memorial.

Sir Adam was one of the ' improving ' lairds—a body of men which has never, I think, received proper recogni- tion for the services they rendered to Scotland, though a great deal of what is good in rural Scotland today is due to their labours. ' Improving ' often ran in families, and it did so in Sir Adam's. His father—a Lord of Session— was planting trees, turning moorland into pasture and laying out policies away back in George I's time. His younger brother, also a judge, the amiably impulsive Lord Hermand, became rather late in life an improver in his turn, and farmed in West Lothian with a zeal which was almost fanatical. Sir Adam's own improvements were business-like and thorough. A full account of the earlier ones is given in Andrew Wight's *Recent State of Husbandry in Scotland*, whose author, when he visited Carrick in 1777, ' saw various operations of husbandry carried on with industry and attention, the inclosures in perfection, both hedges and stone walls,' and praised the ' progress of agriculture in that part of the country ' as being ' chiefly owing to Sir Adam himself.'

Sir Adam, in a letter to Wight, recalled the backward state of agriculture in Carrick a few years earlier, ' when there was scarce an inclosure in it but some few round the gentlemen's houses, when there was not a pound of grass seed sown from one end of it to the other, and when the whole attention of the farmer, and the whole dung of the farm, was applied to a few acres, while the rest was totally neglected.'

I can give no better account of Sir Adam's improvements than his own, which is more directly and economically expressed than many of his private letters :

' My object has been to turn the farms in my own possession into good grass as soon as possible. . . . The trouble and expense that I have bestowed on this object has been much greater than any person would conceive from the quantity of ground that I have improved, without considering what it was in its natural state. You cannot fail to have observed the multitude of large stones upon the uncultivated fields in this country ; most of these are of such a size as to require being blasted with gunpowder before they are carried off. As the soil runs naturally to wood, there is a necessity of clearing the fields of shrubs and bushes before they can be properly ploughed. If to this is added the expense of draining, you will not be surprised at my saying that many fields cost more than their original price before the plough is put into the ground.'

By the 1780s, however, all the farms on the estate were enclosed, and the wasteful old run-rig system was a thing of the past. Pasture had greatly improved, and the farmers had learnt, by example, the importance of keeping their land in good heart. Lime was made available in large quantities from a quarry on the estate. The breed of sheep also had been much improved by the importation of Dorchester and Bakewell rams. Elaborate draining had been carried out on the lower ground, and hundreds of acres had been planted with trees.

At the end of the century Sir Adam's correspondence

shows him busy with road-making, linking up his neighbourhood with Maybole and Ayr to the north and Girvan to the south, and providing an outlet for the coal which Hamilton of Bargany and Kennedy of Dunure were working on their respective properties on the north side of the valley. He built two high stone bridges over the Water of Girvan, of simple and beautiful design, which still stand today as good as new. In these days, when Government and local authorities make roads with public money, it is often forgotten how much, a hundred and fifty years ago, was left, and sometimes very successfully left, to private enterprise. When I watch the buses speeding northwards beside the Water of Girvan, I often recall with a secret pleasure that their unconscious passengers are travelling not only beneath Sir Adam's trees and beside his fields, but over one of his bridges and along his road, made by his initiative, according to his plan, and largely at his expense.

To these activities Sir Adam devoted his declining and gout-ridden years, combining with them the care of a large family of nephews and nieces of two generations who looked up to him as to a father. He owned himself ' heartily tired ' of Parliament, and declined the offer of Henry Dundas (suggested by George III himself) that he should go to India as Governor of Madras. With an occasional grumble of a kind grown more common since his day—' this Income Tax is a galling one '—he settled down to spend the rest of his life at home. ' *Ille terrarum,*' he might have quoted, ' *mihi praeter omnes angulus ridet* ' ; and he found everything about it perfect, even the climate. ' There is not probably a milder air in the winter months than that in which I now sit,' he wrote in January 1809 ; and in another letter, written in a similar season, he sums up the contentment of his quiet but still active life :

' We have had a delightful winter . . . without snow, of which we have not had three days during the whole season. The air is now delightful, and the birds singing as in spring. Five or six large trees were blown down here ; among which one of the largest beeches above the house. But enough remain : and I think, upon a moderate computation, for every one blown down, I plant 5,000.'

Scotland 1938

Scotland

Here in the Uplands
The soil is ungrateful ;
The fields, red with sorrel,
   Are stony and bare.
A few trees, wind-twisted—
Or are they but bushes ?—
Stand stubbornly guarding
   A home here and there.

Scooped out like a saucer,
The land lies before me ;
The waters, once scattered,
   Flow orderedly now
Through fields where the ghosts
Of the marsh and the moorland
Still ride the old marches,
   Despising the plough.

The marsh and the moorland
Are not to be banished ;
The bracken and heather,
   The glory of broom,
Usurp all the balks
And the fields' broken fringes,
And claim from the sower
   Their portion of room.

This is my country,
The land that begat me.
These windy spaces
   Are surely my own.

And those who here toil
In the sweat of their faces
Are flesh of my flesh,
   And bone of my bone.

Hard is the day's task—
Scotland, stern Mother !—
Wherewith at all times
   Thy sons have been faced :
Labour by day,
And scant rest in the gloaming,
With Want an attendant,
   Not lightly outpaced.

Yet do thy children
Honour and love thee.
Harsh is thy schooling,
   Yet great is the gain :
True hearts and strong limbs,
The beauty of faces,
Kissed by the wind
   And caressed by the rain.

Gossip

PRINTED IN GREAT BRITAIN AT
THE PRESS OF THE PUBLISHERS